Locating Cultural Change

Thank you for choosing a SAGE product! If you have any comment, observation or feedback, I would like to personally hear from you. Please write to me at <u>contactceo@sagepub.in</u>

—Vivek Mehra, Managing Director and CEO,
SAGE Publications India Pvt Ltd, New Delhi

Bulk Sales

SAGE India offers special discounts for purchase of books in bulk. We also make available special imprints and excerpts from our books on demand.

For orders and enquiries, write to us at

Marketing Department
SAGE Publications India Pvt Ltd
B1/I-1, Mohan Cooperative Industrial Area
Mathura Road, Post Bag 7
New Delhi 110044, India
E-mail us at <u>marketing@sagepub.in</u>

Get to know more about SAGE, be invited to SAGE events, get on our mailing list. Write today to <u>marketing@sagepub.in</u>

This book is also available as an e-book.

Locating Cultural Change

Theory, Method, Process

EDITED BY
Partha Pratim Basu and Ipshita Chanda

⑤SAGE www.sagepublications.com
Los Angeles • London • New Delhi • Singapore • Washington DC

First published in 2011 by

SAGE Publications India Pvt Ltd
B1/I-1 Mohan Cooperative Industrial Area
Mathura Road, New Delhi 110 044, India
www.sagepub.in

SAGE Publications Inc
2455 Teller Road
Thousand Oaks, California 91320, USA

SAGE Publications Ltd
1 Oliver's Yard, 55 City Road
London EC1Y 1SP, United Kingdom

SAGE Publications Asia-Pacific Pte Ltd
33 Pekin Street
#02-01 Far East Square
Singapore 048763

Published by Vivek Mehra for SAGE Publications India Pvt Ltd, typeset in 10.5/12.5 pt Adobe Garamond by Diligent Typesetter, Delhi and printed at Chaman Enterprises, New Delhi.

Library of Congress Cataloging-in-Publication Data

Locating cultural change: theory, method, process/edited by Partha Pratim Basu and Ipshita Chanda.
    p. cm.
  Includes bibliographical references and index.
  1. Social change—India. 2. India Social conditions. 3. Popular culture—India. I. Basu, Partha Pratim, 1961–II. Chanda, Ipshita.
HN683.5.L625   306.0954—dc22   2011   2011002885

ISBN: 978-81-321-0576-3 (HB)

The SAGE Team: Elina Majumdar, Shweta Tewari, Anju Saxena and Deepti Saxena

Contents

List of Illustrations

Acknowledgements

The editors would like to thank the University Grants Commission, New Delhi, for extending financial support to Jadavpur University under the 'Potential for Excellence Scheme', which facilitated research for the chapters contributed to this volume by Abhijit Roy, Ipshita Chanda, Sayantan Dasgupta, Partha Pratim Basu, Dalia Chakraborty and Nilanjana Gupta.

Chapter 1

Introduction
Locating Cultural Change: Process and Method

The aim of the chapters in this volume is the study of located cultural processes: but how, if at all, is this different from the existing formulations of Culture Studies and Cultural Studies? Is it the same as both or one (which one?) of them and why? Or is it completely different from either? It is with these questions in view that we might try to outline the focus of this book, which contains a collection of essays on diverse topics that form part of the lived reality of the present.

Can the Real 'Cultural Studies' Please Stand Up ?

Each of the 'objects' of these chapters is constructed and deconstructed by the writers as 'texts' in the sense that Barthes[1] outlines:

> Just as the Einsteinian science demands that the relativity of the frames of reference be included in the object studied, so the combined action of Marxism, Freudianism and structuralism demands in literature, the relativisation of the relations of writer, reader and observer (critic). Over against the traditional notion of the work, for long, and still conceived of in a so to speak Newtonian way, there is now the requirement of a new object, obtained by the sliding or overturning of former categories. That object is the Text.[2]

The text is thus a processual entity in the process of constant formation and reformation through production, reception, use and reproduction. In that sense what we are studying are texts in their dynamism. We could conceive of this dynamism in the words of Deleuze and Guattari, as an 'impulse to meaning'.[3] These writers further elucidate their description by saying that meaning is not necessarily confined by prior structures and feelings—hence the Althusserian position of base always influencing superstructure, as well as the Frankfurt School's claim that culture's role is manipulative, are problematized. The impulse to meaning is, in the words of Deleuze and Guattari, expressive, incarnated and forceful. But the production of meaning is only one part of the story: the actual production of the text whether it is virtual or material, is the complementary part. The process through which meaning and material are produced and conjoined within specific locations could then be the working definition of cultural process. Texts become a part of the cultural field due to this process, and participate in its semiotic and material economy. It is not the sign alone but the sign within this process, the sign-in-process that one attempts to understand in what follows. This is the reason why 'process' as both practice and concept form the focus of the studies included here.

If we return to the questions with which we started, then we can now ask: is this approach different from what we understand as Cultural/Culture Studies in India and elsewhere? To answer this question we may rehearse the history of Culture Studies/Cultural Studies in these locations. As the discerning reader knows, Barthes has outlined the situation in which the transformation from 'work' to 'text' as object of study has become possible. He says:

> What is new and what affects the idea of the work comes not necessarily from the internal recasting of each of these disciplines, but rather from their relation to an object which traditionally is a province of none of them. It is indeed as though the interdisciplinarity which is today held up as a prime value in research cannot be accomplished by the simple confrontation of specialist branches of knowledge.[4]

The foundational moment of modern Cultural Studies probably coincides with this thought, if not with the exact date of Barthes' insight. For in the British perspective, Cultural Studies was a challenge from within to academic value judgements, grading and the hierarchy within English literature as discipline, fuelled by the work of Raymond Williams and Richard Hoggart.[5] It was an 'opening up of the disciplinary structure of the Humanities'[6] and 'one of the first...challenges to the conventional map of intellectual life within the academy'.[7] Indeed, Williams and Hoggart, on the fringes of academia and apparently more closely connected to the class that did not generally populate the university, used it to challenge the 'great tradition' of the Leavises and the 'high culture' of T.S. Eliot. Add to this the inclination for contemporary culture, which different theorists have chosen to see in different forms. Though Matthew Arnold's liberal formulation that 'culture' would save us from 'anarchy', concealed the actual class character of such culture, the Birmingham School for Contemporary Cultural Studies and Williams turned the area of operation of Cultural Studies towards the interrogation of academic institutions and practices identified as 'high' culture in the name of what was 'outside'. In its North American avatar, Culture Studies studies popular mass culture (which the socialist orientation of the British variety of the discipline dubbed 'capitalist') from a pragmatic-liberal and pluralist view. According to Lindloff et al.,[8] the North American version of Cultural Studies concentrated on the 'use' of mass culture. This was taken a step ahead by the Australian theorist John Fiske who argued that cultural objects were interpreted according to the needs and desires of those who received them. This shifted the focus from object/artifact to consumption, from resisting a hierarchy or disrupting a canon or problematizing a point of view to the arena of 'text' as Barthes defines it.

This well-known history may form a background to the inception and institutionalization of the discipline in India. In quite an exhaustive survey of this matter, Radhakrishnan[9] outlines the different views regarding the origins of Cultural Studies in India and then follows this up with a survey of institutions dedicated to activities that are described as 'doing' Cultural Studies, derived from programmatic assumptions about what Cultural Studies actually is. Speaking of the inception of Cultural Studies as a separate identifiable disciplinary entity, he enumerates several categories within which current definitions of Cultural Studies in Indian academic institutions fall. There is the Culture Studies as Media Studies model at the Tata Institute of Social Sciences (TISS),

Mumbai, the Culture Studies as a basket for Humanities and Social Sciences variety at Centre for Social Sciences' Cultural Studies Workshop in Kolkata, Cultural Studies as 'space for doing contemporary theory' at Baroda, etc. Radhakrishnan concludes that Cultural Studies in India bears a 'relationship to local concerns'. But it is clear that here 'local' is an idea rather than a location: it has a vast range and is underpinned by various needs and desires. For example, the birth of Cultural Studies opened a space for studying and 'doing' Continental theory or 'post-colonial'/'third world' literature (in English mainly, and sometimes in translation from Indian languages) in English departments that needed an answer to their own soul searching. Or the fact that the 'subaltern' perspective in the Social Sciences, which had the potential to question established disciplinary practices, was also seen as a cause for the birth of Cultural Studies. These are various narratives describing the foundational impulse for the establishment of Cultural Studies in India, and it appears that there is not much difference between these impulses and those that were seen as primary in 'Western' locations. Rather, the concern and consequent 'opening up' of disciplines in India may be understood as a repertoire of questions and responses from Indian academics exposed to Cultural Studies programmes as oppositional projects interrogating the establishment in 'Western' academia. In that sense, Cultural Studies in India may well be termed as one of the early instances of globalization as a phenomenon. The following of Western models of inquiry is of course not limited to Cultural Studies alone: it is salutary to note that English was the language in which the hierarchy, which some would argue was established by English itself, as discipline and language, was problematized. Alternatives acted upon or articulated tended towards partiality for theoretical inputs and positions derived from Western models. The disciplinary formations to which these were addressed were either English Literature or the Social Sciences, whose chief mode of operation was also that same language. In that sense, a commonality that may be discerned within Cultural Studies, despite its numerous formulations and definitions including the desire to desist from definition itself, may be seen as either of two things. First, an attempt to introduce a variety of Western theory in order to construct an avant-garde or a margin, depending upon the perspective that one takes. Second, to introduce into the mainstream of Indian academia, concerns, positions and objects of study that were again seen either as marginal or avant-garde, depending upon one's perspective.

From this vantage point, reading Radhakrishnan's comment on the 'local' concerns of Cultural Studies takes on another dimension. We may turn to specific cases of Cultural Studies Programmes. The English and Foreign Languages University (EFLU) Programme is described thus:

> Depending upon the number of credits, the student goes away with a Master's degree, in English Literature, Cultural Studies, Linguistics or English Language Teaching. The disciplinary presence of social sciences in the programme is scant in the programming though there were attempts at inter-disciplinary dialogue when a social scientist was employed as faculty. A significant absence in a fully formed institutional space like EFLU is that of attempts at syllabi formation. The making of the syllabi is one that is central to the imagining of a discipline. In a programme like the one at EFLU the immediate translation of research that is understood as Cultural Studies seems to be the default mode of forming the syllabi.... The insistence on the part of the faculty of the Cultural Studies programme in EFLU, that it is a set of research agendas or research programmes including Dalit Studies and issues like gender and community that defines the institution's Cultural Studies programme, is telling in this context.[10]

This seems to connect the goal of the programme to what Radhakrishnan has described as the approach taken by the Centre for Social Sciences. This Centre has been running a Cultural Studies Workshop since 1995, and Radhakrishnan explains the history of this endeavour thus:

> [T]he name Cultural Studies has come to mean, for the purposes of the Workshop, a convenient basket into which most humanities and social science research can be put. This development points to two key issues that can be picked up for our understanding of Cultural Studies—one, that it is a space for interaction between disciplines, and two, that Cultural Studies derives from developments within the social sciences. If we are to look at the institutional structure within which

the Workshop is organised today, we will be able to see that the other disciplines and Cultural Studies are on par with each other. Cultural Studies at CSSS-C is one discipline among many—the former being a space for studies in the wake of developments within English Studies or studies of popular culture. The disciplines as understood in the Cultural Studies Workshops appear to be independent entities that can borrow from each other retaining their basic characteristics and methods. Interdisciplinarity becomes a large field here populated by a number of approaches—from 'inter-' as literally 'between' disciplines and 'inter' as a space for give and take. [11]

The EFLU Programme and the CSS Workshop therefore have a common focus in having no specific focus at all, all the more to allow 'independent entities' or 'research agendas' to define a disciplinary boundary. This is certainly different from the Tezpur (1995) and the North Gujarat University (2002) initiatives which Radhakrishnan describes:

A focus on local culture, on issues related to the forms of expressions in the North Eastern region, is being emphasised upon in this programme. Another initiative of a similar kind at a national level is the Centre for Indian Diaspora and Cultural Studies that was set up in Hemchandracharya North Gujarat University (Patan, Gujarat) in 2002. This centre seeks to study the life of diasporic Indians and thus to redraw geographical boundaries in the understanding of national culture. The initiatives both at Tezpur University and the Centre for Diaspora and Cultural Studies attempt to infuse into a new domain, conveniently called Cultural Studies, concerns of a local nature in dialogue with and contrast to ideas of national culture (as in the case of the former) and of a global nature again in a dialogic and conflictual nature with ideas of national culture.[12]

These two initiatives can certainly be seen as fuelled by 'local' concerns, rather than by academic ones, the latter being the concern with theory, discipline and the relations between them. But also, the institutionalization of these local concerns in mainstream academia is done through Cultural Studies since there is no place for them in any of the established disciplines. In that sense just as the English departments and the Social

Sciences needed Cultural Studies to do theory and post-colonial literature, similarly, different geographical locations in the country demand
that local concerns be addressed and find Cultural Studies a convenient
envelope into which their concerns fit.

Radhakrishnan attempts to bring some coherence to this field when
he says:

> Though the different institutions doing Cultural Studies seem to be
> working within different and at times contradictory paradigms, one
> can discern important similarities between them, although the ten-
> dency so far has been to see them as disparate and unconnected at-
> tempts. For example, all these instances of the emergence of Cultural
> Studies seem to be dealing with an epistemological or political issue
> that has a very close relationship to their institutional locations.[13]

But as we have seen earlier, these 'local' concerns are of varied nature, though all oriented towards a single goal: the introduction of what
was hitherto outside the institution of academia, into the mainstream.
Radhakrishnan sees this as a positive outcome because it 'allows for the
programme to be more inclusive and to address and challenge earlier
disciplinary formations with ease' (ibid., p.12). But he does not ask how
this is to be done. And that brings us to the abiding problem of method
in Cultural Studies: what White and Schwoch (2006)[14] call the 'structuring absence' in Cultural Studies: the absence of a methodology.

Assuming that Cultural Studies is a discipline defined by diversity,
does it have a unified method? In this context, White and Schwoch
(2006) present the argument against methodological rigour in Cultural
Studies by pointing to the implications of 'method' as such. These are
'often, whether accurately or not, associated with an imaginary scholar
devoting an entire career to asking questions and desiring answers with
the same methodological approach over and over again regardless of topic,
regardless of relevance'.[15] And Cultural Studies with its diversity cannot
fall into that trap. So what is the way out? Should Cultural Studies be
content with what these two authors call 'method fragmented within
the context of specific disciplines', rather than 'articulated through Cultural Studies and across disciplines'?[16]

In order to answer this question, we must first point to a difficulty in nomenclature: the terms Culture Studies and Cultural Studies are often interchangeably used. In order to bring a semblance of order into the discussion, let us assume that we are talking about Cultural Studies, which refers to a way of studying material at hand: which is to say we are attempting to do a particular kind of study. We are not, therefore, talking of Culture Studies. Our efforts are not defined by the object of study, that is cultural artifacts met with a collection of material and a cache of theories that are all included within the rubric of Cultural Studies, we come to the conclusion that the object (or subject, depending upon your theoretical proclivities) of Cultural Studies is anything and everything. Given the history of the formation of the discipline, that is probably quite fitting. But then, how is this vast amount of diverse material to be handled, whether 'taught' or 'done'? In other words, is there a method that will distinguish Cultural Studies from ways in which other disciplines, like Comparative Literature, for instance, 'read' 'texts' and have been doing so since the time Goethe wrote *West-eastern Divan* in 1815 ? Having argued that there cannot be a unified method in Cultural Studies, White and Schwoch propose a 'management' or 'negotiation' template, emphasizing possibilities of methodological usage rather than a single model emphasizing boundaries and theories. The final outcome of this is 'a multi-celled cultural studies spread-sheet': 'Visible Cultural Studies spreadsheet cells are those that are germane to the operationalization of that specific project',[17] implying that a smorgasbord of theoretical concepts and tools from a wide variety of disciplines ranging from sociology to film theory is a perfectly acceptable situation. Yet, these same authors pose a counter-argument to the 'no-unified method' position by saying that in the inter- and cross-disciplinary dialogue of the twenty-first century and the advanced communication and information technology systems that we operate and inhabit, a careful rearticulation of method is needed.[18] While we are not unsympathetic to this state-of-the-art argument for method, we are also concerned about the more mundane problems besetting the actual acts of teaching and research without the attendant support of definitive methodological model. Indeed Bourdieu (2001)[19] advises that we must move from a 'mechanics of a model to dialectic of strategies'. We do not claim anything other than a functional necessity, in our desire for 'method'. Hence, it is our attempt in what

8

follows to propose, through individual essays in this collection, a possible formulation of a method, keeping in mind the fact that the object of Cultural Studies is varied by definition.

Our focus is on 'how', rather than 'what'. Why the text has been marked out as the object of study in the beginning of this essay may now be clear. Barthes' definition of the text is constructed at the interstice of a number of frames, from the perspective of a number of entities that stand in varied relations to it. The study of such 'texts' should include the frames of location from an interrelation of perspectives. We have argued that 'process' is the key to this method, and we are studying the production and consumption of meaning and material in conjunction. We may be rightly accused of side-stepping the fraught question of 'what is culture'. Pleading guilty to this charge, we proceed by identifying the 'cultural' as a dynamic field, formed of the interstices of many layers of practice, belief and quotidian living. This field provides a context or a location for the existence, change and operation of the 'text'. It is related, with all its specificities, to other immediate or remote fields constructed and imagined in a similar way. And its dynamism is caused by the fact that the production, reception and re-use of the text that is our object of study occurs within this field. Therefore the production, consumption, reception and re-use of the 'text' has the potential to change the shape and nature of the context/location, even as the 'text' itself is changed and shaped by the context/location. It is through the text's being and becoming that culture is produced and participated in. The processes of being and becoming are those which we have indicated as 'cultural process' and undertaken to study.

We have tried to bring together diverse interlinked moments within the chronotope of the present and populated them with texts. These texts are located in time and space and travelling across times and spaces, beginning from an arbitrary point in the period of their genesis to a projection for the kind of future that they might fashion. Looked at separately, these studies will stand as disparate pieces of writing: viewed from the perspective outlined earlier, however, they constitute a loosely patterned 'present'. The dynamics of change in the internal structures of each of the texts is the object of study here. In that sense, the mystery of the process remains—we are hard put to foretell the direction of change, but we argue that the mapping of the moment will allow us to understand some part of this mystery. We recognize and try to understand the structure of feeling from which the selected texts generated and the changes they are able to make in those structures. Through this, we address various processual dynamics which yield an understanding of some of the dimensions of the specific chronotope chosen.

The processual method attempts to study interrelated processes of textualization located in time and space across the spectrum from concept to embodiment, through language. By language I refer to a medium: the medium of the study, especially if one is writing an academic volume, may be language, but the object of study can be (and has been) expressed/constructed in any medium including language. Changes in the nature and usage of texts, that is changes in their means of production, consumption/reception and re-use, point to a changed 'understanding' of their place and function. This dialectic produces what we have called 'process'. Process may be understood by identifying and understanding this dialectic. As far as antecedents of this form of procedure is concerned, the method that we are proposing may be seen to be derived from Reception and Influence Studies and theories of Contactual Relations. Reception Studies provides methods for understanding the reception of signs within and across specific locations and through time. The concept of influence has been shortchanged by thinking of it as unidirectional: it has been rendered unidimensional as a result. For our purposes, 'reception' includes the dimensions posited by Tartakov and Dahejia (1984),[20] who conceptualize the act of reception as 'Sharing, Intrusion and Influence'. This triad does not exhaust the field, and individual elements here are even not mutually exclusive; but the formulation points out the possibility of variety in conceptualizing reception, and may be seen to occur in various ways in the individual efforts collected here.

At this juncture, we should point out the implications of this method. First, it gives us the opportunity to consider forms of 'understanding' as part of the process too, a condition that we must accept if we do embark upon this route. This means that our conclusions regarding textualization are provisional and located. All stops are wayside stops: of course the stamina, energy and commitment to movement are factors in our continuing this process of understanding as are the actual conditions of the study itself. Underlying this is nothing more than a philosophy

10

that conceives of the enterprise of understanding as *relational* as distinct from *relative*, as social and socially posited, even in the moment of abstract contemplative theorizing. Second, the processual method implies that a theoretical and/or methodological disjunction between studies of production and reception are spurious. Unless this is clearly realized, we shall be unable to move beyond top–down predetermined theory with thematic thrusts: feminism or poco or structuralism. This follows the philosophy of studies 'from below'. Allowing the sign-structure to work out its peculiar and variegated dynamics, rather than imposing some sort of dynamics upon it, thematically, ideologically or otherwise. Paul de Man is supposed to have defined theory as a 'controlled reflection on method'. We have attempted some form of reflection: whether a 'theory' for Cultural Studies emerges out of this may be a subject for the future.

'Locating' Cultural Studies: Outlines of a Possible Method

As an introduction to an account of the essays collected in this volume, we may turn to a 'text': Jorge Luis Borges' 'Pierre Menard Author of the Quixote'.[21] Pierre Menard did not 'want to compose another Quixote—which is easy—but *the Quixote itself*'.[22] Borges proceeds to construct a 'fictitious' Menard writing a 'real' Don Quixote which '(Menard) never contemplated (as) a mechanical transcription of the original; he did not propose to copy it'. Retracing the 'stages' which philosophers go through in the process of arriving at the 'final term', Borges constructs a text of Menard writing the 'Don Quixote by Pierre Menard'. And in so doing, he seems to have outlined a process of textual production. But what of the consumption side? The reader of the Quixote of Pierre Menard will find no difference between this one and the one that is 'originally' written by Cervantes. So how do we understand that this Quixote is by Pierre Menard? This is possible because Menard has revealed the key to his 'method' to Borges:

'My intent is no more than astonishing,' he wrote me the 30th of September, 1934, from Bayonne. 'The final term in a theological or metaphysical demonstration—the objective world, God, causality, the forms of the universe—is no less previous and common than my famed novel. The only difference is that the philosophers publish the intermediary stages of their labor in pleasant volumes and I have resolved to do away with those stages.' In truth, not one worksheet remains to bear witness to his years of effort.

Finding its place in the lives of readers and writers, the book becomes an object whose 'meaning' is now open to (re)textualization and re-use by the consumer. The processual method of studying the text inscribes those stages that Menard has refused to document: these are the stages by which the 'final term in a . . . demonstration' is arrived at. Thus the Quixote of Cervantes can now be 'written' by anyone who holds the book in her hands, with the purpose of reading it. And Menard is one such 'reader', whose Quixote is written because he wants to foreground his own 'reading':

> The *Quixote*—Menard told me—was, above all, an entertaining book; now it is the occasion for patriotic toasts, grammatical insolence and obscene de luxe editions. Fame is a form of incomprehension, perhaps the worst.
> It is ironical (or only natural) that not one word of the Quixote actually changes in the process: it only becomes the Quixote as read and then 'written' by Pierre Menard. How Menard 'makes' this book is the process that we have been referring to.

Like a student of cultural process, Borges follows Cervantes' textualization of Don Quixote in intricate detail. The (re)textualization of Don Quixote by Pierre Menard however is a process of which there are no traces left by Menard. Borges finds only the final product: the Don Quixote by Pierre Menard. And the conclusion that he draws from this 'finished' product is this:

> Menard (perhaps without wanting to) has enriched, by means of a new technique, the halting and rudimentary art of reading: this new technique is that of the deliberate anachronism and the erroneous attribution. This technique, whose applications are infinite, prompts us to go through the Odyssey as if it were posterior to the *Aeneid* and

the book *Le jardin du Centaure* of Madame Henri Bachelier as if it were by Madame Henri Bachelier. This technique fills the most placid works with adventure. To attribute the *Imitatio Christi* to Louis Ferdinand Céline or to James Joyce, is this not a sufficient renovation of its tenuous spiritual indications?

We may answer this question by turning to the essays collected in this volume, to see how they engage with these processes of reception, consumption and re-use. This exercise would also serve to integrate them with the epistemological and ontological contours of Culture Studies as defined earlier.

Abhijit Roy sets out to map the vision of the 'modern' in contemporary television serials to draw attention to the way the 'postcolonial' negotiates the 'global'. Critical assessment of Indian tele-soaps mostly stressed the 'residual' nature of India's feudal order to show how certain values and rituals have sustained their antagonistic position vis-à-vis modernity and resisted their appropriation by the emergent global order. However, drawing on *Jassi*, inspired by a Latin American soap, the author argues that it is more important to investigate the extent to which popular construction of 'tradition' is compatible with the ideologies of globalization, especially how the former doesn't resist but facilitates the articulation of a certain 'modern' through these soaps. His exploration also reveals a gamut of interesting liaison between Latin America and India in TV programming which propels him to talk of a Third World historical condition that seemingly operates in shaping consumer cultures in the broader terrain of the non-West. This, in his view, promises to generate new understanding of how images and narratives travel across continents and how possible cartographies of late capitalism and post-modernity can be charted out through the study of TV serials. Modhumita Roy's chapter examines the intersection of 'fertility technologies' and the global outsourcing of reproductive labour to the less developed world. It argues that the recent breakthroughs in fertility technologies have opened up a 'brave new world' where women can now sell various functions of their bodies to produce a commodity; she has been reduced to a production machine, a 'factory' producing the human body shop's most precious product. This commoditization appears more 'normal' for women for women's bodies in general, and seems much less troubling when coupled with poverty. While women's bodies continue to be subjected to overt and covert forms of property holding, poor women's bodies are deemed even less human for after all they are the 'labouring' bodies of our society. In this backdrop, the outsourcing of reproduction has to be seen as wedged between two somewhat contradictory but linked anxieties: the growing concern over what is perceived to be rising rates of infertility, and, relatedly, to the panic over a sharply falling birth rate in the West. The essay examines a range of social, moral and legal questions including the changing meaning of the term 'mother', complication of the notions of family forms and national belonging as well as the ideology of genetic inheritance, fused as it is with ideologies of race, ethnicity, class and caste.

Manas Ghosh's chapter centres around the commercialization of cricket as a sport and its transformation into 'entertainment' as a media genre. The effects of the global media, and the market for entertainment that is consequent upon it, makes sports a marketable commodity; the chapter addresses the economics of this mediatization as well as the economy of cricket as a marketable commodity. Mediatization and its effects upon sport in general and cricket in particular is explored as a cultural process in this chapter.

Rajdeep Roy's chapter traces the establishment of a hero figure related to the 'underworld' as represented through popular Bollywood films. This is seen in the context of the emergence of terror as a marketable commodity: the composition, operation and influence of the 'underworld' is linked to the cross-national web of funding and control that emerges as Mumbai becomes the scene of communal disturbance. This process of the local reality playing itself out in a global context is represented through the study of a particular genre of film, which merges the documentary with stylized realism to create a contemporary idiom.

Sayantan Dasgupta's chapter captures the overlap of 'local-national-global' spaces by looking at various aspects of translation as a cultural process in the post-colonial Indian context. The author reads translation of regional literature as a site of contest where pressures of linguistic hegemony, decolonization, globalization and cultural imperialism are seen to negotiate among themselves. More specifically, the chapter predicates itself on the notion of 'translation as patriotism' and seeks to grasp how pressures of globalization in contemporary India have impacted the translation of vernacular Indian literature, and more particularly, Bangla fiction, into English. It also contends that translation in India has gone from a state-sponsored activity aimed at constructing a 'national' culture to a more 'marketable' exercise as reflected in the distinct 'boom' in the Indian Literature in English Translation (ILET) industry in the 1990s, when several private publishers were seen to take up ILET seriously, and probes the factors responsible for this visibility.

Ipshita Chanda's chapter considers Farah Khan's 2007 film *Om Shanti Om* in the context of a culture of viewership created by the Hindi film industry itself. Using classical Sanskrit aesthetic theories to read this film, the essay places it within a 'local' constructed through intertextuality, a 'local' that the inveterate Hindi film viewer inhabits, whatever be her actual location within the country or even outside it. The film's visual and situational/episodic texture is nested in Hindi films of the 1970s and the 1980s, and Khan's film utilizes, adds on and reinterprets this tradition as an individual utterance or parole within the larger langue. Though Hindi films are now a 'global' product, the 'local' they operate within is not, as our preface argues, a physical space alone. This chapter attempts to chart a locality of culture without attaching strictly territorial spatial dimensions to the concept, preferring instead to use a tradition as the location of habits of viewership and interpretation.

The starting assumption of Partha Pratim Basu's chapter is that while the part played by the vernacular press in raising the pitch of the majoritarian *Ram Janambhumi* campaign and inflaming anti-Muslim passions in Gujarat has already produced a formidable literature, it is no less important to look at the issue from the reverse, that is how the question of the rights of the minorities have been portrayed in the vernacular press of West Bengal, an Indian state which rightfully claims a liberal and pluralistic heritage. Constitutional stipulations need not necessarily correspond with popular perceptions of minority rights—which Prime Minister Nehru regarded as the touchstone of a democracy—and the regional press' critical role in shaping popular understanding of and responses to the same can be hardly overemphasized. To trace the vernacular media's discourse on the phenomenon, the author undertakes a synchronic as well as diachronic analysis by scanning the coverage of three momentous events—the Shah Bano controversy the 1980s, the riots sparked off by the demolition of the Babri Masjid in 1992 and the carnage in Gujarat in the wake of the Godhra massacre in 2002—in two top-circulating Bengali dailies.

Dalia Chakraborty's chapter focuses on the evolutionary course of medical advertisement—advertisement of tonics, health food and drinks published primarily in Kolkata-based print media between the closing years of the nineteenth century and the present day—to probe the interface of culture and commerce. As medicines turn into 'mass consumption items', and stress on the clients' health, strength, energy, vigour and youth becomes a key marketing strategy, the modernist preoccupation of self, identity and body in the public space, the author notes, creeps into the formulation of the advertisements. While bringing out the unmistakable imprint of globalization, she notes that in order to command the attention and trust of the target audience the advertisers go beyond citing testimonials by public figures or announcement of attractive offers; import of products from the West, recommendations of foreign doctors and manufacture/distribution by multinationals are increasingly played up. Simultaneously, a kind of Third Worldism also becomes evident with the canvassing for ethnic medicines or treatment at the *ayurvedic sala*s which boast of age-old indigenous therapies.

Finally, Nilanjana Gupta and Devlina Gopalan investigate the makeover of club culture in Kolkata, a distinctive component of the city's rich colonial heritage. While the original clubs such as Bengal Club or Calcutta Club, the authors maintain, were set up by the British to recreate the life of London society, their profiles changed after Independence; also, newer social and sports-based clubs such as the Lake Club or Calcutta Rowing Club came in to address the needs of the modern Kolkata *bhadralok*. Again, a new wave of change has begun to redefine club culture in Kolkata in contemporary times, especially the way the membership profile and the kind of events hosted are changing in clubs like Tollygunj Club. It also takes into account the new clubs like the Princeton Club or the Space Circle which have emerged to cater to the needs of the city's expanding business community and stage events markedly different from those in the more traditional clubs. On the whole, the chapter considers the reinvention of Kolkata's club culture in the wake of the emergence of a 'global' culture in city life.

Introduction

Borges' account of Menard's 'reading' of Cervantes' Don Quixote is both a definition of the act of 'reading' and a mockery of its excesses. We offer it here as an example of the practice of studying cultural process. The reader, like Pierre Menard, takes over the text: but the text also resists this takeover because it retains its boundaries. When it becomes the Quixote of Pierre Menard, unless the stages of its becoming are inscribed in it, it is, as Menard desires that it should be, *the Quixote itself.* Conversely, like the disgusted Menard who wanted to rescue the Quixote from what it had become, the reader who re-textualizes has in his mind, like Menard, a text which he thinks *ought to be.* In other words, he desires nothing but *the Quixote itself*: according to his will and idea. In sum, the chapters in this book replicate what Borges attempts to do with Menard, the Quixote(s) and Cervantes. They trace the inscriptions of reception/consumption and re-use of various texts in different media, and study them as situated processes. In so doing, the writers are careful of their own location as scholars of cultural process; they are also equally aware that the circuits of reception, consumption and re-use and the interrelations between them constitute the field we have designated as the 'cultural'. This field constitutes and is constituted by these relations between the 'reader', 'receiver', 'consumer' and 'user' as well as the 'producer' of texts. The detailed investigation of these relations in specific contexts we have named 'Studies in Cultural Process'.

Notes and References

1. Roland Barthes, '"From Work to Text" *Revue d'esthetique*', in *The Rustle of Language*, trans. Richrad Howard (Berkley and Los Angeles: University of California Press, 1971/1989).
2. Ibid., pp. 56–57.
3. G. Deleuze and Guattari quoted in Mieke Bal, 'From Cultural Studies to Cultural Analysis', in *Interrogating Cultural Studies : Theory Politics and Practice*, ed. P. Bowman (London: Stirling, Virginia and Pluto, 2003).
4. Ibid., p. 56.
5. Catherine Belsey, 'From Cultural Studies to Cultural Criticism?', in *Interrogating Cultural Studies : Theory Politics and Practice*, ed. P. Bowman (London: Stirling, Virginia and Pluto, 2003).

6. Bal, 'From Cultural Studies to Cultural Analysis', p. 30.

7. G. Pollock, 'Becoming Cultural Studies: The Daydream of the Political', in *Interrogating Cultural Studies : Theory Politics and Practice*, ed. P. Bowman (London: Stirling, Virginia and Pluto, 2003), p. 125.

8. T.R. Lindlof and B.C. Taylor, *Qualitative Communication Research Methods*, 2nd Edition (Thousand Oaks, CA: Sage, 2002).

9. R. Radhakrishnan, 'Cultural Studies in India: A Preliminary Report on Institutionalisation'. Available online at http://www.cscs.res.in/dataarchive/ textfiles/textfile.2008-07-04.3578111600/file (accessed on 30 August 2009).

10. Ibid., pp. 9–10.

11. Ibid., pp. 7–8.

12. Ibid., pp. 11–12.

13. Ibid., p.15.

14. M. White and J. Schwoch, *Questions of Method in Cultural Studies* (London: Blackwell, 2006), p. 2.

15. Ibid., p. 4.

16. Ibid., p. 3.

17. Ibid., p. 6.

18. Ibid., pp. 6–7.

19. P. Bourdieu, *Outline of a Theory of Practice*, in *Cambridge Studies in Social Anthropology* (Geneva: libraire Droz 1972 and London: Cambridge University Press, 1977).

20. Gary Tartakov and Vidya Dehejia, 'Sharing, Intrusion, and Influence: The Mahisasuramardin Imagery of the Calukyas and the Pallavas', *Artibus Asiae* 45, no. 4 (1984): 287–345.

21. J.L. Borges, 'Pierre Menard Author of the Quixote', in *Labyrinths and Other Writings*, eds Borges & James E. Irby (New York: New Directions,1962/1964), pp. 36–44.

22. Ibid.

Chapter 2

Jassi Jaissi Koi Nahin and the Makeover of Indian Soaps

Abhijit Roy

In the media reports and numerous internet forums discussing the television serial *Jassi Jaissi Koi Nahin* (DJ's Creative Unit, Sony Entertainment Television India, 2003–06), one could clearly see the audience sharing an air of 'freshness' about the serial before losing interest towards the end. Many suggested that the audience were greatly 'relieved' to have something that was not premised on the feudal domestic context. Some went to the extent of suggesting a 'paradigmatic shift' in programming in India.[1] In this chapter, I shall investigate how perceptions of originality and uniqueness are constructed in culture industries, and in what ways the existing ideological frameworks of a range of popular tastes are negotiated to create the 'new'. With respect to the particular serial under examination, the key aspects of concern will be the generic trope, the market, consuming patterns and the narrative. *Jassi Jaissi Koi Nahin* (henceforth *JJKN*) is particularly important in understanding what is projected as a novel tendency in popular culture, because the serial itself is thematically premised upon the idea of the 'makeover', one key form of 'change' that has found major currency in consumerist perceptions. I refer to the much hyped 'makeover' of Jassi, the central character, but not only that. A close examination reveals that with *JJKN*, at least two aspects of Indian television got a makeover: marketing strategies and the genre of soap. If one includes the context of adaptation from the Latin American telenovela, itself possibly a process of makeover, and the transformation of image that 'SET India' as a channel accomplished through the serial, one possibly has a chance of examining 'makeover' as a much wider category in studies of global consumerist cultures. It was indeed interesting to note how the serial triggered a context of reception in which the central thematic of the bodily makeover resonated with a broader thematic of societal and representational changes. The opportunity here for Television Studies is to examine how the public domain is suffused with a certain image of TV itself as a change-agent and how interfaces between global television formats conjure the 'local' narratives of transition. The location of issues in gender at the centre of this theatre makes the whole investigation a major imperative of our times.

The name of the serial, translatable as 'no one is like Jassi', is catchy and apparently paradoxical. If the nervous, fumbling and 'less-than-ordinary looking girl' is so rare or almost an exception, how do the viewers identify with the character? Why did the channel at all venture into the project of making a popular programme based on an exceptional character while soaps have always notoriously relied on stereotypes? The fact that there are indeed millions like Jassi is what indeed creates the paradox and should draw our attention to, more than the nomenclature, a certain mode-of-address that characterizes consumerist propaganda, 'commercials' for instance. We can look at the way the SET India website introduces the serial:

> 'Jassi Jaissi Koi Nahin' is the story of a sweet, simple and less-than-ordinary looking girl with a heart of gold and a persevering nature. Born to ordinary middle class parents, Jassi's simplicity and clumsy ways make everyone fall in love with her. Like millions of middle class Indian girls Jassi too aspires to make a mark for herself with her never say die attitude yet gullible nature. The show brings out the eternal conflicts between the middle class and the high society; simplicity and glamour; artificial facades and true inner beauty. 'Jassi Jaissi Koi Nahin' has all the ingredients to make it connect well with its viewers—a contemporary setting, a metrosexual male and fashionable socialites contrasting with a plain, ordinary girl aspiring to be accepted in high society and determined to make it big one day. The show is sure to click with the Indian viewers, as most of them with similar values will strongly relate to Jassi, her aspirations, her attitude and her never-say-die spirit.[2]

So, in spite of Jassi being like 'millions of middle class Indian girls', appearing in a show that depicts 'eternal conflicts between the middle class and the high society' and that 'is sure to click with the Indian viewers, as most of them with similar values will strongly relate to Jassi…' the show is called 'there is no one like Jassi'. This, I think, is typical of the global consumerist rhetoric of advertisement that, to generate mass acceptance, always addresses the individual as exception. Advertisements, in this era of atomization of brands and fragmentation of desiring consumer-subjects, always address the consumer as somebody who is special. The pleasure that the consumer is expected to derive from such mode-of-address is of 'exercising my *individual* choice' and of 'not being influenced' by advertisement. This is like a fallacious statement: 'since you are upright, self-made, not so easily impressionable, and hence different from other consumers, you will buy this'. Valorizing multiplicity and difference surely amounts to a logic of enhancing consumption. I think *JJKN* is the first major Indian television serial that overtly engages with the typical mode-of-address of the post-liberalization advertisement, thereby making each of the 'millions of middle-class Indian girls' identify with Jassi in one's own 'exclusive' way, virtually raising the impression 'there is no one like me'. The earlier two major phases of Indian soaps, the first of the 'progressive melodrama' and the second epitomized by the *saas–bahu* tales, both largely called for identification with the 'common'. *JJKN* is not doing anything different, but is aligning to a new language. The suggestion here is not only of the difference between a *Kyunki Saas Bhi Kabhi Bahu Thi* (*Since mother-in-law was also daughter-in-law once,* Balaji Telefilms, Star Plus, 2000–08) referring to generational continuity or *Kahanii Ghar Ghar Kii* (*The tale of every household,* Balaji Telefilms, Star Plus, 2000–08) claiming universality and a *Jassi Jaissi Koi Nahin* that claims exclusivity, but of an emergent framework of representation that claims to be novel while trying to keep ideological ties with 'tradition' somewhat intact. It will be my precise argument that the formal changes presented by *JJKN* are of the specific order of the 'makeover', a change of face and the corresponding 'image' in the public domain, but never a paradigmatic shift in ideology, particularly vis-à-vis the institutions of patriarchy like family. In fact sustenance of a certain order of 'tradition' appears to be a key condition in discourses of makeover. We will have occasion to discuss the politics of the makeover later in detail. It is more important at this point to delve into a brief analysis of the earlier generation of television serials in India which majority of *JJKN*'s audience bracket as clichéd compared to *JJKN*'s novelty.

The bunch of serials mostly produced by Balaji Telefilms,[3] and shown on the channel Star Plus, representing a major and influential trajectory of soaps in India, has been considered as a site of 'traditional' Indian values, a constituency of the Feudal to be more specific. I think it is more important to investigate the extent to which the popular construction of 'tradition' is compatible with the ideologies of globalization and how the former doesn't resist but facilitates and crucially conditions the articulation of a certain 'modern' in this soaps. We should undertake, with reference to questions of gender, the rather unconventional task of mapping the vision of the 'modern' in these serials in an effort to complicate the popular binary of tradition/modernity and to draw attention to the way the post-colonial negotiates the global. 'Tradition' is projected as synonymous with performance of Hindu religious rituals in these serials. The seemingly positive charge of progressiveness that emits from the performance of these rituals can possibly be related to a certain upsurge of conservatism all over the world during globalization as a *reaction* to the radical movements and ideologies of the 1970s. I propose that such 'traditional' practices bear more an impression of 'opposition' than of 'universality' and can therefore indeed be projected as signifiers of a new radical vision of the modern. The institutions of modernity like the nation state can, on retrospection, thus emerge in these discourses as perfectly compatible with what was previously projected as the 'pre-modern'. The popular image of the Indian software engineer in the US working with the idol of a Hindu deity on the computer desk, the image and appeal of the radical Hindu *sanyasin* like Sadhwi Ritambhara and the whole phenomenon of Smriti Irani, the main actress in *Kyunki Saas Bhi Kabhi Bahu Thi* (henceforth *KSBKBT*), joining the Bharatiya Janata Party, the political wing of the Hindu right in India, can all possibly be related to such an oppositional (even militant) self-image of the tradition that wishes to address a desire for modernity.

The portrayal of women in a somewhat 'naturalized' masculine sphere of property and law in these serials aspires to negotiate a modern that demands active participation of women in the new social order. But such roles are always as a rule determined by the horizon of possibilities offered by patriarchy where the transformative capability of the woman is limited by the finitude of masculine stereotypes. In *Saarthi* (Neela Telefilms, Star Plus, 2004–08), the woman heading the Hindu joint-family *Business*, in control of a substantial share of family property, becomes eligible for inheriting the family business shares only because her husband is physically challenged. She keeps consulting her husband on business issues and keeps reminding us that she is not ambitious and merely deputing for her husband. In *KSBKBT*, Mohini's fight for property for *herself* is taken as a signifier of a degraded woman. The point is to note how a patriarchal feudal order, dependent upon manufacturing the consent of women, presents itself as perfectly capable of accommodating 'modern' desires of women for which it suggests some 'formal' adjustments to itself. However, these adjustments stop short of questioning the basic structure of traditional institutions, implying that such questioning is absolutely unnecessary. The whole architecture of a predominantly feudal set of familial relations in these serials strains to negotiate the contemporary forms of global corporate culture, but nonetheless articulates strongly what it thinks the ideal way(s) of this negotiation. A major proclamation is made particularly on the post-colonial state-form. *Hindutva* as a global tech-savvy rightist ideology should be related precisely to this dimension of the global in India and probably broadly in the non-West.

Let us look at the crucial juncture of *KSBKBT* when Tulsi's daughter-in-law files a case of marital rape against her husband, Tulsi's son. We see Tulsi going against her family to support her daughter-in-law and fight for what she calls the 'self-respect' of her daughter-in-law and the family in general. This is not simply a situation of a traditional woman taking an exceptionally radical position on contemporary issues but of clearly articulating that such a position is quite possible from within the confines of a 'traditional' family, that the ideal *bharatiya nari* can easily come out with such a 'radical' reaction. Tulsi, in addressing the issue more in terms of 'family prestige' than of woman's rights and identities beyond family, makes it a point to reckon Hindu marriage far superior to the legal system of modern democracy. She clearly mentions in the court room that the Hindu scriptures are sensitive to women's self-respect, while the juridical order of the modern nation state is not. Her questioning of the authority of the state significantly allegorizes *Hindutva*'s claim to the post-colonial state-form.[4]

The category of 'feudal family romance' in the Hindi popular cinema, proposed by Madhava Prasad, as making possible the pleasures of 'romance' (in the sense of heterosexual couple formation) under the patronizing gaze of the feudal family, can effectively help us understand the ideology at work here. The joint business family doesn't really mind (in fact it actually promotes) the romance with consumerism as long as a social machinery for pre-empting the threateningly secessionist potential of such romance is at work.[5]

The television apparatus itself has been theorized as a grand site of the 'familial' particularly because of the TV's primary location at home. We would see that *JJKN* and some of the new serials inspired by it, featuring for the first time in a major way the 'young woman in the workplace' and apparently providing a relief from the typical *saas–bahu* sagas of the family soaps, don't deviate much from the familiar moral boundaries of the earlier form of soaps and especially from a certain trope of the familial that so canonically defines the genre. In *JJKN*, we see a middle class educated woman, Jassi, moving out of the confines of a protective home and caring family to join a fashion house. The complexities of interpersonal relationships in the corporate office look quite similar to the *saas–bahu* hostilities in the family soaps; Jassi and Mallika play the sisters-in-law; Armaan and Raj the brothers like Ram and Laxman; the head of the fashion-house, 'Gulmohar', is cast in the role of the grand patriarch of the family. The crucial turns in the narrative also centre around Jassi's 'romantic' relationship with her boss, Armaan, and around the broader question of inheritance of the family business and property through heterosexual couple formation. Along with this are allied ups-and-downs in the relationship of Jassi and Armaan with Mallika, Armaan's fiancée, with Aryan, the villainous brother of Mallika, and with Pari, the wannabe secretary of Armaan. Though the family located in Jassi's home is shown quite often, the main constituents of the drama—the wedding, the runaway bride, the makeover—all sprout basically in detours away from the 'actual' home, in the office, the theatre for the performance of the familial. Even when Jassi has severed all connections with Gulmohar, her characterization in the new incarnations of Jessica and Neha revolves around either what is happening back in Gulmohar, or around her new business ventures.

As the serial progresses, however, more non-office (though not completely domestic) situations arise, like situations with Purav and her brother, situations in Nainital. However, I want to focus more on the implications of the cultural space of 'workplace' here, since that is the space that the audience thought gave them fresh air to breathe, rescued them from the self-enclosed claustrophobic homes of the erstwhile soaps. The office becomes more a site of personal than official relationships, echoing all the components of a perfect home drama. Interesting to note here is the ways in which a certain idea of the 'corporate family' (as in 'STAR Parivar' or 'Sahara India Parivar') has gained currency in India in the recent years. The familialized corporate space, the 'workplace', in the new global order, may be looked as the symptom of a process of reproducing the values of the family in the space of the emerging capital. We are attempting to study this process here, with its implications for the local production of a globalized culture, and the consumption of that culture by the television audience. The 'workplace' has to be projected as the new 'home' for the emergent workforce not only because of the extended working hours but more crucially because of the need to cast the woman in a variety of her traditional 'familial' roles, albeit in a displaced manner, in the face of increasing requirement of women labour for the circulation of global capital.

So the distinction between a *KSBKBT* and a *JJKN* is not that between tradition and modernity, but primarily between two spaces, both of which can articulate visions of the modern compatible with global consumer cultures. I don't mean that the location of gender in these two sets is the same since both advocate versions of 'women's empowerment' within the structure of global capital. There is in fact serious difference between the 'housewife-at-home' and the 'unmarried woman-at-office' modes of serial drama as the latter doesn't go by the former's majoritarian logic of conceiving the nation. *JJKN* is more close to the inclusivist logic of consumerism. Also from the perspective of gender, *JJKN* looks more radical because it reflects the aspiration of home-bound women to work outside. However much the housewife, in the earlier generation of serials, tried to fight for women's domestic rights from within the home by occasionally inhabiting the public space, they failed to address the aspirations of women (particularly of the middle class) working outside home.

25

The links between the domestic/private sphere and the woman were underlined in such representations, contrary to the increasing dilution of such ties in the era of multinational capitalism. From patriarchy's point of view, the advantage in the representation of woman in *JJKN* is that the 'ontologically feminine' can now be shown as productive both at home and in the office. This representation appeals particularly to the middle class, a class empirically much larger in the audience than the feudal-turned capitalist. But more than the numbers, what is at play here is the relation between the middle class and realism in general.[6] The middle class has emerged in globalization as possibly the only class that can be *narrativized*, in the sense of figuring a journey towards the global nation, as the only body that mutates and makes possible a *realistic* story of transition.[7] The realism at work draws its force not only from the reality of the middle class joining the machineries of capitalism, climbing up the ladders of economic success and social prestige, but also from a certain unreality, in the earlier brand of serials, of still sustaining an exclusionist and majoritarian vision of nation and culture in an essentially inclusionist (though highly hierarchical in terms of representation of class) consumerizing world.

This doesn't mean that identification with the Balaji brand of earlier serials would diminish. 'Identification' as a spectatorial engagement is almost always with spaces of both aspiration and experience, none of which has substantially waned from the earlier brand. The aspirational identification, I would say, has found a major continuity in elite settings and high life, the signifiers of a certain mode of consumption. But what was for long, despite a huge difference in class, a major basis of experiential identification with the Balaji brand of serials for the middle class, that is the reality of familial tension between the in-laws, had to come of age after sometime. This is not only due to the social reality of increasing female participation in sectors of global business like the Information Technology (IT), faster erosion of traditional joint families or rise in single parenthood, but also due to two other reasons. One is definitely the near-exhaustion of narrative possibilities of this mode, connected with the logic of fast obsolescence that operates possibly most intensively in highly competitive markets like that of popular software. The other is a visibly fast and steady increase in youth programming in television across the world. Shanti Kumar and Michael Curtin suggest that in post-liberalization India '...an emerging satellite class of young women is exploring progressive notions of femininity via new forms of popular media that the process of transculturation makes available to them'[8] and 'popular media texts around the world increasingly feature female characters that resist or reformulate conventional gender roles...'.[9] So, the currency of the middle class, youth and the young woman in particular across the global televisual-scape, both in terms of figuration from the perspective of production and of experiential identification from the perspective of spectatorial engagement, has created the context in which the realism of this brand of serials works. Kumar and Curtin particularly examine the workings of the global music industry in India. But the way they locate in this industry 'heterogeneous articulations of race, class, gender, sexuality, and age, even as they perpetuate the homogenizing tendencies of capitalist institutions and patriarchal power'.[10] A broad correspondence can be drawn possibly with the genre of the soaps in India. This correspondence can be figured in the Indian soaps featuring, e.g., alternative sexualities (Maddy in *JJKN*; Bobby in *Big Boss*, Season 1 and Rohit in *Big Boss*, Season 3 (the Indian version of *Big Brother* that claims to be '*Har Daily Soap Ka Baap*', that is 'the father of all soaps'). Also, television formats and genres can fit well in this theorization as inhabiting a truly 'trans-cultural' space, from which *JJKN* itself emerges as the adaptation of the globe-trotting Columbian telenovela *Yo Soy Betty La Fea* (RCN, Columbia, 1999–2001). *JJKN* does appeal a lot to the 'Indian young women' and there must have been a certain degree of deviation from the original Columbian version in narrative strategy to fit the Indian audience. However, the serial particularly signposts the futility of the logic of a predominantly inward, territorialized or 'national' vision of the social in explaining the concerns of the emergent generic form. The point to be noted is that the earlier form of soap opera in India could be understood to an extent through this approach. For instance, the idea of *Streeshakti* (women's power) or 'tradition' in discourses of *Hindutva* did lend a certain charge to these serials. One should not, however, have much difficulty in discovering the 'colonial modern' in the genealogy of such an apparently 'rooted' idea of the national.

Without considering *JJKN* as largely inhabiting a transcultural space, we cannot possibly understand the implications in the serial of the confused and substantially demasculinized hero like Armaan, the representation of the global milieu of fashion industry, the travels of the story to Malayasia and Mauritius or the makeover of Jassi. This of course is not to suggest that the ideology of the earlier form doesn't at all resonate with the femininity represented here. In a sense *JJKN* appropriates the erstwhile configuration of the 'traditional' woman in the form of Jassi's religious and patriarchial family (the *saas–bahu* relation is particularly amicable here), Jassi's recurrent praying in front of *Babaji*, the exotic 'Indian' marriage between Armaan and Jassi and so on. But these signifiers of a constructed Indian-ness are not only used to define the home but are also largely relocated to the domain of the 'woman-at-workplace' as the moral basis of a work culture. The feminization of the genre of soap, due essentially to the familial context of soap narratives and television's reception at home, is sustained this way. Once the home is defined, enter the world; the woman is shown as being at the centre in both the spaces. Without a *KSBKBT*, we cannot possibly understand a *JJKN*. In the serial *Radha Ki Betiyaan Kuch Kar Dikhayengi* ('Daughters of Radha will do something in life', NDTV Imagine, episode dated 14 February 2008), as Radha accompanies her three daughters on their journey from 'outside' to the city of Bombay, aspiring for college admissions and jobs, she says: 'I pray that your wishes come true. Education after all happens to be the only weapon for us middle-class people.' As the daughters bow to offer the mother *pranam*, the word 'education' raises a double semantic register in the context of the *mise-en-scène*: education that tells you how to be 'traditional' (respect to elders, etc.) that the daughters have gained at home and the education of the modern institution of the school ('weapon') that gets one jobs or helps one struggle in the job market. This I think is precisely how the 'woman' as a sign operates in *JJKN* and such serialized fictions, in the neoliberal popular discourses connecting the middle class, the workplace and youth (especially female youth), carrying semantic imports from both the home and the world.

A brief analysis of the connection of *JJKN* with the Latin American genre of telenovela can help us further complicate the interplay of class, gender and realism in the popular discourse of makeover that *JJKN* presents. One can't help remembering here that *Hum Log* (Doordarshan, India's public television, 1984–85), the first 'mega-serial' on Indian television, had an interesting connection with the Hispanic 'underdeveloped' world. In the era of state television's first major commercialization drive in India post-1982, the attempt was to negotiate the emergent market through a balance between melodrama and progressivist messages of the welfare state. *Hum Log*, modelled on the Mexican television format of the 'progressive melodrama', was a great success leading to a whole set of such serials in Doordarshan in the 1980s and early 1990s. *Hum Log* reflected the state's effort to intensify the family planning campaign as part of the international drive by bureaucrats and social planners to devise educational soap operas.[11] Though the 'progressive melodrama' sub-genre is usually taken to be congruent more with a Statist mode of programming, the Market played a crucial role in shaping the concerns of the genre, as I have also suggested elsewhere.[12] *JJKN* definitely offers a context that is very different from that of 1980s India, but it should be a serious question on the agenda in Indian television studies to ask why the legacy of the media culture of another Third World context plays a key role in conceiving popular serial narratives at two key moments of Indian television, when debates on societal transformation in general were raging. While a thorough examination of this is outside the premise of this chapter, I would simply draw attention to the discourse of 'progressive-ness' or broadly of 'development' that is associated with the popular reception of *JJKN*. *JJKN* doesn't appear to the majority of the audience as providing only entertainment, but appears to be also offering a role model for an ordinary middle class girl or for an earning woman, exemplary roles for daughters-in-law and mothers-in-law, the lessons of corporate success, etc. *JJKN* and a host of subsequent television serials seem to have been guided by the ethos of 'corporate social responsibility' in the context of a popular culture that is primarily defined by privately owned satellite television channels. The 'don't drive drunk' message from Maruti or Shabana Azmi's call for saving two buckets of water in the Surf Excel commercial exploits the popular idea about such responsibilities, but more than that, it is a certain texture of the consumerist popular that enacts the mapping of the Nation in terms, albeit displaced, of the Welfare State.

Particularly from the 1980s in India, the concept of 'development' widens to incorporate the agency of the corporate sector, with television exhibiting this semantic expansion much more than any other medium. Television, or Media in general, becomes the grand agent of benevolence and epistemological superiority embodying a perfect collaboration between the state and the market, enacting the original historical liaison between democracy and capitalism. This of course became more transparent in the 1990s in India, obscuring the somewhat intensified social power that the Statist values have enjoyed post-liberalization. From the 1990s the Indian State seems to have shrugged off the self-image of being essentially antagonistic to the codes of the market, an image it used to nurture largely till the 1980s. But the crucial history of the mutual constitution of these two ideological frames manifested in a certain super-image of the Media (in the 1990s) most certainly started post-1982 with the commercialization of public television and has since been demonstrated most efficiently by television itself. That the juridical redefinition of the 'public' in India in the historic Supreme Court judgement in 1995 involves television, does not, in this sense, seem to be a coincidence.

All this is to suggest that the transnational legacies of both the 'progressive melodrama' of the 1980s and that of the contemporary youth-based serials like *JJKN* can be connected to possibly explore the consistently renewable images of both the state and the market and the dialogues which they engage in to incessantly produce fictions of 'change'. The Indian Post and Telegraph department's release of a stamp[13] featuring Jassi can be read probably as an acknowledgement of *JJKN*'s quasi-Statist claim to social welfare. The popular perception of television's (or soap opera's) notoriety in injecting 'bad education' is seen to be largely non-existent in the serial's marketing and reception as we mark books titled *Jassi's 7 Steps to Success* and *My Jassi Colouring Book*, both in English and Hindi, brought out by Popular Prakashan, Mumbai, and mobile phone games that teach managerial skill this way: 'Armaan has an important meeting. Jassi realizes that he's forgotten his file. Help her reach the file in time and deliver it to him before the meeting begins.'[14]

The *KSBKBT* mode of serial drama undoubtedly also emitted socially relevant messages, but its notion of development was truncated by a certain exclusivist (hence limited) vision of the nation and by a certain valorization of the *re-contextualization of the old*. *JJKN*'s appeal, on the other hand, is predominantly of a 'present' that one aspires to *arrive at*, that is of 'change', key to any discourse of development. *JJKN* is also connected more closely with the present in its eruption from a contemporary history of transnational television-format exchange. It should be however simultaneously remembered that the reception of a foreign format evident in *Hum Log* is of a different nature than that in *JJKN*; *Hum Log*'s was an instance of copying or remolding a form rather than of a direct purchase of rights of a particular programme as is the case with *JJKN*. It was only at the end of 1980s that the telenovela industry in several countries of Latin America started experiencing an important transnationalization, mainly through export.[15]

One possible way of understanding the relationship between Indian soaps and the Latin American telenovela can be an analysis of the common conditions of the developing nations or engaging in a comparative study of the socio-economic contexts and trajectories of the particular countries in question. The other could be examining the particular context of transnational exchanges in the global media industry, its history and politics. We will very briefly try to engage here with the latter to stick to our agenda of the implications of *JJKN* in signposting a new mode of televisual programming in India. So much is common between the soap and the telenovela, that one is tempted to use the terms interchangeably, especially if one analyzes some key elements in the narratives of both genres, like complicated family relationships, love, hatred, murder and jealousy. But we are more interested in the specific inclinations of the telenovela for understanding *JJKN*'s claim to novelty in the Indian context. Rosalind C. Pearson tells us about some features that appear 'new' compared to the Indian experience of the earlier generation of prime time soaps. These are, first, the theme of 'the poor striving to be rich', then, the fact that they are 'closed narrative texts' with 'a very definite beginning, middle, and end', and finally, that their lengths vary 'from as little as three months to occasionally, if successful, perhaps eighteen to twenty months'.[16] While some of these traits can be clearly associated with *JJKN*, it is worth remembering that the telenovela itself is not homogeneous and has evolved over time. The standard reaction of *JJKN* being more 'realistic' than the earlier *saas–bahu* form perhaps has its roots, as Pearson suggests, in a certain 'cultural verisimilitude' peculiar to the telenovela, 'something that roots telenovela narratives in *the* world, a world separate from fiction but identifiable immediately with what is real'. In the Mexican instance, Pearson suggests, this is particularly the case, with the 'new-style' telenovelas seen on TV Azteca towards the very end of the last century.[17] Clifford also confirms that 'Since the arrival of TV Azteca on the scene, the telling of stories in this genre has acquired a new perspective, often called "realism." All telenovelas are now classified into two general kinds of melodrama: Cinderella style or realist.'[18] Pearson complicates such binaries by invoking the findings of a survey where:

> [T]hese 'new-style' telenovelas were viewed by focus group members as "more realistic" and as entertaining enough to 'make you forget reality for a moment.' Themes were considered to be 'realistic', but the handling of situations was not. What is presented and identified as a lifelike situation to begin with then moves into exaggeration and extreme circumstances, moving it away from reality. Themes hitherto considered unsuitable for telenovelas—or indeed television in Mexico—are now being treated, but at the same time, the stereotypical good and bad characters are still present.[19]

This means not only that the Cinderella-type can combine with the realist mode, but also that the themes hitherto considered unsuitable, like homosexuality, can be easily narrativized within a conventional representational framework.

The diegetic world of *JJKN* from all these perspectives seems to be resonating with a variety of narrative and formal concerns of telenovela. The category of 'identification' that is so centrally invoked in all discourses of realism in the telenovela seems also to have worked fine in case of *JJKN*. And that precisely is what seems to pose a problem to understanding international flow of television formats, something that Daniel Mato tries to analyse in relation to the 'strong local flavor of numerous Colombian telenovelas'. He concludes:

> *The success of telenovelas, to a great extent, depends on the possibilities of audience identification with the characters, stories, actors, and actresses...*
> It is a point that appears also in press statements by many others, such as the Colombian Fernando Gaitán, author of two of the most

successfully exported Colombian telenovelas, *Café con Aroma de Mujer* (exported to seventy-seven countries) and *Betty, la Fea* (exported to thirty-five countries), who recently declared that 'Betty confirms that one has to make telenovelas of one's own country, with its own particular humor' and later added that 'one has to be clear in that the success of the telenovela depends on the degree of the collective's identification with the characters' (...). Producers point out that because of this, it is highly risky to homogenize products when thinking of potential export markets.[20]

According to Mato, the main concern of the big production networks and the distributors of the telenovelas is the respective internal market and not export, as the latter adds a meagre 'plus' to the internal revenue. He underlines the importance of internal advertising sales and particularly mentions in this connection *Betty La Fea*, *JJKN*'s source-text as 'the most watched telenovela in recent times', that according to him was a 'record breaker in Colombian advertising history'.[21]

The question therefore is that if the telenovela form is so territorialized and rooted to the local, what explains its global success? Mato makes an insistent effort to show 'how contemporary processes of globalization present territorial marks—they have a transterritorial character but are in no way deterritorializing'.[22] He can therefore perfectly explain the popularity of telenovela in the US, which has a considerable Hispanic audience, or the large-scale production of telenovela in Miami, near the Cuba border. But when it comes to explaining the phenomenon of the telenovela's export to as far as India or Japan, the argument looks strained, and takes recourse to an ahistorical account of 'emotion' as the 'common denominator of the human species'.[23] I think that the telenovela's capacity of being adaptable to various national situations may be definitely attributed to its deterritorializing dimensions that play at the level of the global currency of consumerism at a certain moment in the career of capital. Mato's meticulous theorization certainly helps us comprehend the reasons for the telenovela's heterogenous forms at the site of its production and even for its movement across territories that have cultural affiliations to the Hispanic. For explaining a wider and a qualitatively different form of circulation, one possibly needs to undertake an arduous investigation into key transnational actors like the one that Mato himself significantly hints towards, that is the advertising industry. The investigation in this area must delve into a comparison between Jassi and Betty in the light of the present global history of consumerism located in the intersection of various identities: middle class, youth and women. Also, the stories of 'transformation' that may have a special currency in the third world or in the non-West, significantly shape the trajectory of such an interconnected history. The 'under-developed' can definitely be traced territorially in the geopolitical map of the global but this does not imply that it has to be antagonized with the deterritorializing trope. The point is to note how new territorialities are being produced through a deterritorializing process and how 'indigenization' becomes a key route for globalization.[24]

Not only Mato's category of 'emotion', but other much-cited factors behind the movement of telenovela also exhibit what we could now name 'the territorial dimension of deterritorialization'. This becomes clear if we examine the gamut of reasons for the import of the telenovela even in the US, the very space that rightly gives Mato the opportunity to exemplify 'trans-territoriality'. Bielby and Harrington suggest 'research on the international market for television points also to the importance of technical quality, visual style, and other aesthetic considerations in attracting audiences'. They refer to the host industry's need and desire for novelty and also to the imperative that 'any new product be framed as familiar or otherwise knowable in some way' in the context of an industry where 'the commissioning or purchase of new programs is made in a business context of ambiguity and uncertainty'.[25] This interplay of the 'familiar' and the 'new' in the imported cultural product is I think particularly suggestive of a certain negotiation between the territorial and the deterritorializing. They also refer to the 'declining domestic profits' as a result of which, network decisions are increasingly oriented to the global marketplace. This finds an interesting parallel in the widespread perception of a recession in Indian television industry before importing the format of *Yo Soy Betty La Fea*, as Kunal Dasgupta, the CEO of Sony TV, said in May 2002: 'The reality is many producers don't know what to do. Advertisements have been reduced due to a recession. Sony did not want to be encrypted, but ads could not sustain us.'[26] In fact in the financial year 2002–03, the state of national economy presented a rather gloomy picture with the GDP growth at 4.4 per cent, lowest since 1996. Novel products are desperately sought at such times. One should note that the crisis of the media industry is not an *essential* and universal reason for import of the telenovela in a national context. However, the interesting parallel between the Indian and the US contexts in this regard indicate a possible condition for transnational movements of media formats across the world. What, however, followed almost immediately, fortunately for *JJKN* (or may be it didn't matter, since the plans to adapt *Betty* by SET India was surely already in place by that time), was an overtly euphoric atmosphere about the Indian economy in general, with the July–September period of 2003 recording a growth of 8.4 per cent (*JJKN* started on 1 September 2003), the sharpest since economic liberalization in 1991.[27] In India, the time of *JJKN*'s launch was also the time when the Bharatiya Janta Party was starting to launch its campaign based on what it called the 'feel good factor' in the country in the run-up to the parliamentary election of 2004. Despite the party's booming confidence that it would sweep the elections, the election results proved to be playfully deceptive. This however draws our attention to the complexity of India's electoral politics where the perception of the upwardly mobile 'educated' middle class and an equally middle-class news-media, with their eyes glued to the signifiers of global consumerism, emerges as unreliable for understanding a democracy that predominantly requires a rural franchise. *JJKN* quite evidently features a self-enclosed world, where the middle class, terribly amnesiac about its leadership role in many social movements for change, only wishes to look *up* and never down.

So, even when we compare territorial considerations for import of the telenovela, there emerge categories that are truly global in their affiliation to the Market. Jesus Martin Barbero, in his analysis of the cultural changes introduced by modernization in Colombia and their link to the development of media, talks of 'spheres of life that, in the images of the media, are being affected most profoundly by contemporary transformations. There are five: family, consumption, free time, public opinion, and aesthetic tastes'. No doubt India has also experienced key changes in these areas. Among the key strategies for inciting consumption that we can connect to *JJKN*'s backdrop of a fashion house, and youth cultures, Martin-Barbero refers to fashion and 'the new heroes that emerge with the elevation of youth—from sport and music idols—as the supreme value of the modern'.[28] A specific question regarding territoriality should, however, be asked at this point; put simply, the question is: why Latin America as the key source of import? Or why not the US, that has established itself as a key exporter of other genres like the game show? Bielby and Harington refer to a key reason: 'One of the biggest drawbacks to the export potential of US serials is their open-ended format. While providing a large pool of episodes for buyer selection, with long-running, domestically successful products, the text literally becomes unwieldy to export.' The *Bold and the Beautiful*, by far the most popular soap export of US, one of the tops in India too, has a relatively short history and is a half-hour programme.[29] The shorter length of the telenovela becomes increasingly compatible with multinational capitalism in its portability, its compliance with the logic of obsolescence, its non-dependence on long-spanning audience loyalty in the age of sharp competition within the media industry, etc.

The categories like realism, identification, emotion thus can definitely have territorial affiliations, but would remain largely inconceivable unless we examine their global connections. One significant characteristic of the telenovela that makes the genre contextual in the global marketing network is its ability to generate a large degree of public participation. Interactivity, however, has long emerged as the basic condition for consumerist television, to realize its goal of enhancing consumption. The genre that perhaps most effectively exploits the interactive potential of the televisual network is Reality TV. Classically, the genre of soap has been averse to the practice of directly addressing its network of audience, as is evident in the earlier mode of serial fiction in India. *JJKN* in this sense presents unique marketing strategies corresponding more to the telenovela form which 'offer audiences a type of public forum that frequently allows the articulation of citizenship and political emancipation'.[30] The idea of the 'Jassi Pals' club on the internet, '*Jassi Dekho Zen Jeeto*' contest, and connecting Jassi with fans of 13 different cities live through video-conferencing by an arrangement with Reliance WebWorld[31] are fitting examples. But much more effectively than this, *JJKN* triggers intense debate in the public domain through blogs, groups, and other forums on the internet. Topics include whether and in what sense *JJKN* is 'fresh', why should Jassi, if at all, be considered an icon for middle-class earning woman, what constitute a perfect work culture, whether Jassi's turning 'beautiful' through makeover does justice to the uniqueness of the serial in addressing the problems of an ordinary-looking girl, whom should Jassi choose to marry between Armaan and Purav, is it fair on Jassi's part to run away from her marriage ceremony, and so on. What was particularly noticeable in the reception of *JJKN* is a relatively high degree of male viewership compared to the standard soap that has been defined as a predominantly 'feminine' genre. Traditionally constructed as the tracker of public spaces, that is as avid watchers of news, the male television audience became inquisitive about the genre when the woman enters the 'workplace', hitherto seen as the 'male' territory. Such a high degree of viewer participation in the public domain, however, cannot be simply attributed to the specialty of narrative (*JJKN* does deploy a fair number of clichés as we have suggested earlier in this chapter), but should be connected to the serial's unique strategies of selling and branding that Indian television witnessed for the first time. In fact *JJKN* is the first major instance in Indian television of phenomenal success in terms of advertising sales and branding despite a TRP that can be at best called decent. As Rohit Gupta, SET's then Executive Vice President (ad sales and revenue management) reminds us: 'There is life beyond numbers'.[32] The Colombian original of *JJKN* also demonstrated the importance of advertising sales in the internal market. Mato gives the figures:

> …an advertising minute for this telenovela billed at US$15,600, so each chapter represented US$124,000 in advertising sales for RCN… This is without taking into account the product placement strategy whereby products were promoted within the telenovela itself, which in this case reached extremes never before seen in this genre. Indeed, *Betty* was a record breaker in Colombian advertising history.[33]

So is *JJKN* in India, and its success has to be measured more in terms of advertising sales, product placement, brand equity and the ability to trigger vibrant debates in the public domain, than in terms of the number of people consistently watching the serial. This is due to a certain ethos of advertising in the era of late capital that lays more value on the possibility of reaching the 'target audience', the product's compatibility with the serial's theme and the ripples in the public sphere, than simply on the numbers actually watching. Within a few weeks of its launch, *JJKN* drew 12 sponsors that included cosmetic brands like 'Fair and Lovely', 'Emami's' beauty secrets and 'Ayur cold cream', the young woman's scooter 'Kinetic Zing', the new generation drinks that claim to combine health and fun like 'Frooti green mango', elements of partying like 'Royal Stag' whiskey and 'Hutch' mobile phone connection, the new 'must carry' gadget for the youth. Besides these were brands that associate themselves with tradition, like 'Mother's recipes' and 'Ashirbad' salt. Even when it is something like 'Moov', the ointment for joint pain, that doesn't apparently connect with youth cultures and traditional legacies as other brands do, the advertisement shows the daughter in her teens advising her mother to apply the ointment. The point is not to establish thematic correspondence with every sponsoring brand but *JJKN* definitely offered the sponsoring brands a new thematic space, hitherto largely unexplored by Indian soaps, to associate with Jassi's public image of a young, simple and intelligent woman working in a key sector of global business with strong roots in 'tradition'. 'Godrej No.1' soap made Mona Singh, the actress playing Jassi, its brand ambassador for she was a 'simple, unpretentious, down-to-earth girl-next-door'. Godrej soap that tops in the soap-market of Punjab and Haryana,[34] may have also valued the actress's real and fictional surnames, Singh and Walia, both of which can have Punjabi origin, and particularly Jassi's family that is deeply religious. The 'Jassi' brand has in fact a great appeal as it proliferates over a wide range of products: Jassi games by Nokia N-Gage and Ericsson, cellphone ringtones featuring the soap's title music, the '7 steps to success' and other books mentioned earlier, music albums, Jassi dress line by the designer chain Satya Paul, the 'Kurkure' advertisements featuring Juhi Chawla as Jassi (interestingly, Kurkure had earlier spun advertisements around the character of *Tulsi* from *KSBKBT* and *Anarkali* from the original film 'Mughal-e-Azam')—testifying to *JJKN*'s uniqueness in being successful as a brand without drawing a not-so-exciting TRP. The serial, however, didn't let go of any opportunity for raising its visibility; one important strategy was inculcating popular ingredients: hit 'item numbers' from Hindi films, cameo appearance of the Hindi film hero

Saif Ali Khan as the character he plays in the film *Hum Tum*, singers from the popular show *Indian Idol*, the detectives from the serial *CID* investigating Jassi's alleged murder by Jessica Bedi, etc. In fact *JJKN* took the trend of a programme's referring to other programmes on the same channel, pioneered by *Star Plus*, to a new height. If we particularly consider *JJKN*'s role in rescuing SET from the rough patch of much lower popularity than *Star Plus*, the reason why *JJKN* became the site of cross-programme references becomes clear. By presenting an idea of the oeuvre of programmes on SET, *JJKN* acted as a space for showcasing the channel as a whole. It is interesting to note how a particular programme can become a sort of logo for the 'new look' of a channel. This becomes evident in the battle over scheduling that at this point was fought between Sony and Star Plus. Clearly it was the second incarnation of *Kaun Banega Crorepati* (*KBC 2*, hosted by Amitabh Bachchan), offering double prize money than the previous season, that was projected as the logo of Star Plus. The episode of the long awaited and much-hyped wedding of Jassi with Armaan was slated on the very day and time of the return of *KBC 2*, in August 2005. One smells planned scheduling here particularly because the *JJKN* episode was a one-off Friday episode breaking the show's usual Mon-Thu weekly cycle and *KSBKBT* on that day was to appear first on a Friday as by that time some of the popular serials of Star Plus had been stretched to Fridays. As the channels fight for ratings, the possibility of intertextual references by the mascots of the channels increases.

But above all this, the success of the *JJKN* brand lies in its craft of 'product placement', the practice of integrating products in the narrative. *JJKN*'s grabbing the Apsara Film Producers' Guild Award for the 'best marketing for an entertainment product (film and television)'and the EMVIES award for the 'best media marketer' in 2004 owes a lot to the serial's publicity campaigns and the ways it made possible placement of a wide range of products in narrative. Sony tied up with 'Maruti Suzuki Zen' to show Armaan gifting Jassi a Zen in one of the episodes. A contest titled *Jassi Dekho Zen Jeeto* was also launched that gave the viewer a chance to win a Zen by answering a question related to the story in February 2004. Kellogg's, through a special arrangement, was connected with a particular moment in the narrative. In one scene, while Jassi the intelligent girl is busy doing calculations in the office, Kellogg's Corn Flakes intrudes right into the scene with its catchline *'Dimag Chalega Nahi, Daudega!'* (Your brain will not walk, it will run!). One of the officials of Mindshare, the brand manager for Kellogg's said:

> When we were looking for something innovative to do in the media, only *Jassi Jaisi Koi Nahi* came to our mind because all the other programmes which come on television are 'saas-bahu' sagas. On the other hand, *Jassi...* was one programme where the story was about this intelligent girl and it well fitted with the tag line of our brand. [35]

Another such vignette was woven around Intel which was soon to change its brand tagline from 'Intel Inside' to 'Leap Ahead'. Other brands placed strategically in the narrative are L'Oreal, 'Mauritius Tourism' and VLCC.[36] Special occasions such as Jassi's wedding and makeover provided immense opportunity for product placement. During the wedding, Armaan donned a dress designed by fashion designer Neeta Lulla and Jassi's jewellery came from 'Neelam Jewels'; the wedding as a whole could also be taken as a promotional for tourism in Malayasia. The widely publicized makeover provided the greatest platform for product placement, connecting almost every aspect of the makeover to various fashion designers: Mehra Kola (make-up), Seema Khan and Ruksana Karimi (outfits), Nandita Mahatani (footwear), Shaan Khanna (bags). Other brands associated with the makeover were 'Raih—Hair Reinvented' (hair), Kaya's Skin Clinic (skin), Bausch and Lomb (glasses)—all this under the supervision of Queenie Dhodhy, *Mid-Day*'s makeover guru, and Vandana Luthra of VLCC.

The practice of product placement lends a certain order of 'plausibility' to the realism of a show. When the products, tangibly used on a day-to-day basis or desired as elements of consumption, are represented in a text as major agents of change, not only the 'change' looks real, but the whole *mise-en-scène* of the text starts emitting an air of corporeal genuineness. It is not only in this sense, but in many other, that *JJKN* can be said to offer an impression of 'real life'. What immediately comes to mind is of course the genre of Reality TV which, I propose, provides a definitive legacy to the particular form of soap opera we are discussing. While it is not possible to discuss all the elements of Reality TV within the premise of this chapter, one does not need much effort to see the correspondence between *JJKN* and the reality shows' ability to inspire audiences to discuss and participate in the show. This has sometimes been indirectly provoked as can be traced in *JJKN*'s phenomenal currency in the media, particularly in the new media. In fact *JJKN* seems to be the first soap in India to have extracted such huge discussion and debates across cyberspace. This possibly points towards the show's uniquely large viewer-constituency among internet users, among the net-savvy new middle class in general. The impact on this section of people can be gauged by the case of India-Forums, which was started by a fan of *JJKN* as the website containing daily update of the show and gradually, flooded by numerous comments and queries, went on to become the first internet discussion forum on Indian television.[37] Fan activity was also directly invited by the programme through, as mentioned earlier, '*Jassi Dekho Zen Jeeto*' contest, the '*Jassi Pals Club*' and the unique promotional strategy of making Jassi meet fans from 13 cities of India 'live' through 'Reliance WebWorld', all being instances of using the New media. In the last instance, viewers could advise Jassi, through SMS, website submissions and video messages, on whether to forgive or punish Armaan for his deviousness. Viewers could also tune in to Red FM in Mumbai, Delhi and Kolkata to advise Jassi. The best messages were selected by Red FM and played out across all their stations. The lucky winners were treated to an exclusive chat with Jassi herself through video conferencing organized by Reliance WebWorld on 11 January 2005. The response was overwhelming: 'Reliance WebWorld' got 600 video messages, SET website received 10,539 messages, and the number of SMS messages were 26,676. The majority of respondents voted for Jassi's revenge over Armaan.[38] As the subsequent development in the narrative shows, Jassi indeed becomes relatively assertive after this and her demure and nervous demeanor begins to change gradually. This was a sort of character-makeover for Jassi in the new year of 2005, 'Naya Saal Nayee Jassi' (New Year, New Jassi), as the SET India press release says 'thanks to the support and advice of millions of fans across the nation'.[39] This clearly parallels the convention of participants returning to a reality show by 'public demand', or more generally the 'democratic' practices that the Media purports to stage in the era of consumer-driven satellite television. The publicness that we witness here has to be connected to the quasi-state functions of the media in general: news media particularly, in their invocation of daily polls on hot topics and reality TV as well.

The way the serial tried to construct the public image of Jassi was indeed unique as a marketing strategy. This can particularly help us understand the element of the Reality TV genre in it. The whole idea was to establish Jassi not as a character but as a 'real' person. The convention of pasting a face on a billboard or playing on TV a scene from the show with the name and character was avoided. Instead, the plan was to create an intrigue, an exciting buzz around the character: Who is Jassi? What does she look like? The execution took the form of little blurbs where anonymous people were talking to each other about Jassi. Also used were flash mobs, PR, email marketing, radio, SMS, leaflet messages, etc.—all of which successfully built up curiosity around the character and the show. The biggest mystery of all was of course the identity of the actress playing Jassi. SET strategically created a veil of secrecy around the actress, and fuelled media speculations, a strategy it sustained for months after the show started. Press conferences were organized in which Mona Singh would appear and pose as Jassi; 'Jassi' appeared at the Miss India pageant and anchored a part of the Lakmé India Fashion for SET's telecast;[40] 'Jassi' was interviewed live in the studios of Aaj Tak and Red FM, was felicitated by the Delhi Secretary's Association;[41] people ('flash mobs', as they are called in advertising jargon) were seen holding placards for Jassi at the domestic airports of Mumbai, Delhi and Kolkata at the time of key flights in the mornings and the evenings;[42] before her wedding, in select areas of high footfall, musical bands were placed with placards inviting everybody to come to the marriage ceremony;[43] flash mobs also travelled with pink umbrellas in local trains discussing Jassi[44] and gathered in marketplaces calling 'Jassi' loudly.[45] Thus if one looks closely at the marketing strategies of *JJKN*, especially at those that aim to create a large degree of public participation, one does find interesting clues to how the realism attached to the character of Jassi and the show in general hinge upon the Reality TV format. One can trace the legacy of such strategies in the generic scope of the telenovela which tries to use the audience-network unlike the traditional soaps. Crucial to our understanding should be an overarching transformation in the Media in general that has undergone what can be possibly called a 'reality-tv-isation' in all respects. Jesus Martin Barbero, investigating the Columbian cultural scenario from which *JJKN* sprouts, suggests:

> Public opinion appears as the transformational sphere executed in/by the media. In replacing the public plaza or the bar as 'fora' for debate and for citizens' opinions in the past few years, the media, through surveys and opinion polls, have become the most powerful 'source' of public opinion. These forms of knowledge are eloquent about the capacity for construction (and imposition) of opinion. But they tell little about inquiry and debate over the diversity of opinions that are really at play in society.[46]

Surely the processes of formation of public opinion and the complex of injuries inherent in them remain largely unrepresented in the frenzy of public participation that is premised in the format of limited multiple choices offered by the Media. Both reality TV and telenovela are engaged in representing such configurations of public opinion. But the publicness attached to contemporary television has brought many genres, for instance the new soap opera and the Reality TV, closer to each other in many other respects. Graeme Turner draws our attention to some of the emerging similarities:

> There are explicit links between soap and the construction of reality TV narratives, and they were often discussed publicly by those working in television production. The closeness of these programs' relationship with and appeal to their audience is not difficult to explain either. Both formats are especially sensitive to audience responses to narrative lines over time; both are usually produced sufficiently close to broadcast time to enable these responses to influence at least some narrative lines or outcomes (although this is much more the case for *Big Brother*, of course). Both aim at a high level of cultural visibility and interest; despite their serial nature, they must aim at becoming in some sense public 'events'. (Soaps tend to do this only from time to

time rather than constantly, but they still work at regularly constructing such moments.)[47]

Talking of generic transactions at play in *JJKN*, we should also not
ignore what has been called 'Makeover TV', a sub-genre within the Reality repertoire, which has gained tremendous popularity particularly
in the US and in Britain. This is not only because *JJKN* tells the story
of Jassi's gradual makeover from an ugly duckling to a swan, from a
nervous secretary to a confident entrepreneur, but also because *JJKN*
resonates with Makeover TV's primary concern for staging the societal
theme of 'transition' through complex engagements with categories of
gender, body, middle class, publicness and realism. Reality shows involving celebrity-participants, to a certain extent, make famous people look
ordinary, engaging in a reverse order of makeover, a practice opposite
to the usual practice of making ordinary people famous. However, reality shows that do not feature celebrities contain a strong element of
makeover in the *dominant* sense. This includes a considerable degree of
grooming that the participants have to undergo in their journey through
the glossy lanes of fame towards acquiring the status of celebrity. But the
makeover genre, as in programmes like *Extreme Makeover* (ABC, 2002),
makes the bodily makeover the very centre of all attraction and aspiration, with much investment in the exhibition of the gradual mutation
of the body under the guidance of cosmetic surgeons, beauty experts,
dieticians and fashion designers, and in a concurrent discourse on makeover as facilitating 'confidence', hence an increased social acceptability.
The idea of the makeover has been so popular that it has extended to
sites other than the human body, instances ranging from home (*Extreme
Makeover: Home Edition*, ABC, 2003), to recipes, toys, pets, gardens
and financial planning. But surely makeover of the human body, particularly of the female body, remains the iconic representative of the
genre, something that should concern us here. Dana Heller looks at the
genre as the 'paradigmatic example of reality television's prominence and
far-reaching mass appeal'.[48] Caroline Dover and Annette Hill connect
the makeover genre to lifestyle programmes in a way that must remind
us of *JJKN*'s primary location in a fashion house and obsessive concern about dress and beauty.[49] The peculiar mélange of a fairy tale-like

transformation and a representational style that claims to be 'real', probably give these programmes and the likes of *JJKN* a quality of 'faireality tales', as Bratich terms them.[50]

It is in these contexts of global consumerism, marketing strategies, audience networks, family, middle class, urban youth, earning women, realism, identification, emotion, Indian soaps, telenovela, Reality TV, and the makeover sub-genre, *JJKN* has signposted a set of new trajectories in Indian television and has been able to present an all-pervasive discourse of makeover. The point is to note how the serial makes possible deployment of the idea at multiple levels of social register and how a study of its ideological, stylistic and generic legacy calls for a semantic expansion of the idea. The bodily makeover of an ordinary-looking young woman definitely remains at the centre of the narrative, but the discourses associated with this makeover seem to derive their arguments from a larger societal order of conceiving 'change', of negotiating the emergent orders of gender politics, class identities, nationhood, citizenship and publicness. At a time, when India's economy was increasingly being projected by the new globalist incarnations of the Indian Media as booming with unprecedented growth rate (judged as capable of bringing 'welfare for all' through the misleading indices of the sensex), when the political alliance ruling at the centre was trying to trickle a certain 'feel good' impression down to all spheres of public life, when the debates on women's beauty, body, sexuality and autonomy, pitched with issues of representation in the face of globalization, had drawn tremendous popular interest (particularly after the 1996 Miss World beauty pageant in Bangalore[51]), when a tech-savvy new middle class had more or less ossified its self-image based on patterns of consumption, and when a certain form of home-drama was coming of age, appeared *JJKN*. The idea of 'change' that *JJKN* presents remains to be understood in the light of these historical trajectories.

What we can suggest from our limited survey of some of the representational tropes that lend their ideological contours to *JJKN*, is that the pleasure of witnessing the gradual unfolding of a makeover is always accompanied by the pleasure of being a possible *object* of makeover. Since it is the woman who is mostly made over in such shows, she, as Kathryn Fraser suggests, '...must be able to imagine herself in both images, as simultaneously the subject *and* object of transformation'. Fraser further argues: 'Such dialectic can be understood as determining women's narcissistic relation to consumerism: commodity acquisition, which usually distances subject from object, is here conflated. The woman, it seems, is incapable of separating herself from the commodity she buys.'[52] While this can shed some light on the possible reasons for the woman's identification with and a seemingly realistic look of *JJKN*, the broader politics of the makeover seems to have been articulated in the way Mary Ann Doane theorizes the relationship between femininity and consumer cultures. She suggests:

> Commodification presupposes that acutely self-conscious relationship to the body, which is attributed to femininity. The effective operation of the commodity system requires the breakdown of the body into parts—nails, hair, skin, breath—each one of which can constantly be improved through the purchase of a commodity.[53]

But more than only consumerism, it is the key location that the woman has to occupy almost as a rule in narratives of societal transition that is at stake here. It is my precise argument that the central thematic of the makeover in *JJKN* derives much of its appeal from larger discourses of makeover that have a significant dimension of continuity of the old; in fact that is the very condition for a transformation to be called 'makeover'. In the popular discourse on the makeover of Jassi, the person *basically* doesn't change; it is only the look and the public image that undergo a transformation, though the latter, we are always reminded, has an effect on the person underneath. But the transformation of the underneath doesn't bring about a basic change in the person in the sense that the person's basic beliefs and values, that is one's faith in tradition and the 'roots' of one's identity are not affected. The underneath changes only as far as the 'surface', the terrain of the contemporary, demands. The reverse is also no less true in the sense that the mind requires to endorse certain consumerist propaganda to endorse the makeover of one's body. The politics of the makeover is not premised grossly on the body–mind distinction that hinges upon the distinction between nature and culture. In the case of the makeover, these categories are thought to have an interconstitutive relationship, *to the extent consumerism permits such a relationship*. If a certain dimension of the 'change' in the mind, hence of the contemporary, is reflected through the change in the made-over body, another dimension of non-change, of tradition, also lends itself to the same body. The idea of the 'true inner beauty', mentioned by SET in its webpage on *JJKN*, that gained great currency in popular discourses on Jassi's makeover, plays precisely this role of representing the order of non-change or of allegiance to 'tradition'. 'Inner beauty' or for that matter 'true self' that the makeover claims to bring out is nothing but a displaced idea of an abstracted tradition that the person going in for a makeover should stick to. When it was suggested by many that Jassi was already quite visibly beautiful and her pre-makeover look almost seemed like a masquerade, the reference was to a certain traditional notion of beauty attached to salwar-kameez, long hair, coyness, faith in religion, family and social hierarchies in general. But this was not enough for a global corporate workplace where the masculine gaze demands a different attire and make-up. It is only through the mediation of consumerism's transformative capability that the 'incomplete' woman can become perfect for joining the global workforce of transnational capitalism. The popular critique of the makeover in the public domain suggested that it was unfair on the part of the serial to push Jassi for a makeover because that went against what was anticipated as the message of the serial: that an ordinary 'ugly' girl can make it big in the corporate world. But we tend to forget that the serial does exactly that. The less-than-ordinary ugly-looking girl does make a fortune out of her life *only when she decides* to change her looks and thus shed her ordinariness. The most crucial ability of such a girl should be to transform herself from 'such a girl' to a beautiful confident woman. The story was never meant to be about an ugly girl succeeding in life but about how a girl, ordinary in all respects, can succeed *only by transforming* herself in certain respects. And since she never *basically* changes, the allegation of deviation doesn't really hold good. The ability to align with the values of a consumerist ethos—adjusting to circumstances generally—was always there in Jassi and it is precisely that potential, coupled with her ability to resist change at certain levels, that defines a key aspect of her character. The overlapping nuances of change and stability in contemporary tales of transformation are therefore what make a complex of subjectivities compatible with the inclusivist ideology of consumerism. The female subject, as she carries the home to the world, has to play the special role of bearing the burden of representing the array of negotiations between tradition and modernity. But her agency is significantly limited by the patriarchal definition of beauty and womanhood where her desire for the makeover becomes a desire to be desired. This, however, should not be underestimated since the orchestration of such desires within serial narratives offers the first major instance of representing the middle-class earning woman on Indian television and of creating a scope for debating this in the public domain effecting a necessary politicization of this representation. Beyond the tale of women, the makeover discourse becomes a tale of societal transformation that cannot present itself without bringing the woman to the centre of its narrative.

Notes and References

1. 'Viewers are relieved to find an ordinary girl as the central character—a welcome change from glamorous and wealthy heroines that have become soap opera staples.' (Deepti Priya Mehrotra, 'Jassi—India's New Icon!'Available online at http://www.boloji.com/wfs2/wfs286.htm, accessed on 1 September 2007). Seema Pherwani comments in indiantelevision.com ('Jassi Bids Adieu; Long Overdue but No Denying her Impact', available online at http://www. indiantelevision.com/special/tellyscope/y2k6/may/tscope15.htm, accessed on 1 September 2007): 'All said and done, the primetime soap adapted from the South American telenovela format of *Betty La Fea*, did fantastically well not just for the channel but also defined a paradigm shift in terms of programming on the general entertainment channels' and 'Going back in time, trying to really analyse the success story that was *Jassi*. I think the serial came at a time when television seemed to be at the mercy of saas-bahus.' See also the article by Sangeeta Barooah Pisharoty ('Plain Jane Jassi a charm for Sony', *The Hindu*, Delhi, 20 October 2003):

   Despite having 'saas-bahu' flavoured large family soaps like 'Kkusum' and 'Kutumb', the channel was not doing so impressively against Star

TV's gamut of family-oriented serials. But in the first week itself, 'Jassi Jaissi...' made an impressive opening with a rating of 3.6 on that Sunday and consistently climbed the ratings chart to reach 4.2 by the following Thursday.

2. See http://www.setindia.com/shows/shows_inside.php?id=14 (accessed on 5 May 2004).
   This particular passage has been reproduced in numerous websites. See for instance the serial's 'daily update' page on india-forums.com: http://www.india-forums.com/topic_index.asp?FID=5 (accessed on 22 July 2005).

3. Balaji Telefilms Private Limited is a media production company based in Mumbai, primarily owned by the Kapoor family, the most famous face of which is Jeetendra, the Hindi film star from the 1980s. Conceived and produced by Ekta Kapoor, Jeetendra's daughter, its soaps are sometimes called K-serials, since almost all of them have names starting with the alphabet K.

4. I am grateful to the 'Women and Media' project of School of Women's Studies at Jadavpur University, Calcutta, for helping me with valuable information on these serials and particularly to Nandita Dhawan for sharing her insight on the topic.

5. Madhava Prasad, *Ideology of the Hindi Film: A Historical Construction* (New Delhi: Oxford University Press, 1998), pp. 30–33.

6. One of the major categories that emerges in the popular discourse on *JJKN* is its realism. Everybody from the anonymous blogger to the writers in media was of the opinion that *JJKN* was more realistic than the 'K-serials'.

7. In this connection, one can look at the way post-Liberalization Hindi popular film narrativizes the middle-class mediaperson hero and represents mobilization of a middle-class public in a film like *Phir Bhi Dil Hain Hindusthani* (Aziz Mirza, 2000) or *Nayak* (Shankar, 2000). For a detailed treatise on the issue, see Abhijit Roy, 'Live(li)ness and Network Publics in Post-Liberalization Indian Popular Films', *Journal of the Moving Image* 5 (2006): 86–110.

8. Shanti Kumar and Michael Curtin, '"Made in India": In Between Music Television and Patriarchy', *Television & New Media* 3 no. 4 (2002): 346.

9. Ibid., p. 347.

10. Ibid., p. 346.

11. See Veena Das, 'On Soap Opera: What Kind of Anthropological Object is It?', in *Television: Critical Concepts in Media and Cultural Studies*, vol. III, ed. Toby Miller (London: Routledge, 2003), p. 147 for an elaboration on how the educational soap opera, since the mid-1970s, was expanding its territory especially in the third world, from Peru through Mexico to India, and how a whole range of bureaucrats and social planners were involved in making *Hum Log* a reality in India.

12. See Abhijit Roy, 'Bringing Up TV: Popular Culture and the Developmental Modern in India', *Journal of South Asian Popular Culture* 6, no. 1 (2008): 38–39, for an account of how a serial like *Hum Log* remains largely inconceivable without invoking the transformative dimensions of the market in the emerging frameworks of liberalizing state policy and consumerist television's audio-visual form.

13. *The Times of India*, 'Jassi Jaisi on a Stamp? Just Ask'. Available online at http://timesofindia.indiatimes.com/articleshow/835209.cms, (accessed on 5 December 2004), quoted the Chief Post Master General (Maharashtra Circle) K. Noorjahan elaborating on the criteria: 'Special covers are generally issued on special occasions or to honour prominent personalities who have had an impact on people's lives socially and morally.'

14. 'Advertisement for the Game'. Available online at http://www.tonebase.com/ericsson_games/ (accessed on 17 May 2008).

15. Daniel Mato, 'The Transnationalization of the Telenovela Industry, Territorial References, and the Production of Markets and Representation of Transnational Identities', *Journal of Television and New Media* 6, no. 4 (2005): 426.

16. Rosalind C. Pearson, 'Fact or Fiction? Narrative and Reality in the Mexican Telenovela', *Journal of Television and New Media*, 6, no. 4 (2005): 400–01.

17. Ibid., p. 405.

18. Reginald Clifford, 'Engaging the Audience: The Social Imaginary of the Novela', *Journal of Television and New Media* 6, no. 4 (2005): 362.

19. Pearson, 'Fact or Fiction?', p. 405.

20. Mato, 'The Transnationalization of the Telenovela Industry, Territorial References, and the Production of Markets and Representation of Transnational Identities', p. 427.

21. Ibid., p. 428.

22. Ibid., p. 441.

23. Ibid., p. 441.

24. M. Madhava Prasad, 'Television and National Culture', *Journal of Arts and Ideas* 32–33 (April, 1999): 126.

25. Denise D. Bielby and Lee C. Harrington, 'Opening America?: The Telenovelaization of US Soap Operas', *Journal of Television and New Media* 6, no. 4 (2005): 393–94.

26. http://www.thefreelibrary.com/Video+Age+International/2002/May/1-p5222

27. See *The Telegraph*, 'Happy India Year…but Watch the Figures…', 1 January 2004.

28. Jesús Martín Barbero, 'Cultural Change: The Perception of the Media and the Mediation of Its Images', *Journal of Television and New Media* 4, no. 1 (2003): 87.

29. Bielby and Harrington, 'Opening America?', p. 393.

30. Mauro P. Porto, 'Political Controversies in Brazillian TV fiction: Viewers' Interpretations of the Telenovela *Terra Nostra*', *Journal of Television and New Media* 6, no.4 (2005): 355.

31. See the Media Release of Sony Entertainment Television (India) dated 11 January 2005. Available online at http://www.seindia.com/press

32. Sonali Krishna and Hetal Adesara, 'Jassi Jaisa Branding Nahi!', Indiantelevision.com's Media, Advertisement and Marketing Watch Special Report posted on 14 March 2005. Available online at http://www.indiantelevision.com/mam/special/y2k5/jassi_branding.htm (accessed on 1 August 2006).

33. Mato, 'The Transnationalization of the Telenovela Industry, Territorial References, and the Production of Markets and Representation of Transnational Identities', p. 428.

34. See *The Hindu Business Line* (Internet edition), Thursday, 12 May 2005. Available online at http://www.blonnet.com/2005/05/12/stories/2005051201760400.htm. Punjab incidentally also happens to be a major repertoire of male protagonists of the post-colonial Hindi popular film. Being the exclusive site of agrarian reform in India, a province that was partitioned during Independence and also the land from which a large diasporic community emerged, Punjab has consistently exhibited an ability to represent a certain idea of citizenship particularly in narratives of transition that requires to enact appropriation of modern desires by traditional institutions.

35. 'Jassi "Zen"s along with Kelloggs Corn Flakes', Indiantelevision.com's Media, Advertising & Marketing Watch, 23 February 2004.

36. VLCC, the company founded by Vandana Luthra in 1989, is presently India's largest health and beauty brand. The category of 'makeover' that we would soon try to analyze, can be interestingly understood by the company's vision published in the company's website: 'The guiding vision of VLCC Group is "Transforming Lives". By "Transforming Lives", we imply transforming self, spreading happiness and transforming future....VLCC's services provide holistic wellness, as a service, marrying scientific research and traditional therapies.' See http://www.vlcc.co.in/about.asp

37. See http://www.india-forums.com. This website, developed by a Kolkata-based software professional Vijay Bhatter, had a dedicated reader base of more than 30,000 in September 2005. Bhatter is quoted as saying 'Initial reason was my enthusiasm to discuss the serial *JJKN* which I believed was something different than other shows and started daily updating show. Soon we got so many users coming on to the site regularly checking the updates.'
Sujoy Dhar, 'When Jassi Meets Jassi in the Cyberspace'. Available online at http://www.bhatter.com/jassi/2005/09/when-jassi-meets-jassi-in-cyberspace.asp (accessed on 18 November 2006).

Abhijit Roy

38. Media Release of Sony Entertainment Television (India) dated 11 January 2005. Available online http://www.seindia.com/press
39. Ibid.
40. See http://www.gourishukla.com/id13.html
41. Krishna and Adesara, 'Jassi Jaisa Branding Nahi!'.
42. Viveat Susan Pinto, 'Jassi Jaissi Koi Nahin: Lessons in Marketing'. Available online at http://www.agencyfaqs.com/news/stories/2003/12/15/7889.html (accessed on 10 July 2004).
43. Chandrima S. Bhattacharya. 'KBC on Comeback Runs into (Bride) Jassi'. Available online at http://www.india-forums.com/forum_posts.asp?TID=40332& TPN=5 (accessed on 21 October 2005).
44. Deepa Kumara, 'A Case Study on the Indian Soap: Jassi Jaisi Koi Nahin'. Available online at http://www.indiabschools.com/sparkjournal_m6.html (accessed on 5 October 2005).
45. See http://www.tribuneindia.com/2004/20040912/spectrum/main3.htm
46. Barbero, 'Cultural Change', p. 88.
47. Graeme, Turner, 'Cultural Identity, Soap Narrative and Reality TV', *Television & New Media* 6, no.4 (2005): 421.
48. Dana, Heller, 'Reading the Makeover', in *Makeover Television: Realities Remodelled*, ed. Dana Heller (London: I.B. Tauris, 2007), p. 3.
49. See Caroline, Dover and Annette Hill, 'Mapping Genres: Broadcaster and Audience Perceptions of Makeover Television', in *Makeover Television: Realities Remodelled*, ed. Dana Heller (London: I.B. Tauris, 2007), pp. 23–38. One of the major propositions here is that the makeover genre, as it has evolved, has, unlike lifestyle programmes, started to premise itself more into the framework of 'entertainment' and 'emotional experiences' than 'lived experiences', something that brings programmes like *Extreme Makeover: Home Edition* closer to the form of family melodrama. This can connect interestingly to the correspondence that we are trying to establish between the reality genre of makeover and the new breed of soaps.
50. Jack Z. Bratich, 'Programming Reality: Control Societies, New Subjects and the Powers of Transformation', in *Makeover Television: Realities Remodelled*, ed. Dana Heller (London: I.B. Tauris, 2007), p. 17.
51. See Rupal Oza, 'Showcasing India: Gender, Geography, and Globalization', *Signs* 26, no. 4 (2001): 1067–95 for an account of how 'the pageant was considered iconic of globalization by the state and the organizers as well as by the opposition to the pageant' referring to a consistent and widespread topicality of the issues of woman's beauty and fashion at the very heart of popular debates on globalization in India.

52. Kathryn, Fraser, 'Now I am Ready to Tell How Bodies are Changed into Different Bodies... Ovid, *The Metamorphoses*', in *Makeover Television: Realities Remodelled*, ed. Dana Heller (London: I.B. Tauris, 2007), p. 184.

53. Mary Ann, Doane, 'The Economy of Desire: The Commodity Form in/of the Cinema', *Quarterly Review of Film and Video* 11, no. 1 (1989): 22.

Chapter 3

Foreign Babies/Indian Make

Outsourcing Reproduction in the Age of Globalization

Modhumita Roy

Baby Manji Yamada was born in India, carried to term in the womb of an Indian mother, Pritiben Mehta, who gave birth in October 2008. The baby was commissioned by a Japanese couple Yuki and Ikufumi Yamada. The embryo implanted in the surrogate was created with Ikufumi's sperm but the egg was bought from an anonymous Indian woman. Unfortunately, the Yamadas divorced before Manji was born and Yuki relinquished all claims to the baby. After fulfilling her obligation, the gestational mother, too, gave up any claim to Manji. The infant's birth certificate left blank the space where a mother is named. Instead there is a handwritten instruction which tells us that egg 'donor'[1] must not be identified.[2] Who, then, is Baby Manji's mother? And how might we identify the baby's nationality? Is she Indian or Japanese? Is her mother the egg donor, the woman who carried her in her womb, or the former wife of Ikufumi, who had commissioned the baby? Or all three? Due to the unusual circumstances of her birth, Manji, paradoxically has three mothers—gestational, genetic and social—yet legally she has none. Why, one might ask, should this matter? In the first place it mattered because Baby Manji needed documents to travel. She was identified as Indian by the Japanese Embassy which meant that she could not be issued a Japanese passport. The Indian authorities as well as some NGO groups raised a whole host of questions about the circumstances and legality of commercial surrogacy; the chief objection however was the ineligibility of Ikufumi to 'adopt' a baby girl as a single man. A six-month court battle ensued and Baby Manji was issued a 'certificate of identity'—a piece of paper granted to people who are deemed stateless. The identity paper, like her birth certificate, leaves blank the name of her mother and her nationality.

Baby Manji's case allows us to raise critical questions about a number of issues that relate to artificial reproductive technologies in general and commercial, outsourced surrogacy in particular. For one, it allows us to re-examine the ideology of genetic inheritance, fused as it is with ideologies of race, ethnicity, class and caste. Such surrogacy arrangements also complicate notions of family forms, of national belonging and boundaries. One should recall that the word 'nation' is derived from 'natio' (to be born) and our legal claims to citizenship are often connected to being born in a specific place. Will the outsourced, cross-border reproductions challenge such legal definitions? We might also ask how race, religion and caste systems, to mention just three, will now be calibrated for babies born to poor, non-white gestational surrogates for affluent 'white' infertile couples. But most importantly, we should ask whether contracts to 'make' babies (by egg 'donation' and via surrogates) can be legally enforceable. Last, but not least, whether property and contract laws are the most appropriate means of understanding these relationships.

The advent of commercial surrogacy or what has been less glamorously termed 'womb renting' is the latest in a series of New Reproductive Technologies (NRT) or Assisted Reproductive Technologies (ART) which are creating babies and families in unprecedented ways. They raise a number of moral, ethical and legal questions including the one with which I started—that is, our understanding of motherhood and the changing meaning of the term 'mother'. These medical innovations have fragmented reproduction dividing motherhood into discrete components—genetic, gestational, legal and social, rendering the gestation period culturally ambiguous and raising difficult ethical and legal questions about the concept of 'mother'. In the late 1980s Katha Pollitt wrote a series of provocative articles in which she pointed out, 'To a small and curious class of English words that have double and contradictory meanings...the word "mother" can now be added.'[3] Pollitt argued that with the advent of scientific interventions to 'cure' infertility the 'natural' realm of motherhood has been rendered problematic. Specifically referring to the famous (and at the time, the first ruling of its kind) in *Calvert vs Johnson* in which the presiding judge ignoring California law which deemed the woman who gave birth to a child as its mother, had ruled that Anna Johnson, the 'gestational surrogate' was not the baby's mother but was in the words of Judge Parslow, 'an environment'. The judge decided that the rightful mother was the woman whose fertilized egg Anna Johnson had 'merely' carried to term. In an earlier and equally infamous case of another 'surrogate' Mary Beth Whitehead, the judge had determined that the 'real' mother was a woman who had no biological connection with the baby.

The *Calvert vs Johnson* case was precedent-setting since it overturned, in a sense, the 'settled' definition of a mother in Western jurisprudence where 'of woman born' had been the standard for determining motherhood. In one of the most expensive and infamous inheritance battles that gripped late eighteenth-century Europe waged by the powerful Dukes of Hamilton against the Douglas family, the central question was whether or not the twin boys that Lady Jane Douglas had produced as her children were 'born of her body'—an essential condition for determining rightful inheritors of property. In the *Calvert vs Johnson* case where Anna Johnson was the non-genetic gestational surrogate, her lawyer had unsuccessfully argued that, 'the act of giving birth and the inevitable bond a woman makes to the fetus confers the rights of a mother.' The Calverts' lawyers took the opposite view—and one that ultimately prevailed in court and has now, in the marketplace of baby-making, taken root—that a couple's sperm and egg 'are the most precious thing they have…[it is] their genetic heritage'. And that by staking a claim to the baby, Anna Johnson was in fact attempting to steal the Calverts' child. Indeed, Judge Parslow concluded that a non-genetic birth mother was not a real or legal parent—'she and the child are genetic hereditary strangers'.[4] Referring to Crispina Calvert as the 'natural' mother, Parslow broke new legal ground by separating the gestational from the genetic. California's Supreme Court upheld the decision, defining Anna Johnson's role as a 'service' and protecting the interests of infertile couples, fighting for 'their' children. The California Courts, thus, became the first to hold that a baby's birth mother has no parental rights—that she cannot even be called a mother. She was 'a gestational carrier…a host in a sense' thus rendering the labour of reproduction incidental, reducing women to 'interchangeable fetal containers'.

Fertility technologies have also opened up a 'brave new world' of reproduction where women can not only sell various functions of their bodies to produce a baby, each component of reproduction—egg, sperm, embryo, womb, can be locationally separated.

As technology develops, the 'surrogate' becomes a serviceable (maternal environment) a production machine or factory for the purposes of bearing the 'customer' couple's child. One should point out that IVF etc. are not (cures) for infertility nor are they 'treatments' as such. They are, as Pollitt argues, methods, technological interventions with big price tags—to 'provide the wealthy but childless access to the fertility of others.[5]

My interest in the subject began with reading a news item in an English newspaper on a recent trip home to India. Under the intriguing heading, 'Foreign kid, Indian make',[6] was the picture of two rows of women dressed in surgical robes and face masks, huddling uncomfortably in front of the camera. They were collectively identified as 'women of Anand, carrying babies for couples around the world'. The author noted that 'womb renting' is a growing enterprise in India estimated now to be half a billion dollar a year business and counting. Alongside the more recognizable outsourcing of Information Technology (IT) in the form of 'call centres' and 'cyber coolies', India is also the centre of a ghoulish market for replacement body parts, primarily kidneys. It is reported that in India, the going rate for a kidney from a live donor is roughly $1,500, $4,000 for a cornea and about $50 for a patch of skin. To this ignominious list, one can now add labour of biological reproduction.

The brisk trade in eggs and wombs globally should be seen in the intersection of a number of factors: first, the increasing commoditization of the body, what Andrew Kimbrell calls the 'Human Body Shop'.[7] Trade in blood, tissue, DNA samples, egg, sperm, organs, body parts and other substances derived from the body some of which (like aborted foetuses, cord blood, placenta, etc.) is a worldwide profit making industry. There are now more than a dozen new ways to make a baby, all of which, as Jeremy Rifkin points out, 'involve sophisticated technological intervention into the reproductive process'.[8] He argues that 'in the not-too-distant future...the entire process—from conception to birth...will be brought under the watchful eyes of technicians and be made both an efficient production technology and lucrative commercial enterprise.' It is, he argues, 'the final stage of a five-hundred-year journey to enclose, privatize and commodify the Earth's ecological commons'.[9]

But perhaps more immediately, the outsourcing of reproduction ought to be seen as wedged between two somewhat contradictory but linked anxieties: one the one hand, the growing concern over what is perceived to be rising rates of infertility and relatedly, to the panic over a sharply falling birth rate in the West. Emerging in the 1980s infertility among married couples seemed to have reached epidemic proportions in the West. Though most experts concluded that no such epidemic existed the perception of an alarming climb in infertility remains palpable, aided in no small measure by sensational media stories and the active fear mongering by pharmaceutical companies. On the other hand, is the opposite anxiety of 'the population bomb' or the fear reiterated in every decade for the past 50 or so years that the darker races are having too many children who will eat through the planet's food supply, wreck the planet's fragile ecosystem and cause our collective demise. The anxiety over falling birth rates and the downward trend in population are often seen as a 'white' phenomenon occurring across the North American and European continents. Demographers have introduced the term 'lowest low' as a short hand to indicate that birth rates in significant parts of Europe have fallen below replacement rates of 2.1 which is widely accepted as necessary for maintaining a country's current population level. To encourage couples to get pregnant, governments are actively considering awarding—and some already giving out—cash awards. Overpopulation, of course, is associated with the global south where women for decades have been subjected to unwanted, experimental and sometimes illegal procedures including forced hysterectomies and sterilizations to stem the overpopulation of brown and black bodies. Globally speaking, if we put the two together—scarcity on the one hand, and abundance on the other—we will find no falling birth rate, only the panic over the paucity of very particular kinds of racial and ethnic reproduction; that is, the right kinds of babies are not being born in the right numbers. Enter, reproductive technologies which now make it possible to buy eggs from Romania, sperm from Denmark, implant the embryo in the womb of a destitute Indian woman and presto you have your dream baby which allows you to send out your announcement: 'Oh it's a Viking!' Reprotech baby-making via outsourcing is part and parcel of a familiar scenario of globalised circulation of commodities, trade and profit and the increasing outsourcing of labour to the third world. 'It is a win-win', says S.K. Nanda a former health secretary in Gujarat. The outsourcing is 'a complete capitalistic enterprise. There is nothing unethical about it.'

While surrogacy falls within the ambit of infertility treatments in the West, it is still relatively rare and relatively well regulated. Britain, for example, has outlawed payments for serving as a surrogate who may only be 'reimbursed' for her medical expenses. Commercial surrogacy is banned in most of Europe, though interestingly egg donations, especially from eastern European countries both for use in research and for fertility treatments are approaching alarming proportions. Surrogacy is banned in Japan, one reason why the then married Yamadas travelled to India to 'make' their baby. In addition, there are strict guidelines governing *in vitro* fertilizations in most parts of Europe. The British Human Fertilisation and Embryology Authority (HFEA) allow a maximum of two fertilized eggs to be implanted while the rest of Europe is moving towards a single embryo transfer. Italy bans the procedure altogether on religious grounds. Furthermore, under British and Canadian laws the woman who carries the child is considered to be the mother whether or not the child is genetically linked to her. With some variation this is true in almost all Western countries—'born of her body' still remains the criterion for determining motherhood.

India, by contrast, has seized the global moment and turned commercial surrogacy into a thriving industry. Rapid advances in 'reprotech', the pursuit of profits by intermediaries. Absence of regulations and regulatory bodies and liberalization of the economy has resulted in the mushrooming of ART facilities in India. In 2002, the Indian Council for Medical Research (ICMR) issued guidelines for ART thereby permitting surrogacy and opening the floodgates. A search of websites in 2004 yielded few that were 'devoted exclusively to *in vitro* fertilization (IVF) and fertility services'.[10] But a similar search two years later revealed that the number had more than quadrupled.[11] Rudy Rupak, co-founder and President of a medical tourism agency Planet Hospital, has seen his business grow from about 24 clients in 2007, the first year he offered his services to 100 in the first six months of 2008. And he is not alone in raking in the profits. India recognized medical care as an industry which allowed for financial arrangements such as raising capital at low interest rates, reduction in import duties on high-tech medical equipment, joint ventures with insurance companies. In one of the most significant and telling moves, the External Affairs Ministry introduced a 12-month medical visa for 'patients' and families and agreed 'to fast track clearance of medical patients...to facilitate medical tourism'.[12] The stage was set, in other words, for making babies for the global market for 'biological' children.[13]

So why has India become the fertility tourism capital? First, and most obvious, is cost. Surrogacy in the US is extremely expensive costing up to and sometimes over $80,000. The success rates of these procedures remain low so that the process has to be repeated several times. Health insurance companies are reluctant, when they do not refuse outright, to pay for the repeated attempts which can quickly add up to several million dollars. By contrast, in India the total cost of surrogacy, including medical costs, two trips to India, hotel, sight-seeing amounts to $25,000—a fraction of what it would cost in the US.[14] In commercial surrogacy arrangements the surrogate in the US gets somewhere between $10,000 and $15,000 for her labour, with brokers charging as much as $30,000 to $40,000. Indian surrogates get somewhere between $2,000 and $5,000—but since there is no regulating body or any oversight it is difficult to ascertain whether this money is actually paid out. As we know, the success rate of ART is low and the process has to be repeated several times with medical insurance paying a fraction or not at all for any of these procedures. It is little wonder that eager would-be parents have sought to reduce the labour costs and turned to outsourced, cheap womb renters in India who wait in line, primed and ready in their surgical masks and gowns.

In India, like other kinds of outsourced labour, commercial surrogacy is mostly unregulated; the few guidelines that exist are mostly observed by their breach. Indian Council for Medical Research guidelines, ignoring entirely any health concern for the surrogate, allows for the implantation of up to five embryos at a time, making womb renting in India more economically attractive: 'more bang for the buck' as it were. This disregard for maternal health is all the more egregious since India accounts for 20 per cent of the world's maternal deaths—six times worse than China and 8 times worse than Cuba. An estimated ½ million women die yearly as a result of pregnancy and childbirth and this rate, not surprisingly, is the highest among poor, illiterate women in rural areas: precisely the population from which surrogates are most often recruited. It is ironic—but tragically not surprising—that the very same ministry (of Health and Family Welfare) which propagates the state policy of 'one or two (children), no more' permits three cycles of embryo implantation for a surrogate. The 135-page 'Assisted Reproductive Technology (Regulation) Bill and Rules 2008' to be put before Parliament continues this dangerous disregard for the health of poor women. Not only does the draft bill legalize commercial surrogacy, it essentially reduces the surrogate/birth mother to a 'fetal container' by mandating that she will have to relinquish all legal parental rights to the baby. Furthermore, doctors and not the 'surrogate' will make medical decisions, including some of the most wrenching decisions about the pregnancy: foetal reduction or selective abortion to reduce the number of births.

Unlike other industries, however, where profits margins are announced with great fanfare, what one hears again and again (mostly from those who are making a handsome profit) that 'this is a mutually beneficial process' in which money is not the primary motivator. 'If you say it's a business of emotions, I would say yes…And if a female is just doing this for business, I think this is not the right thing to do' claims Naina Patel, the medical doctor turned innovative entrepreneur who is generally credited for having put India on the womb-renting fast track. She has become, of course, wealthy by conducting the 'business of emotion'. There is a glaring disconnect between the rhetoric surrounding the value of children and the cost of producing them. While commissioning parents and intermediaries are constantly attesting to the emotional value of children, (tagged 'priceless') even a cursory examination of compensated surrogacy reveals that these widely held sentiments are used as a factor in attempting to reduce the relative bargaining power of potential surrogates in order to safeguard profit margins. This is done first by rhetorically framing surrogacy as rewarding in and of itself, as a gift from one woman to another. In most studies, even women who mention money as their primary motivation for entering into the agreement feel the need to say 'I'm not doing this just for the money' at the same time that they express their displeasure with the amount being paid for the service rendered thereby laying bare the contradiction between the socially hegemonic ideology of 'priceless children' and the hard bargained, market-price of womb-renting services. Also noteworthy is the actual demographic background of surrogates which is in stark contrast to what is advertised in surrogacy websites which claim surrogates are solidly middle class and never on welfare. In her research Liza Mundy has found that that surrogacy in the US is divided into two kinds of women: highly educated, slim, economically and culturally privileged (white) women who provide the unfertilized eggs and a working-class 'overweight', stay-at-home mum, who may be a woman of colour who carries the pregnancy to term.[15]

But cost alone is not the reason why couples are turning to India for commercial surrogacy. There is also the question of control. In a recent National Public Radio programme report focusing on outsourcing of surrogacy arrangements, we are introduced to Julie, who is described by the reporter as 'a slim attractive woman in her mid-30s', and who after five failed attempts to have a biological child has turned 'in desperation' to paid surrogacy, a world away, in India. One reason for doing so is obviously economic: at Anand she is getting a baby made up for a fraction of the price she would have to pay in the States. But perhaps of greater moment, the degree to which in India the balance of power is tilted towards the buyer.

Poor, often illiterate women are recruited and kept ready by wealthy, well-educated, often medical professionals who act as intermediaries for their wealthy (often white) clients from the US, Europe, Israel, Japan and Taiwan. Dr Populo Rama Devi's state-of-the-art clinic, whose English-language website set up three years ago invites us to 'Come as a couple… Leave as a Family' is globlization incarnate. She imports all essential biomedical components from the high-tech zones of the 'first world':

her microscopes from Japan, incubators for the fertilized cells from Germany, the artificial culture medium from Denmark, the Petri dishes and test tubes are from the US, the pipettes and needles are from Australia. Her labour force, alone, is 100 per cent Indian. As an efficient global service provider she takes special requests into account—Hindu couples often ask for Hindu surrogates, a Muslim couple from Dubai had asked for a Muslim egg, and sometimes couples request vegetarians. The 'Criteria for Selection of Surrogates' handed out to all customers assure them that their planned children are all 'in good wombs'. Dr Patel, in her Akanksha Clinic, similarly assures her clients that the women she provides as surrogates are 'free of vices'. Dr Rama Devi's specifications for surrogates are precise: surrogates are between the ages of 22 and 30, no smaller than 1.60 metres, weighing between 50 and 60 kg, married with children, has regular menstrual cycles, free of sexually transmitted and hereditary diseases and has been tested for ovarian problems. Hormonal and chromosomal analyses are also provided. The surrogate, clients are assured, does not have parents or grandparents who died young (accidental deaths are not counted). The skin colour is not too dark, with pleasant appearance. Once the candidate has passed all medical examinations, she is selected via a final personality test. It should be noted that Dr Rama by her own admission has never found a candidate mentally unsuitable, opining that 'usually there aren't that many psychological problems in India'. Surrogates at her clinic are not entitled to terminate the pregnancy at her will. If she does, she is required to refund all certified and documented expenses, which, given the number of expensive (not to mention invasive) mandatory tests to which she is subjected, is far beyond the surrogate's means to reimburse.

This ability to control the surrogate is one of the most significant issues in outsourcing to India. The surrogates are kept under surveillance, living in supervised homes, their diets strictly regulated, tested regularly for disease and other medical conditions. They are also prohibited from having sexual relations during the time of gestation and have to undergo a battery of tests to ascertain the health of the foetus. Such close monitoring would not be legally permissible in the US. For all the syrupy sweetness of how much 'this' (that is the ability to have a baby) means to the women/couples in question, what is undeniably a major factor in outsourcing to India is the inordinate difference of power between the transacting parties. Julie's demand that the surrogate be tested for drug use, disease, etc., will be fully met by the surrogacy agency in India. In the radio report, Julie admits her anxiety about American surrogates: 'You have no idea if your surrogate mother is smoking, drinking alcohol, doing drugs. You don't know what she's doing. You have a third-party agency as a mediator between the two of you, but there's no one policing her in the sense that you don't know what's going on.' Her phrase 'there's no one policing her' tellingly reveals the nodal issue. It belies the many strenuous denials issued by clients and intermediaries alike and missed entirely by the media reports which make the surveillance sound like fun bedtime at Mallory Towers: 'Every night in the quiet western Indian city of Anand [Joy], fifteen pregnant women prepare for sleep... ascending the stairs in a procession of ballooned bellies, to bedrooms that become a landscape of soft hills.' The surrogates themselves, however, are mindful of the economic investment and confess, 'I am being more careful now than I was with my own pregnancy.'

Perhaps the most significant factor of all, surrogates have no legal rights in India. Commissioning couples in the West wish to bypass custodial challenges in court. The laws regarding commercial surrogacy vary from country to country in the industrialized north and are negligible to non-existent in the global south. It is banned in France where the highest court ruled in 1991 that 'the human body is not lent out, is not rented out, is not sold'.[16] By its ruling, France put on par commercial sex (and sex trafficking), slavery and womb renting. In Canada, it is the pregnant woman and not the commissioning party who is allowed to make all medical decisions. In the US, the laws are murky and ambiguous, creating 'extensive legal confusion with no federal guidelines'. Each state seems to have its own set of laws which surrogacy agencies attempt to exploit. Arkansas and Texas have drafted legislation to negate parental rights of the surrogate while Kentucky and Indiana declare commercial surrogacy contracts void. Agencies capitalize on this legal morass and attempt to reassure nervous commissioning parents with advertisements that amount to 'product warranty': 'All our gestational cadres reside in California...this allows us to benefit from favourable laws concerning who may be declared the parents of the child and enforceability of gestational surrogacy.' Brokers and clients in the US are now actively soliciting poor women and non-white women as non-genetic surrogates since it is highly unlikely that such women will have the resource to lay legal claim to the children. It is also believed that judges in the US would be less likely to award non-white surrogates custody over white and well-to-do couples—as was the case in *Calvert vs Johnson*. Despite these claims, so-called surrogacy 'contracts' are subject to costly and lengthy legal challenges, with unpredictable outcomes. There have now been more than 80 such court battles and the numbers are growing.

In India, conveniently for Julie, not only is the whole process available at a cut rate, there is the added value of no legal trouble from pesky surrogate mums demanding rights to the foetus they have brought to term and given birth. Indeed, surrogacy websites reduce the woman to her function. PlanetHospital.com, for example, refers to the women simply as a 'host'. And in India, the 'host' signs away her rights as soon as the baby is born. 'It is a big relief for the foreigners who come to us', says Dr Patel. 'The whole experience places a strain on the couple and they do not want to be worrying about these things.'

Whereas for surrogates in the developed countries the narrative of altruism is dominant, for the poor, dark-skinned woman half a world away—the narrative constructed is not one of exploitation but empowerment. It should come as no surprise that the reserve army of reproductive labour comes from the most abject of families—women who see so other way of making a better life. More ominously, there are hints of coercion from employers and male relatives, mostly husbands crippled by debt who see womb renting as their way out. Dr Rama's surrogate mothers, for example, are recruited from relatives and friends of people who work for her. Upon being asked by a journalist why she became a surrogate, 'Geeta' replies, 'It was my husband's idea.' A second surrogate, 'Saroj' has turned to womb renting in order to be able to afford rainproof housing.[17] Most reports, however, focus on the gratitude of the surrogate and the difference the money will make in their lives: 'From the money I earn as a surrogate mother, I can buy a house', or 'It's not possible for my husband to earn more as he's not educated and only earns $50 a month.' It is undeniable that a windfall of $2,000, indeed, makes an appreciable difference. Womb renters whether in the US or in

India, are economically vulnerable and socially powerless women and in consenting to engage in this form of commercial transaction they are not, for the most part, displaying an instance of 'women's legal authority to make decisions regarding the exercise of her reproductive capacity' as some have argued. Perhaps the more troubling argument is the one that tends to 'normalize' the market transaction as 'freedom'. Margaret Radin, though opposing commercial surrogacies, is nonetheless troubled that prohibiting payments would create a 'double bind' since womb renting would 'enable a needy group—poor women to improve their relatively powerless oppressed condition, an improvement that would be beneficial to personhood'.

What is being obscured in these discussions is, of course, the fact that commercial surrogacy does not occur in some race and class neutral environment. Far from acknowledging or improving their 'personhood', Indian commercial surrogates are constructed as a species apart with little, if any, attention paid to their health beyond the immediate and limited concern over foetal health. Nor is there any attention paid to their feelings or the psychological cost the surrogacy may entail. Instead, the women are constantly told to think of their pregnancy as 'someone else's child come to stay at your place for 9 months'. The women, thus, become in the words of Judge Parslow, 'an environment'—no more than the labour they perform.

Reports about womb renting focus so relentlessly on their abject poverty (which seems sufficient rationale for exploitation, it would appear), it is difficult to know how these women actually feel or whether there *is* a person beyond their instrumentality. What is also evident in all of these reports is the splitting of the parental function: parenthood as a deeply meaningful event is reserved for the commissioning couple and reduced to mere bodily function for the surrogate. Once in a rare while do we hear of their sadness and depression to remind us of their humanity: 'I used to weep at the thought of having to give up the baby'; or as another said repeatedly in an interview, 'I want to hold the baby in my arm.'

In India, ART has been transformed into an efficient, industrial process. A veritable supermarket of baby-making one-stop-shopping makes it the most sought after place for womb renting. As a savvy global service provider, Dr Rama, and others, offer bargain packages that includes up to three cycles of *in vitro* fertilization. In one instance, reported by

Der Speigal a 45-year-old British woman 'has ordered egg cells and a surrogate mother'. To improve her chances and 'to speed things up' she is planning on two parallel pregnancies. Two or three embryos will be implanted into her own womb and just as many into the womb of the surrogate. If both attempts fail, she will be entitled to a third as part of the package deal. *The International Herald Tribune* ran an article describing a gay Israeli couple who travelled to Mumbai, India to 'make' their baby: 'Yonatan Gher and his male partner eventually plan to tell their child it was made in India, in the womb of a woman they never met, with the egg of a Mumbai housewife they picked out from an internet line-up of candidates.' In the case of this couple—and one could infer, for others, as well—'no contacts between egg donor, surrogate mother or future parents were permitted.' The combination of strict surveillance, worry-free legal transfer of rights, not to mention well-trained, English speaking medical personnel, give India the edge in a competitive market. There are now plans to open franchises throughout India, says Dr Rama and then overseas. Not in Europe—since it has too many regulations and laws, but in the Caribbean so Americans will not have to travel far.

As I noted at the outset, the commercialization of pregnancies raises a number of deeply disturbing social and ethical questions. In the first place, says Dr Lantos of the Centre for Practical Bioethics, it raises the spectre of 'baby farms in developing countries'. Are we not in the process of creating a 'breeder class' of poor, brown women without any legal rights to the baby they produce, nor, indeed to their own bodies while they are gestating? We might also ask what underpins this 'market' for commercial surrogacy? Does this expressed desire—even hunger—for babies not what Raymond calls a creeping essentialism which assumes that women (and men) have a deep *biological* need to have children? It also reifies the idea of genetic inheritance as the basis of parenthood, obscuring the fact that motherhood (or fatherhood) is a relationship that is created through and exists in variable social, political and historical contexts and is not/should not be reducible to a biological imperative or basic instinct. The prospects of a complex articulation of 'parenthood' which includes the gestational mother is especially dismissed for poor Indian women. *The Telegraph*, one of the leading English dailies in Calcutta begins its report on the phenomenon of 'womb renting' in this way: 'Shilpa Mehta is visibly pregnant. But the baby she is carrying is *not hers*. The *real or genetic* parents are a Scandinavian couple…' The article goes on to say, 'Mehta is, in fact, renting her womb out to a couple for a *cool* Rs. 4 lakh to Rs. 5 lakh.' (Emphasis added) In the space of a few sentences, the writer not only fails to consider that the surrogate, too, can be the 'real' parent, it diminishes the complicated factors involved by claiming the surrogate is making a 'cool' bundle.

Equally troubling are the eugenic undertones of ART. Indians, for example., want well-educated sperm donors ('We assure patients that we are not getting sperms from rickshawallahs' says one provider), and the most consistently mentioned characteristics for egg donors are 'fair' or light skinned and 'high class'. Laura Mamo, in her recent study of 'queer reproduction' describes lesbian couples poring over sperm—donor catalogues selecting everything from hair colour to SAT scores, choosing among doctors, musicians and computer programmers. For the Israeli couple, profiles of egg donors were sent via e-mail: 'We picked the one with the highest level of education', Gher tells *The Tribune*. In addition, a factory worker was rejected in favour of a housewife who is presumed to have less stressful lifestyle. [Odd conjunction of hi-tech procedures and low tech superstitions about genes!!]

Commercial surrogacy is one in a long line of service industries which cater to the rich. As Rothman has pointed out, 'the baby like any other commodity does not belong to the producer but to the purchaser'. By putting their thumbprints or signatures on pieces of paper, these anonymous women, herded into group homes for the purpose of producing babies are signing away 'rights' they barely have: 'the right to legal custody of their children, the right not to be bought, sold, lent, rented or given away'. It is worth noting that some of the women who fight for choice and for privacy rights in the US, at best ignore and at worst deny the same to women whose wombs they rent. While in the US, in most cases, others (fathers) do not have the right to make certain private intimate decisions about a woman's body: she cannot be forced to have an abortion or not have one, or be subjected to invasive medical procedures, and yet they demand that the surrogates be put through precisely such control. Since the relationship is contractual, one should also ask what if the baby so produced is defective…Do the commissioning couple have a right to return the product and demand a refund? Can the surrogates be forced to have abortions? Do commercial surrogates have any say at all about their medical treatments? If we travel down the road of legal contracts, where would we stop? Would Dr Patel and others like her have the right to produce *en masse* babies with 'donated' eggs and sperms for childless couples who are eager to adopt? How far away are we from the spectre of a veritable WalMart of eggs and uterus, all racing to the bottom of the price scale?

The commoditization of pregnancies or 'womb renting' is a direct progeny of 'what passes under the euphemisms of "liberalization" or "globalization"' which, in India, is reversing 'the trajectory of economic development on which the Indian state was initially based in the formative years of the Republic'.[18] Instead, the state has become, in the memorable phrase of Marx, 'the managing committee of the bourgeoisie as a whole' and has disappeared as the guardian of the social good.[19] Instead it mutates into representing 'the interests of "globalization" *to* the nation'[20] In the current conjuncture, we are witnessing capitals' power to penetrate any and all borders *on its own terms*. In this instance, as in the case of most manufacturing—be it shoes, clothes, automobiles or babies— labour is made to disappear spatially. George Orwell had noted, almost a half a century ago, that 'the overwhelming bulk of the British proletariat does not live in Britain.' The current structures of global capital and exploitation have, if anything, rendered labour cheap, invisible and easily disposable. Wombs are the latest, and perhaps most troubling in a series of resources that link the seeming discrepancy between development for the few and despair of the many. The women in Anand, we are repeatedly told, bring boundless joy to couples who intensely desire a child of their own but are unable to conceive. Therefore, we should not view them crassly as 'incubators on legs' nor the clinics as 'baby farms'. We are reminded, as well, that the women are carefully trained not to feel any maternal attachments. It begs the question: why not train the yearnings of the childless *not* to desire a baby?—or at least, not to associate the joys of parenthood with genetic transference? That the women at Anand are trying to guarantee a modicum of financial security for their families is undeniable. But one needs to ask a prior question: in what kind of social and economic desperation are women's choices reduced to renting or selling their reproductive capabilities? And should that be the rationale for exploiting them?

Commercial surrogacy raises profound questions about what it means to be human. Most ethical, political, legal and philosophical debates have sought to argue that the human body ought to be 'the boundary of inviolability'. The Comité Consultative National d'Ethique in France, for example, has not hesitated to proclaim that French law 'does not accept that the human body should be used for commercial purposes. The body is not an object and cannot be used as such'. Commercial surrogacy, by contrast, encourages the view that body parts, the womb in particular, are separate components of a person, thus commodifying the body in new ways. Perhaps this commodification seems less outrageous since women's bodies continue to be subjected to overt and covert forms of property holding. This commoditization (of women's bodies in general) thus appears more 'normal' and seems much less troubling when coupled with poverty. Poor women's bodies are deemed less than—less protected, less worthy, less human. After all, they *are* the labouring bodies of our society. They clean our houses, cook our food, bring up our children, look after the sick and frail and through all of it we manage to render them invisible. But gestation, I want to argue, is a very different form of labour whose product is another human being. The sale of an element of reproduction is unique among all commercial transactions. Implicitly or explicitly, it is the sale of a potential person. It represents the invasion of the market into our most intimate selves. For feminists, especially activists, these ought to be questions of great moment. We need a charter that will uphold for all what the French high court has affirmed: 'A woman's body is not lent out, is not rented out, is not sold'—especially not for the profit of others.

Notes and References

1. 'Donation' is a euphemism for what is a market transaction. This benign term also helps cover-up what is a painful, time-consuming and physically risky medical procedure. It should be noted that where no payment is permitted (for example in Britain, Canada and most states in Australia), 'Donation' is an apt term.

2. All of the information has been culled from various newspapers. See, for example, 'Japan Hints at Visa for India Surrogacy Baby' Inquirer.net, 15 August 2008; 'Surrogate Baby Stuck in Legal Limbo' CNN.com. Available online at http://www.cnn.com/2008/WORLD/asiapcf/08/12/surrogate.baby/index. html; 'Surrogacy orphan trapped in red tape after mothers abandon her' in *Timesonline*, 7 August 2008.

3. Katha Pollitt, 'Checkbook Maternity: When Is a Mother Not a Mother?', in *Reasonable Creatures: Essays on Women and Feminism* (New York: Vintage Books, 1995), p. 100.

4. Quoted in Susam Markens, *Surrogate Motherhood and the Politics of Reproduction* (Berkeley: University of California Press, 2007), p. 117.

5. I take this point from Marilyn Strathern, *Reproducing the Future: Essays on Anthropology, Kinship and the New Reproductive Technology* (Manchester: Manchester University Press, 1992), p. 38. 'New techniques of 'fertilisation' do not remedy fertility as such, but childlessness; they enable a potential parent to have access to the fertility of others.'

6. Telegraph, 'Foreign Kid, Indian Make,' *Telegraph*, Calcutta, Tuesday, 1 January 2008.

7. Andrew Kimbrell, *The Human Body Shop: The Engineering and Marketing of Life* (San Fransisco: Harper, 1993).

8. Jeremy, Rifkin, Foreword, in *The Human Body Shop : The Engineering and Marketing of Life*, ed. Andrew Kimbrell (San Francisco: Harper, 1993), p. viii.

9. Ibid. p. ix.

10. Shree Mulay and Emily Gibson, 'Marketing of Artificial Human Reproduction and the Indian State', *Development* 49, no. 4 (2006): 84.

11. Ibid.

12. Ibid., p. 85.

13. 'The most glaring indication of the marketing intent of the websites is the specialized links for "overseas" or "international" patients.' Fee structures on the websites are in rupees and in dollars. See Mulay and Gibson, 'Marketing of Artificial Human Reproduction and the Indian State', p. 86.

14. These numbers are reported widely in newspaper reports. See, especially, *International Herald Tribune/ NY Times*, 'Foreign Couples Turn to India', Tuesday, 4 March 2008. The use of the term (tourism) is especially telling.

15. Liza Mundy, *Everything Conceivable: How Assisted Reproduction Is Changing Our World* (New York: Knoff, 2007).

16. Quoted in Anastacia Mott Austin, 'Wombs for Rent: Outsourcing Birth'. Available online at http://www.buzzle.com/articles/wombs-for-rent-outsourcing-birth.html (accessed on 7 November 2009). See also *New York Times*, 2 June 1991. World Section.

17. 'Childbirth at the Global Crossroad', *American Prospect*. Available online at http://prospect.org/cs/articles?article+childbirth at the global crossroads.
18. Aijaz Ahmad, *Lineages of the Present Ideology and Politics in South Asia* (London: Verso, 2000), p. 210.
19. Ibid., p. 213.
20. Ibid.

Chapter 4

Nationalism, Television and Indian Cricket in Global Mediascape
Where Has the Local Gone?

Manas Ghosh

Introduction: Marking the Boundary

Televised cricket since late 1980s has emerged as the most popular media show in India. The massive popularization of cricket and the advent of global television in India are closely related. In fact they appear as two apparently different parts of a single phenomenon. Watching the live telecast of a cricket match and watching cricket sitting in the gallery trigger two different structural forms of perception. The form of cricket is radically transformed when represented on television. This chapter explores the general history of media representation of cricket in India in order to understand the changes and transformations in structural forms of perception. The different forms of perception often invoke different psychic dimensions, marking out varieties of reception. This chapter traces the rapidly shifting scenes of representation of cricket on global television, and studies the implications, thus exploring a cultural process that embraces the commercialization of sports, its reception and use in the context of global media and capital.

The game cricket was shipped in to the Indian subcontinent as a part of colonial modernity. It is no surprise that cricket in India primarily was a game played by British civil servants, government administrators, Royal army officers and few native elites. The educated middle class of India started taking interest in cricket as cricketers from India, mainly the young members from Indian royal families in England, performed well in English County cricket and some of them were selected in England Test team. By early 1930s the idea of 'Indian cricket' had been taking a shape in popular parlance as the names like C.K. Nayadu and Lala Amarnath came into discussion after they had shown their class in first-class cricket and Test matches in home and abroad.[1] In the post-colonial era Indian cricket was elevated to real 'national' status as Indian Cricket team sent by the sovereign country started taking on other national sides. In this period All India Radio would broadcast the running commentary of cricket matches to the people of India. Often people would attend to running commentary in BBC and ABC relayed by Radio Ceylon.[2] Till early-1980s cricket was popular but not as popular as football and hockey were. Since mid-1980s cricket, riding on nationwide live telecast programmes of satellite television coupled with 'aggressive' nationalism outsmarted football and hockey in the measure of popularity.

In this chapter the history of cricket in India has been seen in four temporal phases based on the nature of spectatorship, public interest and exposure in the broadcast media. This temporal development of four phases was related to the different stages in the trajectory of nationalism. The colonial and early post-colonial period framed the first phase when watching game sitting in the arena was most important, and hence limited number of people could avail the scope of watching a live cricket match. Yet the enthusiasm was great. We can remember at least three occasions when people of Bombay and Calcutta raised voices like 'no Nayadu no match', 'no Mushtaque no Test' and 'no Durani no Test' in protest when they came to know that their favourite player had been dropped from the side falling victim to princely dirty politics. And the selectors had to bring them back under public pressure. Running commentary of cricket matches started on the radio in the early 1930s but not very regularly; and moreover the number of radio sets was few even in the cities.[3] The newspapers would carry belated news of cricket matches. The prolonged second phase consisted mainly of listening to radio commentary of matches taking place in India and abroad. The third phase was heralded by the development of nationwide television network at the time of the New Delhi Asiad in 1982 and was realized in the live-telecasting of cricket with Kerry Packer's new approach of using multiple camera exposure on Channel Nine.

In the initial phase, cricket, introduced by the colonial rulers, was played mainly by government employee sides like the Railways eleven, or by teams sent from army regiments, etc. Later different provinces of British India like Bengal province, United Province, Central Province, Sind, Bombay, Poona and princely states like Baroda, Hyderabad, Holkar, Patiala, Vijayanagara would sent their teams. Though club cricket except in Bombay and to some extent in Calcutta, unlike club football, was not that popular all over the country, cricket-lovers of India were interested in news of English County cricket. In fact cricket was not much played by the educated middle class of India in that period. The game was mainly played by anglicized elites of India and native princes, though Parsees of Bombay took interest in cricket since its advent in India.[4] But the game attracted the enlightened middle class as it was perceived as a part of Western modernity. From Swami Vivekananda to Jawaharlal Nehru, Tagore and Satyajit Ray, a fairly long list can be produced in support of this claim.[5] Cricket was very much a part of drawing room *adda*s and a part of enjoying leisurely midday watching a delicate battle between bat and ball in the winter sun.[6] In spite of its 'foreign' connection, watching and taking interest in cricket were 'local' experiences in both senses territorial as well as political in the milieu of colonial/colonized dynamics.

In the post-colonial era, Indian cricket was mainly played in the form of Test matches and 'domestic' matches. Running commentaries of Test matches became popular and local stations of All India Radio would air running commentary of domestic matches in vernacular languages. But as nationwide commercial television network followed by satellite television and global television in 1990s came to hijack radio's popularity entirely, representation of local/domestic cricket in audio-visual media vanished very quickly. This article would like to place an argument how the triad of nationalism-global television-commercial interest actually makes this sea change possible. Currently under the rubric of Indian Premier League (IPL), the world is watching haughtiest cricketing showdown in the small screen of global media. Definitely IPL explores a realm outside so-called 'national'. This chapter also attempts to briefly examine the way IPL 'reconfigure' the representation of 'local' in global television.

Manas Ghosh

Cricket Calls the Nation...

'The virtue of all-in wrestling is that it is the spectacle of excess.' This is a comment made by Roland Barthes.[7] But is it right to say that cricket is also a kind of spectacle of excess? I prefer to answer: 'Yes, partly true.' Cricket is a game less dependent on content and more on form. The form of the game hardly provides continuity, generating new spectacles in each ball delivered to the batsman. In addition to this, however, the time needed to reach a clear result in a cricket match of the classical mode leaves the possibility of generating pure spectacles out of it.

Cricket, as argued by Nandy, is a game that depends more on chance and style and less on *purushakar* and rationality.[8] A comment made by late Mushtaque Ali, who represented the Indian team in the 1930s, 1940s and early 1950s, could be recalled. He said: 'One cannot be a successful cricketer unless he accepts the game as a religion.'[9] The game, exported by the colonial rulers, was adored and adapted by the native Indians for its capability of producing excess that exerts chance over rationality. The essence of the game favours the non-rational natives than the rational rulers.

Despite the victory of Mohunbagan Club in the soccer shield final in 1911 over an English team, and despite the Hindu reformers' emphasis on football, cricket gradually gained popularity in the decades of 1930s and 1940s. The logic behind this popularity of cricket might have been: 'When we dominate a *sahib* in cricket, we dominate him at his chosen game.' This may be applied to understand the native cricket-lovers' joy in the success of Ranjit Singhji and Iftikar Ali Khan Pataudi in England. Cricket, at this popular plane, has represented the 'unbound seriality'[10] of hopes, ambitions, fears and anxieties of the people caught within the system of an emerging nation state. In the first three decades after Independence, cricket was a signifier of the nation's prestige, the later depending less on the result of the matches and more on the display of style, recalled Salim Durani's stormy spectacle or Pankaj Roy's courageous resistance against fast bowling, or the magical spells bowled by the Indian spinners, often condemned by the Western people in orientalist terms as 'Asian black magic'.

But a new kind of nationalism fuelled by cricket, which is not like the earlier, emerged in the mid-1980s. Nandy thinks that it surfaced in the Reliance Cricket World Cup in 1987, organized jointly by India and Pakistan. And this second wave of nationalism presumes a sharp distinction between the Self and the Other. Nandy notes how the police bigwigs of Calcutta, who were anxious anticipating the deterioration of the law and order situation as a result of a possible Indo-Pak encounter in the final to be held at the Eden Gardens, were relieved after the semifinal matches, as both India and Pakistan were eliminated. But the nationalist euphoria based on the will to demolish the 'other' surfaced as Indians massively celebrated the defeat of Pakistan at the hands of Australia.[11] Victory and defeat, in this way became more important than the splendor of the game. The late Vijay Hazare, Indian captain who played in the 1940s and '50s wrote in his biography:

[C]ricket has now become an issue of national prestige. In my opinion too much importance is attached to the result of a match. A win is a sign of supremacy while defeat is regarded as disaster. In this respect at least, cricket has changed. In my time we were still sorry to lose but did not attach undue importance either to a victory or to a reverse. [...] Our attitude was that as long as we did our best either individually or collectively, a defeat was no disgrace.[12]

In fact, victory or defeat was a rare occasion in Test cricket as most of the Test matches ended in a draw. So, shaping national cricket in the binary of win/lose is not inherent to the game but is a type of representational binary proposed by television and fuelled by the nationalism. A conjunctural relationship may also be imagined between television and neo-nationalism in India, mobilized around the sport since 1982. That year marked the watershed in the history of Indian television broadcasting when the Asian Games (held in Delhi) and national television came together in a permanent bonding.[13] As the national television network spread out in different corners of India in the mid-1980s, the live telecast of cricket became more and more popular. This popularity was boosted with statements made by the then sports-loving Prime Minister Late Rajeev Gandhi in favour of investing much to the performances in sports as a carrier of the national prestige. And as live telecast of cricket on television became popular, a new kind of spectatorship developed. Spectatorship before a television set becomes different from the spectatorship in the sports arena. Televised cricket has an economy of representation that creates an experience different from viewing the game sitting inside the arena. Let us remember that the spectator-position invoked by the radio relay of the cricket matches is not close to the televisual spectatorship. Radio commentary constructs a spectator-position that is more open in terms of an excess of imagining the visual by listening to the description and ambient sound of the arena. The age of radio commentary in India, incidentally, marked the age of old nationalism of the Nehruvian liberal type while the age of entertainment television coincides with the age of neo-nationalism characterized by an aggressive regimented communal politics. The televisual style of representation, that narrows down the 'excess' of the game, contributes largely to this nexus of 'regimented nationalism' and the success of the national team in international cricket.

Nation Calls Cricket ...

The history of the development of cricket telecast has been a journey towards an 'economy of representation'. The history of television, as indicated by Umberto Eco, has undergone two distinct phases—Paleo-TV and Neo-TV.[14] In the age of Paleo-TV that marked the pre-1970 era, telecast live cricket followed a 'primitive mode of representation'. The single camera visuals, with an editing pattern marked with compulsory jump cuts was like early cinema. The mode of representation in Paleo-TV provoked spectatorship that was, to some extent, resembled the spectatorship in the arena, as it provided a single viewing position similar to a viewer seated in the gallery. Paleo-TV thus emphasized the actuality of the game-event. The scenario first changed in the late 1970s when Kerry Packer, after being barred by the authorities from telecasting the test matches played by the national team, organized a World Series Cricket spectacle in Australia and broadcast it through the Channel Nine owned by him.[15] Packer's private channel was the first to show cricket on television with the use of multiple cameras equipped with powerful zoom lenses that could get close-ups and reaction shots of the cricketers in action. Packer, in an interview, made the interesting comment that he planned to set cameras at both ends and in different positions on the cricket field as he did not want to see 'cricketer's bums'.[16] This reveals the fact that the Australian media tycoon was much more interested in representation than the game itself. The reception of Packer's package had another interesting aspect. The star-studded show failed to draw people to the arena but became popular on television. On the other hand, people were gathered in the arena to see the performance of their weak and broken national team led by veteran Bobby Simpson. Packer's real success came when he got the right to telecast the performance of the national team through Channel Nine. Thus nationalist euphoria and the discreet charm of televisual representation merged into a single stream.[17]

The Indian audience experienced Packer's magic in 1983 as Channel Nine got the sole rights to telecast the matches of Benson and Hedges (Mini) World Cup held in Australia, all over the world. The star-studded Indian team won that tournament and Channel Nine showed the spectacle of the celebration by the team after they won.[18] The Indian audience who experienced that event on television can remember the last lap of the spectacle which showed the players of the victorious national side in the arena on a luxury car gifted to a member of the Indian team by a big corporate company. The representation of that victory lap with minute dramatic details asserted the 'everywhereness' of the subjective camera in a cricket field. This event had a symbolic value as the omnipotent camera, nationalist spirit and corporate involvement—all three determinants of present day cricket broadcast came to a point of convergence for the first time in the history of sports.

Packer's mode of representation influenced televisual cricket all over the globe. And within four or five years, Indian national television adapted this new mode of broadcasting cricket. As far as broadcasting sports are concerned, the experience of Neo-TV in India became synonymous with the Packer mode. However, as a result of the advent of Neo-TV equipped with high-tech devices and an omnipotent look, the spectatorship before television now differs markedly from the spectatorship in the arena. A crowd in the gallery, for example, creates a real public sphere which forms a real community; a spectator before television though lacks a communal reality yet feels him/herself part of a community—a community which is virtual, not real. A television spectator viewing a live telecast of a cricket match in this way imagines a community[19] based on a pseudo-mass watching cricket in different unidentified corners of the country, unknown to each other but thought to be bound together by the same national allegiance.

It may sound too obvious but one should mention that the audience in the arena is much more plural in nature than a spectator viewing television. An Indian crowd in the stadium, for example, prefers to see their national player scoring a century, but may not be unhappy when they find a foreign player, for example, Salim Malik or Steve Waugh scoring points. Let us remember the last match played by Asif Iqbal at Eden Gardens, Kolkata, in the early 1980s. He received a five minutes' standing ovation from the crowd as a farewell tribute. This kind of reaction is propelled by direct interaction between the cricketers in the field and the crowd in the gallery. On many occasions, while fielding on the fence for example, the players interact with the crowd, chat with them, pass comments or respond to the jokes made by the people, even sign autographs to them. It is evident that there are some foreign cricketers who are extremely popular with the crowd in the gallery not much for their cricket skills but for their relationship with the mass. Some unpleasant incidents did happen, but generally these are due to some gesture or short-temperedness from the player. Inzamamul Haque, for example, dislikes the crowd as people often pass comments on his bulk. But these incidents rarely entail nationalist sentiments.

A foreign player after scoring a century customarily lifts his bat to the gallery; the crowd applauds in return. But for a viewer watching television, the image (close up or medium close up) of lifting and waving the bat by a foreign player is a 'distant signifier' which rarely affects the emotions. The gesture, made by the foreign player, the viewer supposes, is not addressed to him but is directed at his 'imagined other'. The gesture, which I call a 'distant signifier', is also a 'mythic signifier' at the same time. In myth the meaning of the signifier is distorted by the concept, as Roland Barthes explains.[20] Here the meaning of the sign of waving and

80

lifting the bat by a foreign player is distorted by a concept of nationalism which claims a transcendental cultural identity, and is based on othering too. Barthes suggests that the mythic signifier has two aspects: one, full, which is the meaning and the other, empty, which is the form.[21] What the concept distorts is of course what is full, the meaning—at this level, history and contexts are reduced to mere gestures. On the other hand, the empty aspect of a signifier, that is form, is here cricket as a game. The distortion doesn't occur at this level. So, in mythical signifiers, form is empty but present (the game itself), but meaning is absent but full. A flesh and blood cricketer, thus, is constructed as an 'other' to a television spectator. The 'concept', that is nationalism, manipulates and 'distorts' the meaning of the signifier. As far as broadcasting cricket is concerned Palio-TV's capacity to 'distort the meaning of signifier' in comparison to Neo-TV's was much less as it lacked the proper cinematic devices in its form of representation. The later has achieved immense power to manipulate the meaning with the use of, for example, options produced by multiple cameras, employing the technique of continuity editing, using tele-lenses for big close shots, and capturing bird's-eye view of entire locality, etc. Let's have an example of the method of manipulating the meaning of the signifier. The post-Kerry Packer standard style of cricket telecast shows, say the celebration of a century scored by a batsman or the fall of a crucial wicket with the constellation of shots made up with, for instance, an intimate view of the stroke that brings the 100th run or of the ball hitting the stumps followed by the face in big close up of the overjoyed batsman or bowler celebrating the moment; and shots of national flags being waved from the gallery or a poster displayed there, and even the close shots of viewers in gallery with faces painted with colours of the national flag and the big smile of a jubilant filmstar in VIP box are often inserted in the scene.

Dreaming Nation, Viewing Cricket...

The relationship between televisual cricket in the era of global media and the spectator-subject posited by it invokes a psychic dimension which is ambiguous in nature. A heavy investment of nationalism in televisual cricket must indicate a kind of displacement of emotion and feeling which is clearly manifested in the mass media. The nexus among cricket, nationalism and television can be defined and modeled in a framework of 'mediawork', a coinage inspired by Sigmund Freud's 'dreamwork', where, we know, a 'latent content' is represented in the form of a dream as 'manifest content'. I borrow this Freudian interpretation to explain the ideological and formal functioning of media from Hamid Naficy's article 'Mediawork's Representation of the Other'. Naficy writes:

> Mediawork, as an agency of hegemony, acts similarly to 'dreamwork': it manifests in its representations the latent or 'deep structures' of beliefs and ideologies. But in the interests of maintaining consensus (and a sense of free choice) it conceals its own operations, and reformats or disguises those deep structures and values. Thus the deep structures, the dominant ideologies, remain latent, beneath consciousness, are taken for granted and considered normal.[22]

In this framework, cricket broadcast as entertainment television in India must fit into the role of manifest content which actually is a projection of the latent content constituted by a special kind of nationalism that emerged in the mid-1980s. And this nationalism, based on the distinction of self/other, desires the other to perish, and the desire is manifested in the disguise of a game, to be more specific, in the victory/defeat of the national team in cricket. Television in India in the global era, in this process, plays the role of a dream factory, which produces the manifest content, refining, channeling and displacing its desired messages in the pretext of live telecast of cricket.

Live telecast of cricket matches of the national side, as compared to the manifest content, invokes a certain kind of 'economy of representation' that actually leads to a structure of narrative. 'Sport on television demonstrates particularly clearly an aspect of narrative on television … sports promises a live narrative', comments John Ellis.[23] But it must be taken into account that televisual narrativization of sports, somehow has a different effect altogether. One basic aspect of cinematic and literary narrative is iconicity, which television lacks ontologically. On the contrary, the effort to narrativize a televisual nonfiction programme contributes to its flow'.[24] The experiences of television in the UK and the US lead to the conclusion that the 'flow' of television dislodges the stability of images and in this process destroys the aura of iconicity largely. But the Indian experience with television is slightly different. Television in India resolves the binary of flow/iconicity through a synthesis. Televisuality here works within a 'flow of iconicity', the process which destabilizes the so-called stasis of iconicity and restabilizes it by repeating it constantly. 'Iconicity' here is not embedded in a single text but dispersed within the form. And this dispersion is caused by the overproduction of iconic images, and often by evoking the 'mode retro'.[25]

So, television in India, despite its immense 'flow', won't destroy iconicity, rather it establishes a new kind of iconicity, which I refer to as a unique phenomenon of 'flow of iconicity'. The logic that backs up the proposition is simple: television in India cannot conceive the signs of nationalism if it loses iconicity completely. Because, in a postcolonial nation like India nationalism as a discourse and iconicity as its visual signification are tied together in an umbilical bond. The nationalism that has been generated as a reaction to colonialism needs an image of iconic value that can shore up identity. It may be ambitious but not unjustified to say that a postcolonial nation appropriates an apparatus of postmodern de-iconization on its own terms without being carried away by the mere dynamics of 'flow'.

In order to restore iconicity, if one part of television in India converts itself into a 'nostalgia industry', another part, which consists of phenomena like broadcasting live cricket, works through the overproduction of iconic images, even though the essential flow remains undisturbed.

Consuming Cricket, Consuming Nationalism...

Thus basic features of television in India in the era of global media can be summarized as (*a*) mode retro and (*b*) telecast of live and recorded sports. Sports on Indian television in the pre-open-sky broadcast era were a kind of live spectacle shown occasionally in a very selective manner. But the advent of global television, which introduces a number of twenty four hour sports channels, locates sport events in a continuous 'flow' of televisuality. The images of live or recorded sport events generated by always available sports channels are so naturally identified with and seamlessly sutured within the 'flow of iconicity' constituted with films-on-television, soap opera, advertisement and song/dance spectacles that televisual sport shows a 'pseudo-play mode' subjugating the 'record mode'[26] beneath the flow constituted by the apparatus. Thus, global television transforms the sanctity of 'live' sports telecast to a pleasure of representation. The documentary effect of 'liveness' and fictionality of the play mode are so homogeneously mixed that the line of demarcation often vanishes.

I would like to refer to the recent betting scam in the cricket circuit that became an event in print and electronic media but rarely affected the viewership of cricket as entertainment television. We have a very clear statistics in support of this statement. According to the survey report of Television Audience Measurement (TAM), the viewership of satellite television in India increased fantastically in between the year 1999 and 2003, though some major betting scams were exposed in those years. The viewership of sport programmes in 1999 was 22 million in India. In 2003 it reached an estimated 45 million.[27] This statistics provides a cue that in televisual cricket, representation and televisuality are much more important than the credibility of the game itself.

Margaret Morse in her article 'Sports on Television: Replay and Display' comments: 'Sport is, however, not only a stadium event and an institution, but also a television genre, and, in the convergence of sport and television, it is clearly television which is the dominant partner.'[28] Morse's seminal article explained some of the important discourses related to televisual sport. But she studied the US Television and consequently reached conclusions which are specific to the US experience of sports broadcast. One proposition made by her is: 'advertisements do not endanger the "live" framework of sport by offering a realistic contrast....'[29] This remark needs rethinking as far as the experience of consumer television, particularly in India, is concerned.

The massive boom in the advertisement industry inspired by and made for 'nationalist' cricket on television in India and the insertion of those advertisement capsules in the body of a live sports programme largely destabilizes the demarcation between the live world of the game and the fictional one of advertisement texts. The fictionality of advertisements, which sometimes includes the same characters that are on the field, casts doubt on the non-fictionality of the representation of the game, thus inflicting the play mode onto a 'live' show. The 'perfect' blending of advertisement texts with the game creates continuity. But a representation is not self-sufficient to convey the message that it wants to. It must generate consent, at least partially, from the spectator. Only the consumer subjectivity of the spectator could legitimize the blending of an advertisement text with a live show.

Ava Rose and James Friedman, in their article 'Television Sport as Masculine Cult of Distraction', note:

> Today's family of consumers has access to diversion in their own home. Perhaps the strongest—certainly the most consistent—lure to the screen is televised sport. Nowhere there is a more spectacular celebration of the surface sphere, a more explicit correspondence between enterprise and entertainment, or a more pervasive reiteration of dominant values.[30]

They further suggest that televisual sport as 'a cult of distraction' in the US should be viewed not as a 'national cultural phenomena', but as 'textual and historical peculiarities'.[31]

But the problem regarding televised sport in India ought to be addressed within the context of nationalism and consumer subjectivity offered by some other social determinants. Television in India in the era of global media uses nationalism to supply a proper matrix in the development of the broadcast of cricket, which again offers enough space for the germination of a phenomenon: the 'overdetermined' spectator subject. Unlike televised sports in the US, the reception of cricket broadcast on television in India lodges largely outside the text, though textual experience and representation matter considerably. In the US and UK even the telecast of local and club matches are immensely popular. But in India the massive craze related to the performance of the national team beneath which the popularity of local or international sports is lost, clearly indicates that the major element of attraction is nationalism, something that is performed outside the text. As a result of that, in India, cricket broadcast on entertainment television creates a kind of transtextual experience where textual meaning is overcharged and distracted by apparently disconnected discourses which encircle the text.

As television in India transformed itself into entertainment television, and later on into a global medium, a new citizen subject emerged that I would like to term the 'consumer citizen subject'. This new citizen subject is different from the old one posited by the national media (All India Radio and Doordarshan). Doordarshan posited a citizen subject which was directly inspired by the so-called welfare state. The national television in that era used to convey the emblems of welfare state which, borrowing Eric Hobsbawm's term, can be described as signs of 'symbolic nationalism',[32] signs which helped the production of the 'authentic effect' of the citizen subject. The advent of global media, on the contrary, defines the citizen subject within the contours of 'consumer nationalism'. I would like to interpret the phrase 'consumer nationalism' as a form that develops and works outside the domain of 'symbolic nationalism'.

'Consumer nationalism' is a product of what is called globalization in India. But the ideology of globalization accepted by a government ought to appear abstract to the people until and unless it is symbolized recognizably through the mass media. And it is taken for granted that satellite television in India performed this role as it was the first among the media that adopted a global idiom. In this sense satellite television in India in itself stands for 'symbolic globalization'. I would like to recall Marshal McLuhan's famous comment, 'medium is the message',[33] to substantiate the argument. Global television itself is a signifier, if we think in Mcluhan's terms that indicate a specific relationship between the symbol and its meaning. The content of mass media, McLuhan argues, is less important than their structures, since the content lies at the level of structure.[34]

The proliferation of global television by its specific nature and structure posits a subjectivity which is different from the single-citizen subjectivity; it can be identified in an analogy with the 'dual-citizen' subjectivity. The constant experience of viewing CNN, BBC, Hallmark, Star TV programmes along with Indian channels multiplies the citizen self—one part of the subjectivity relates to the national and another relates to the extra-national. Entertainment television in the global era posits 'dual citizen subjectivity'[35] on a virtual plane. The virtual 'dual citizen' subjectivity symptomatically surfaces through cricket broadcast. When television, with its global reach, shows the spectacles of non-resident Indians watching cricket matches sitting in the gallery in Dubai or Canada or in the US, and supporting the Indian side by applauding, greeting and shouting, a viewer in India before the small screen identifies, at least partially, with them.

And finally, I would like to discuss the Apple Singh phenomenon in order to address the issue of 'dual citizen' subjectivity more specifically. Remember the world cup cricket held in England in 1999. Apple Singh, who was present at Lords and Headingly, appeared before the television cameras regularly. The image of Apple Singh actually drew upon people of north-Indian origin, unsophisticated, dressed queerly in turban, misfit *kurta* and massive *nagra* shoes. He was not scared, though fully aware of the big city, London or the *sahibs* around him; he ardently desired the victory of the national team. This image clearly was targeted at a large number of very ordinary people of north-Indian origin, who were settled in cities like London, Melbourne or Montreal, selling their labour as tram conductors or taxi drivers or run small business like motels and inns. The structure of global television and its potential to posit virtual 'dual citizen' subjectivity surface through these images. And this is not actually an exceptional incident. Apple Singh's performance was a staged one; but Navjot Singh Sidhu's rise as a very popular yet hard line 'patriot' in the commentary box is to be underlined. The self-image which he has been presenting before the television camera, unlike M. L. Jaysimha or Sunil Gavaskar's rational and sophisticated projection, is the popular idea of a quasi-rustic Punjabi. The jokes which Sidhu shares with other speakers in the panel and the viewers are a conscious effort to fit him into the assigned stereotype. Compare this to Gavaskar's sharp wit or Boycott's restrained comical comments.

As opposed to the 'English-speaking' international image epitomized by Gavaskar or Jaysimha, global television has constructed a 'local-Indian' image played by Apple Singh or N.S. Sidhu. Though these two images apparently oppose one another, they are not really antagonistic. We can identify two major problems in the contraction of this 'local-Indian' image. The image somehow recalls the 'shining India' campaign.[36] 'Local-Indian' here very clearly typifies the rich north-Indian farmer. Secondly, the hyphen that links two words local and Indian actually conceals the historical contradiction between 'local' and 'national'.

We do not here go into the orientalist investment in this construction. Hence the projection of 'local-Indian' images in global media is the imaginary of globalization.

Let's elucidate this point by examining the role of commercial interest in global media. Global television's over investment in international cricket has forcefully emptied the place of the local and the domestic in the televisual media. No local or domestic cricket match was represented seriously in television since mid-1980s. Traces of the local were erased from the body of the text but the local has resurfaced massively in the subtexts in televisual cricket. The text is constituted of the images which describe the game in the field and the subtext is mainly constituted of a number of advertisements inserted in the breaks. They form parts of the subtext along with small details of the gallery, panel discussion after the match, etc. In the narrative of advertisements we find the villages, rural landscapes, *mahalla*s and *para*s, an artisan from Hyderabad, a peasant from Uttar Pradesh, and so on. Having been disappeared from the text, the local has only reappeared as a major constituent of the subtext in order to serve the consumerist logic of the globalization. Amir Khan (as model in an advertisement), Sachin Tendulkar, *Pan Parag*, Overboundary, Maruti 800, victory of the Indian team over the Pakistani side, the dream of a peasant, Virendra Sehwag are so neatly and seamlessly absorbed in the 'flow' of global television that images of local cease to function as a sovereign entity.

Televised Cricket and IPL: Where Has the Local Gone...

The coupling of television and cricket was promoted by the huge advertising industry in India. The ideological back up came from the coupling of neo-nationalism and liberalization and privatization of the Indian economy. Indeed the form of the game improvised as limited-over's cricket enhanced its currency in the commercial publicity industry. What national television envisaged by 1982 came to fulfilment as global television entered into the Indian entertainment market. On 24-hour sports channels like Star Sports and ESPN, cricket broadcast emerged as the highest-TRP rated event. We have observed that a new militant nationalistic feeling has emerged riding on the broadcast of cricket in global television. It apparently looks contradictory that the intervention of deterritorialized media helps in generating a territorialized nationalist feeling. But studying the history of the shift from the national to global in television broadcast of cricket in India we have found a very systematic, gradual development to map the complicated journey.

Incidentally, since the introduction of cricket in the colonial period, upto the early 1940s, the 'local' appeared in the true sense, and remained within the domain of nation, despite the native princes' diplomatic oligopoly over the management of Indian cricket. In different princely states the history of origin and development of cricket took different paths. Different styles of cricketing developed from different parts of India. And there were different levels of playing cricket—official Test matches, unofficial international matches, popular tournaments in Bombay participated by Hindu, Muslim, Parsee and Christian teams, matches between two princely states/provinces, school level, office level and club level cricket matches organized at Bombay Gymkhana ground and at Calcutta *maidan*, etc.[37]

After Independence the heterogeneity was largely trimmed. The grant for school cricket was reduced; the average price of a ticket was hiked according to the advice of the Board of Control for Cricket in India. And cricket tournaments at the national level were streamlined through intra-state, interstate, interzone matches at junior and senior levels. The post-colonial statist version of 'domestic cricket' largely ate up the charms of local cricket developed in colonial period.[38] And the local took refuge in the domestic matches of Ranji Trophy and Duleep Trophy. In Ranji Trophy the teams sent by different provinces like Bengal, Bihar, Haryana, Maharashtra, Tamil Nadu, etc., contest while in Duleep Trophy the contestants are Northern Zone, Eastern Zone, Southern Zone, etc. The controversies related to the selection of the national side would usually revolve round under-representation of a province in the Indian team or dominance of one or two particular provinces or zones in the national side. In some way provincial sentiment often became the courier of local sentiments.

The stories of constant and bitter fighting among Bombay lobby, Delhi lobby and South lobby came to the mass through the newspapers and popular magazines along with the 'sad tale' of the deprivation of cricketers from Bengal, Bihar and Orissa. The controversies regarding the national versus provincial/local would take the centre stage in popular parlance at the time of the selection of national side just before the national team prepared to play against a foreign national team. But as soon as the national team started playing against a foreign side in international matches the popular sentiment would go for the national side as a united force. And, in the time of the appraisal of the performances of the players after a bad show of the national side in an international series the controversy of national versus provincial/local would surface again. In this phase print media and radio used to play a very important role.

Till early 1980s it was newspapers and magazines which often initiated, 'exposed' and fuelled the controversies while state-run All India Radio (AIR), as a more sacrosanct and 'unbiased' counterpart of print media, used to broadcast the performances of the provincial and zonal teams and finally the 'united' national side on the field. But as soon as the commercial television became popular, since mid-1980s, the national/local dynamics shifted to a more homogeneous all powerful 'national'. The spectacles of nationalism in cricket have been showcased by Doordarshan since late 1980s in such a massive and aggressive form that the media representation of the domestic cricket in India completely lost popularity within few years. People buying a high priced ticket for a World Cup match is not unnatural. But at the other end the popularity of domestic cricket has receded. A handful of people watch Ranji Trophy matches—the number hardly crosses four digits. Till the 1970s Ranji Trophy was really popular. But today people even decline to avail of a free entry-pass for a domestic match.[39] As far as the representation in broadcast media is concerned the 'local' in this way became silenced and the focus completely taken over by the 'national'. The 'local', losing its autonomy, finally has been subsumed in a mythic quasi-historical 'national'. Ashutosh Gowariker's super-hit film *Lagaan* to a great extent reflects this ideological shift in its form and content.

The advent of global television in the Indian media-scape brought a new dynamics to the national/local dialectics in recent years. With the advent of global media, particularly the open-sky satellite television in India, cricketers are represented as huge stars. Though it is understood that commercial television cannot represent steady iconic images as it is a 'flow' form, an image of Sachin Tendulkar or Sourav Ganguly or

M.S. Dhoni on television is always overloaded with star value. The star value is produced not by a single medium, but it is cooked by the global television, corporate advertisement world and page three. It is true that stardom was there in cricket since before the coming of global media. M.A.K. Pataudi, S. Gavaskar and Kapil Dev were national heroes in the 1970s and 1980s. Pataudi was a star because he was considered as master strategist in the field; Gavaskar was a star as he faced furious fast bowling with courage and success, and Kapil was a champion young fast bowler and an earnest team-man. Though media played a role, star value associated with their name arose from the legacy of cricket itself. I would like to mention a controversy that took place in the year 2009 as vice-captain of Indian cricket team Virender Sehwag said that he did not hear the name of Vijay Merchant, former famous cricketer of Indian team. Pataudi criticizes Sehwag for his ignorance and remarked that a cricketer who represents national team as vice-captain should not forget the history of Indian cricket. Sehwag's attitude is like—'I perform, therefore I exist. Who cares history?' Pataudi's argument is like—without history a nation seizes to exist. This controversy actually marks a divider—a sharp divide between historicism and nationality versus the present and post-modernity. Sehwag and Dhoni, who started playing cricket in last two decades, are more popular as 'individual heroes' than local lads; they represent the triumph of Indian middle class (which is their own family background too) in international cricket; they appear in television and page three as models, playboys and militant nationalists with killer instinct displayed in the field.

This metamorphosis of the image of a cricketer in India from a successful 'local lad' to 'individual hero' started since the Benson and Hedges (Mini World) Cup in 1983. The phenomenon of the rise of Ravi Shastri is crucial in this context. The massive currency of his image as play-boy hero which outsmarted even Kapil Dev's and Gavaskar's national hero image is a contribution of Kerry Packer's Channel Nine. In 1990s Sachin Tendulkar emerged as 'wonder boy' of world cricket. From the very beginning of Sachin's entry in the international cricket his genius in television has been considered to be a discovery in the world cricket, viz. his identity as a Mumbai lad has been addressed very little. But Gavaskar's and Kapil Dev's identities, on the contrary, were always framed in regional-territorial sense respectively as 'Mumbai master' and 'Haryana hurricane'.

Tendulkar's image has been associated with Mumbai only because Mumbai is the city of mega stars. The huge craze of mass media, particularly of page three photographers and entertainment television, in Sachin Tendulkar's wedding can only be compared with no one else but superstar Amitabh Bachchan's son's wedding. Neither his performances in the field nor his personality before mass media is responsible for Sachin's mega star image. Rather his superhero image is constituted with 'phenomena' which themselves were the contribution of television media, page three and advertisement world. Sourav Ganguly in last few years was established as Bengal Boy in Indian cricket. But his 'prince of Calcutta' image was really superseded by his image of an aggressive captain of 'team India'. Sourav was told by the then Prime Minister of Bangladesh after the victorious performance of Indian cricket team in Dacca to speak few words in Bengali. But Ganguly declined to speak in Bengali. In fact the local identity imposed on him was a construction of the local press of Kolkata; in a larger context his gestures to express a kind of aggressive nationalism in the cricket field was much celebrated. Actually global sports television and national press circulated Captain Sourav Ganguly's aggressive attitudes as the successful campaigner of 'team India'.

IPL, the very recent yet truly overwhelming phenomenon of Indian cricket, radically re(/dis)oriented the representation of the global-local dynamics in Indian cricket. Though the participant teams in the IPL are named Rajasthan Royals, Deccan Chargers, Punjab King's XI or Kolkata Knight Riders, etc., they hardly represent the 'local' or regional as most of the players are hired from International cricket and few from national level cricket. Anybody can buy a team in the bid; for example, Kolkata Knight Riders is presently owned by Shahrukh Khan, the mega star of Bollywood who has no connection with Bengal or Kolkata. The IPL can in no way be considered as domestic/local cricket.

IPL has premiered three brand new ideas in Indian cricket; one, a team that usually bears the name of 'local' can be purchased by any Indian multi-millionaire. The IPL is a global spectacle that forged the identity of the local. The 2009 IPL was not even played on Indian soil; it was held in South Africa. Second, Bollywood stardom and glamour world has directly established nexus with cricket. Consequently in the

IPL stardom in cricket field is reciprocated by the stardom in the silver screen. A television advertisement in SET MAX, the channel that owned the telecast right of the IPL 2009, ran a slogan in Hindi: 'Have a bottle of Sprite; get a chance to meet the super-stars—Sourav, Shahrukh and Knight Riders.' The name of a cricket star is aligned with the name of a Bollywood megastar.

Third, as far as its form is concerned, IPL popularized 'Twenty-20' cricket match. T20 form seems very television-friendly as when telecast it's more like a 2/3 hours long TV 'programme' than an 'event' of whole day. Live telecast of the IPL matches completes cricket's Bollywoodization. The camera cuts to the dancing cheerleaders, sort of a band of item girls, after every boundary or overboundary is hit by a batsman, or after a wicket is bagged by a bowler. Even when SET MAX shows the highlight of a match they hardly break the rule. The discreet charm of cricket is divided into two distinct parts—the narrative in the field (in the form of the game) and spectacle just outside the boundary line (in the form of dancing cheerleaders). They establish unbreakable bond with each other. The global television celebrates this new form. The IPL matches draw only a moderate audience in the arena but attract huge number of people on its live telecast. It is quite easy to infer that this new form is being popularized by the global television. The IPL has clearly got centre stage in Indian cricket and to a great extent in world cricket with the help of mass media. The global here appears, as if dressed in local costume. Hence the 'local' has become an empty signifier in Indian cricket. And actually in the IPL the local withers away, the global dominates the stage in the disguise of 'local'.

And finally, as Ashis Nandy remarked, 'Cricket is an Indian game accidentally discovered by the English.'[40] It could be reworked and recycled so that cricket is an epic game which is today reduced to and fitted within a paradigm of Bollywood. The televised Indian cricket, teaming up with Bollywood, has been adapting rhetoric of the 'global' effacing and appropriating the markers of 'local'. Neville Cardus says:

A boy looks upon his heroes at cricket with emotions terribly mixed. He believes they are gods, yet….he thinks they are going to get out nearly every ball…..strangely indeed does a boy think that his favourite are the best but still the most fallible and in need of his every devoted thought.[41]

Once upon a time Cricket was a game of uncertainty. But getting out means little to a boy of today; instead how many fours and sixes the hero hits on the face of the 'enemy' does matter. Global television, as an enormous 'cult of distraction' demands no devotion. Today getting out means only departure of the hero from the 22 yards. But no umpire can declare him out from the domain of televisual reality since the hero is always 'present' in advertisements, talk shows, billboards and page three. Should we mourn—where has the 'brave' little boy gone who feared the fall of his hero with every ball? Perhaps he has gone to the graveyard as the wonder of uncertainty disappeared forever from cricket.

Notes and References

1. See Kumar Prasad Mukhopadhyay, *Dishi Gan Bideshi Khela* (Kolkata: Ananda, 2002), pp. 31–64; also see Boria Majumdar, *Lost Histories of Indian Cricket: Battles of the Pitch* (London and New York: Routledge, 2006), pp. 24–37.
2. See Mihir Bose, *The Magic of Indian Cricket: Cricket and Society in India* (London and New York: Routledge, 2006), p. 142.
3. Parsees versus Mohammedans match at Bombay Gymkhana ground in 1934 was the first cricket match to be broadcast by All India Radio. Legendary cricket commentator and expert Bobby Talyarkhan delivered the running commentary. see Boria Majumdar, *Lost Histories of Indian Cricket*, p. 92.
4. See ibid., pp. 1–7.
5. Narendranath Dutta before he was renamed as Swami Vivekananda was a regular member of a renowned Cricket Club of Calcutta run by natives, situated at south Calcutta. Rabindranath Tagore loved cricket and encouraged Brajaranjan Ray, a pioneer sport journalist of Calcutta. Nehru had a soft corner for cricket. Satyajit Ray's uncle Kartik Bose was a good cricketer and a renowned cricket coach of Bengal. Moreover Ray was attracted to cricket as his poet father Sukumar Ray loved cricket.
6. See Mukhopadhyay, *Dishi Gan Bideshi Khela*, pp. 7–12 and p. 30 where Mukhopadhyay refers to Shankari Prasad Basu's 'Eden-e shiter Dupure'.
7. Roland Barthes, *Mythologies* (London: Paladin Grafton, 1973), p. 15.
8. Ashis Nandy, *The Tao of Cricket* (New Delhi: Oxford University Press, 2000) says 'the continuity between traditions and modernity…and between the "seductive"

West and the "easy", "material", "moral" East', explains Nandy, '… is established not through *purushakar* but through the management of random events. As in cricket, you establish your "success" not through specific successes but through the way you accept and negotiate a random set of challenges' (ibid., p. 45).

9. Sayad Mustaque Ali died on 18 June 2005 at the age of 91. The next day the renowned Bengali novelist and sports journalist Moti Nandy wrote an obituary in *Anandabazar Patrika* (Kolkata, 19 June 2005, p. 15), where he recounted the late cricketer's comment made in 1978 in an interview.

10. Benedict Anderson uses the phrase 'unbound seriality' in *The Spectre of Comparisons* (London: Verso, 1998), to explain a liberal and universal feature of nationalism that stands as an antithesis to a sectarian nationalism based on the ethnicity and othering. Partha Chatterjee, in 'Anderson's Utopia' *Diacritics* 29, no. 4 (1999): 128–29), writes:

> [T]he most significant addition that Anderson has made to his analysis in Imagined Communities is his attempt to distinguish between nationalism and the politics of ethnicity. He does this by identifying two kinds of seriality that are produced by the modern imaginings of community. One is the unbound seriality of the everyday universals of modern social thought: nations, citizens, revolutionaries, bureaucrats, workers, intellectuals, and so on. The other is the bound seriality of governmentality: the finite totals of enumerable classes of population produced by the modern census and the modern electoral systems. Unbound serialities are typically imagined and narrated by means of the classic instruments of print-capitalism, namely, the newspaper and the novel. They afford the opportunity for individuals to imagine themselves as members of larger than face-to-face solidarities, of choosing to act on behalf of those solidarities, of transcending by an act of political imagination the limits imposed by traditional practices. Unbound serialities are potentially liberating.

11. See Nandy, *The Tao of Cricket*, pp. 112–13.
12. Vijay Hazare, *A Long Innings* (Calcutta: Rupa & Co., 1981), p. 247.
13. See Ananda Mitra, *Television and Popular Culture in India* (New Delhi: Sage, 1993), pp. 35–40.
14. See Lucrecia Escudero Chauvel, 'Umberto Eco, the Sixties, and Cultural Studies', *Contemporary French and Francophone Studies* 1, no. 1(1997): 233–43.
15. See 'World Series Cricket', *WORD iQ.COM Encyclopedia*. Available online at http://www.worldiQ.com Encyclopedia (accessed on 20 October 2004).
16. Ibid.
17. Ibid.
18. In the final match India beat Pakistan at Sydney. And Ravi Shastri of Indian team won the Man of the Series award, and an Audi 100 car as prize.

19. The idea of 'imagined communities' is formulated by Benedict Anderson. According to him the modern nation, particularly in the third world, is not constituted by kinship, religion or dynasty. 'In an anthropological spirit,' Anderson proposes, the definition of the nation:

> [I]t is an imagined political community—and imagined as both inherently limited and sovereign. It is imagined because the members of even the smallest nation will never know most of their fellow-members, meet them, or even hear of them, yet in the mind of each lives the image of their communion.

See *Imagined Communities* (London: Verso, 1991), pp. 5–6.

20. See Barthes, *Mythologies*, pp. 132–33.

21. Ibid., p. 135.

22. Hamid Naficy, 'Mediaworks Representation of Other: The Case of Iran', in *Questions of Third Cinema,* eds Jim Pines and Paul Willeman (London: B.F.I., 1994), pp. 227–30.

23. John Ellis, *Visible Fiction: Cinema Television Video* (London: Routledge, 1988), p. 112.

24. See Raymond Williams, 'Programming as Sequence or Flow', in *Media Studies: A Reader*, eds Paul Morris and Sue Thornham (Edinburgh University Press, 1998), pp. 238–39.

25. For 'mode retro' see Fredric Jemeson, 'Postmodernism & Consumer Society', in *Postmodern Culture*, ed. Hal Foster (London: Pluto Press, 1998), pp. 116–17.

26. See Abhijit Roy, 'The Bhadralok and the New Popular' (unpublished paper presented at the international seminar on 'City and the Cinema', Sarai–CSDS, February, 2000, Delhi). He writes:

> It seems that these two aspects of the 'new popular' engage two different modes of address which are not mutually exclusive. We would identify the 'entertainment-popular' best represented by MTV…as engaging primarily a 'play-mode' because things—songs, dance, film, fiction— are 'played' here with the dominant resultant impression being 'it's being played for me/us'. As opposed to this we think of the 'information-popular' (BBC, Star News, etc.) as engaging a 'record mode' generating impressions of things recorded for me/us. These two domains deploy two different kinds of proclamations; the record-mode 'produces' documents of life caught unawares and the play-mode emphasizes 'performance'.

27. See Debashish Dasgupta, 'Cricket & Mass Media', *Journal of the Department of Mass Communication* vol. 2: 76.

28. Margaret Morse, 'Sports on Television: Replay and Display', in *Television, Critical Concepts in Media & Cultural Studies*, vol II, ed. Toby Miller (London, N.Y: Routledge, 2003), pp. 392–93.
29. Ibid.
30. Ava Rose and James Friedman, 'Television Sport as Masculine Cult of Distraction', *Screen* 35, no.1(1994): 22.
31. Ibid.
32. The term 'symbolic nationalism' is used here in the sense in which Ashish Rajadhyakshya, inspired by Eric Hobsbawn's idea, used it in his 'Rethinking State after Bollywood', *Journal of the Moving Image*, no. 3 (2004).
33. See Marshal Mcluhan, 'Medium is the Message', in *Media Studies, A Reader*, eds Paul Morris and Sue Thornham (Edinburgh: Edinburgh University Press, 1998): 38–42.
34. Ibid., p. 40.
35. The last BJP government in the centre promised 'dual citizenship', specially for the NRIs, and both the PM and the Deputy PM declared that they were in favour of it. By virtue of it the NRIs could enjoy the citizenship of India even if they already have the citizenship a foreign country.
36. 'Shining India', an ambitious audio-visual campaign launched by BJP, the then ruling party, as a part of propaganda of their government's achievement in implementation of the developmentalist policy in the general election 2006 placed the image of rich and 'happy' peasants as the sign of economic development of rural people of India under the BJP rule. see Mihir Bose, 'Shining India or Poverty of Ambition?', p. 244.
37. See Majumdar, *Lost Histories of Indian Cricket*.
38. Ibid.
39. Manju Joseph, 'India: An Unnatural Cricketing Nation', in *Cricketing Culture in Conflict: World Cup 2003*, eds Boria Majumdar and A.J. Mangan (London and New York: Routledge, 2004), p. 107.
40. Nandy, *The Tao of Cricket*, p. 122.
41. Bose, *The Magic of Indian Cricket*, p. 230. Bose quotes Neville Cardus at the beginning of 'Gods and Boys', a chapter in his extremely resourceful book on Indian cricket.

Chapter 5

Bollywood and
the Mumbai Underworld

Reading *Satya* in Retrospect

Rajdeep Roy

*The inclusion of Freida Pinto as a latter day 'Helen of Troy' by Vanity
Fair, the American glossy, which has listed the most beautiful women in
the world, is unsurprising.*

*Complexion is in the eye of the beholder. But in London, several British
Indian actresses who have told me that they have been rejected for roles
because casting directors deemed them to be 'too fair'.*

In not so many words, they were told: 'You don't look Indian enough'.[1]

Freida Pinto has become a rage among the Western film-makers after
the success of *Slumdog Millionaire* (Danny Boyle and Loveleen
Tandon, 2008) in the Academy Awards, 2009. The film got
eight Oscars including the Best Motion Picture of the year and the
Best Director award. Incidentally it didn't win any award in the acting
category. However, Pinto, playing the character Latika, an orphan girl
from the Mumbai slums, is redefining Indian beauty (after Aishwarya
Rai, former Miss World and Bollywood actress) in the West, as *Slumdog*
signals the growing presence of Bollywood in the international media
industry.

Slumdog met with mixed responses in India and abroad. While the
Bombay film industry aspires for similar success for its home-made
products, *Slumdog* couldn't impress some big names. Amitabh Bachchan
wrote in his blog:[2]

[I]f SM projects India as [a] third-world, dirty, underbelly developing
nation and causes pain and disgust among nationalists and patriots,
let it be known that a murky underbelly exists and thrives even in

the most developed nations............... It's just that the SM idea, authored by an Indian and conceived and cinematically put together by a westerner, gets creative globe recognition. The other would perhaps not.

The reply to his blog by someone named 'svhayter' acts as an interesting counterpoint. It says:

Slumdog doesn't show a complete picture of India or Indians, but few movies show a complete picture of any place or people, particularly a sprawling, expressive, multicultural city like Mumbai. You see a mere slice. *Slumdog* shows poverty, and it shows wealth, and it shows someone who survives one and is unconcerned with the other. What he is concerned with is LOVE. And that is so Indian.

Bollywood over the years has devised a culture of consumption which can incorporate multiple nationalisms and varied ideas of Indianness evoked by its films. *Slumdog* banks upon this character of Bollywood. Ravi Vasudevan in his essay, 'Meanings of Bollywood'[3] notes that, with the coming of economic liberalization and globalization in India during the 1990s, there is a marked change in its urban life. The period saw the emergence of a consumer economy centred on information and communication technology giving rise to new ways of production, circulation and consumption. The film industry, especially Hindi and Tamil cinema started making systematic inroads into the foreign market. Indian cinema gained the long-awaited industry status at about this time. Vasudevan observes that the popular cinema in order to tap the lucrative diasporic market had to move away from the earlier idea of a territorial nation and project a global brand image of India, Bollywood emerged as the most important category at this point. He noted that although the term, 'Bollywood' was used in magazines and trade journals before the 1990s, it was idiomatic and casual, predominantly used as a Third World imitation of the Hollywood. It was only after the late 1990s with the success of films like DDLJ (*Dilwale Dulhaniya Le Jayenge*, dir. Aditya Chopra, 1995), the term Bollywood came into regular usage and defined the broad culture industry associated with Bombay cinema.

Ashish Rajadhyaksha in his essay, 'Bollywoodization of Indian Cinema: Cultural Nationalism in a Global Arena'[4] defines Bollywood as a culture industry of which film is one element however central to the functioning of its other entertainment and consumer sectors like television, music industry, advertising, fashion and websites. He argues that it is Bollywood which by its narrative of an imagined Indian family and an imagined Indian culture has been able to act as a bridge between the popular mainstream cinema and the nation state. He shows that Bombay cinema which has always been a powerful mass cultural medium in close conflict with the state is getting incorporated into the global consumerist ethos of Bollywood and losing out its democratic potentials. *Slumdog* is perhaps a historical moment in Indian cinema when Bombay cinema (Hindi film industry based in Bombay/Mumbai) finally becomes synonymous with Bollywood.

Moving back to 1998, Ram Gopal Verma directed a film called *Satya* (Truth). This film is about a man named Satya who arrives in Bombay and gets involved in one of the organized crime syndicates in the city. Eventually he is killed in a police encounter. In the same year another film called *Ghulam* (Vikram Bhatt) was released. This film is about a young man who has grown up in a gang community and finally frees the locality from gang exploitation. Both these films are about the city's organized crime but with a fundamental difference. While *Satya* is about a gang community in post-1990s Bombay, *Ghulam* is a story told in the backdrop of 1990s Bombay about the purification of an outlaw on the verge of becoming a criminal. *Satya* tries to recreate a fast changing metropolis under the forces of globalization within the narrative of a gang community headed by a local gangster called Bhiku Mhatre (Manoj Bajpai). *Ghulam* on the other hand stops short of being a love story of an erratic young Sidhu (Amir Khan) living in the criminal underbelly of the city being chastised by love in the presence of a sympathetic state. I think it is *Satya* which becomes the classic model of the Mumbai underworld after 1990s and not *Ghulam* simply because of the former's sense of the changing urban history and its ability to play with stereotypes from previous Hindi films, producing new stereotypes in the process. The genre of underworld films consists of those which represent this change from the days of *Ghulam* to the post-1990s situation, of organized crime in Mumbai representing the culture of the underclass that thrives within it.

Bollywood and the Mumbai Underworld

I consider the term 'underworld' as a part of the complex matrix of relationships between the state, capital and the different communities that organize in some way or other the social and cultural life of Mumbai. The history of colonial nationalism in India shows that the colonized have invested on the 'narrative of community' based on rhetoric of kinship to construct their national identity. Interestingly after Independence as the state enters deeper into the social sphere it has begun to talk about the community in the same rhetoric of 'majority', 'minority' and 'reservations' as conceived of by the colonial state. Since 1970s there was a growing importance of different communities in India's electoral politics and in popular political discourses. The state–community relationships represented in underworld films are based on two primary assumptions. First, the idea of a nation state is increasingly making sense by a constant negotiation with specific communities. And second, the heterogeneous communities act as sites for global-local interactions intrinsic to the global consumer culture. Bollywood uses 'underworld' as a category to produce representations of a specific Mumbai culture which is a hybrid of the regional, national and global forces. It therefore caters to a viewership that receives the 'underworld' as a process of indigenization of global culture and at the same time as an idealized and decontextualized form of a specific element of 'locally' identifiable Mumbai life.

Satya has largely determined the film form for the underworld theme in Bollywood. It presents Mumbai underworld as a means of livelihood, an intrinsic part of the city life and not merely as a romanticized image of crime that thrives in the underbelly of the city. Danny Boyle said in an interview that at least three Indian films influenced him while making *Slumdog*. He believes that *Deewar* (The Wall, 1975) is an 'absolute key to Indian Cinema'. He says that Ram Gopal Verma's *Satya* (1998) and *Company* (2002) and Anurag Kashyap's *Black Friday* (2004) have helped him to recreate the Mumbai of Jamal Malik (Dev Patel).[5] On the other hand Dr Gezim Alpion, who teaches film at the University of Birmingham, while talking about films like *Bend it Like Beckham* and *Bride and Prejudice*,[6] says:

> Asian cineastes try to cater too much for Western tastes. It is the same mistake made by *Slumdog Millionaire*, which is appalling. I can't quite

believe what I've seen in that film, in terms of how the whole of India is trivialized. It deals in stereotypes. There are so many lively places in India. Its culture is as diverse as Europe's. The stereotyping is appalling. Cinema is meant for mass consumption. *Slumdog Millionaire* is sending out the wrong message—that that's the kind of audience and film that we want. I think that what's missing is more sophistication.

What makes *Satya* or *Company* or *Black Friday* which are highly localized in their content, catch the global imagination of Mumbai? In the subsequent discussion I will go on to a detailed discussion of *Satya*, as I believe that the other two films act upon the cinematic imagination of Mumbai underworld produced by *Satya*. I shall attempt to show how the film creates a narrative and a *mise-en-scène* for Mumbai, a Third World city in the global periphery. I will also try to show what elements of the narrative economy in the film are silenced and what gets incorporated in Bollywood.

I will begin by looking at how *Satya* changes the idea of Bombay or the city in Hindi cinema after 1990. The country-city dyad comes as a recurrent motif while depicting the city in Hindi cinema. *Satya* creates characters like Bheeku Mhatre (Manoj Bajpai) who is a second generation slum dweller. To him the image of the original home has already faded away. His new found subjectivity is created by the different spaces intrinsic to Mumbai. I would argue that in a film like *Satya* which forms a distinct sub-genre of city films in Hindi cinema, Mumbai ceases to exist as a 'generic metropolitan other'[7] as the films in this sub-genre do not work on the city-country dyad any more. I would argue that this new breed of city films in Hindi cinema posit an urban spectator subject with no desire to return to an ideal pastoral past. In fact there is no such past for this new urban subject. *Satya* creates a film form to produce this new kind of urban subjectivity.

Judith Wolkowitz in her reading of Henry James talks about two kinds of urban subjectivities. One is that of a 'sympathetic resident' which presupposes 'a privileged male subject' whose identity is stable, coherent and autonomous. He has knowledge of the 'man' and his 'world' through an exercise of reason. He embodies the power of spectatorship of what James called the 'sympathetic resident' who, while residing in one part of the city, is capable 'in imagination' of inhabiting the whole of it. She suggests that the 'sympathetic resident' privileges a set of perspectives about looking at a city—tourism, exploration, social investigation and social policy. She remarks that a powerful streak of voyeurism organizes this activity. She also brings in a second category, that of the *flaneur* as opposed to the bourgeois male whose gaze is reflected in James. The *flaneur* is an illusionist who transforms the city into a landscape of strangers and secrets, a 'dream web' to quote Benjamin where the most ancient occurrences are attached to those of today.[8] I would suggest that *Satya* invites the viewer to inhabit both these subjectivities at the same time in its representation of the underworld. This makes the viewer a citizen-subject, a part of the dominant 'top' in a political community, which relates to the underworld as its 'low other'. The repudiation of the 'low' by the dominant 'top' of the society is paradoxically accompanied by a heightened symbolic importance attached to the 'low other' in the imaginative repertoire of the dominant culture. What is socially peripheral frequently becomes symbolically central to the spectator position in the films based on what I call the 'underworld theme' in Bollywood.

Satya begins in the 'expository mode'[9] of documentary film. The opening sequence introduces Mumbai, in an additive montage of top angle shots of city traffic, 'Queen's Necklace' juxtaposed with a low angle view composed of mainly mid-shots of small fishing boats, slums on both sides of the railway track as the lifeline of Mumbai, the local train passes by, and finally the Victoria terminus becoming visible as the camera suddenly zooms out from a mid-close up of a crowd. In the sequence we also see a series of fictional shots of police encounters and Kallu Mama (Saurabh Shukla) in close-up (pointing a gun towards the camera). On all such occasions, the commentary suddenly stops. These fictional shots get repeated at the end of the film. Their presence in the opening sequence acts as a premonition of the fate that awaits the gangsters. The narrative closure of a moral tale of good and evil, and of a tussle between crime and law, takes place at the very onset of the film. The end of the film is clearly spelt out; we know the ultimate fate of the protagonist. So what holds our interest in the film beyond its opening sequence?

The film from the outset invites us to another narrative—it tells a tale of a city in transition. And the film tries to create the cinematic parallel of this emerging city. *Satya's* beginning lays out the general framework on which its narrative will unfold. True to the expository mode of documentary films, the authorial voiceover in the opening sequence presents Mumbai within a certain frame of reference. And by the very process of its exposition, the attainment of a solution following a cause-and-effect structure delimits the argument it puts forward to the viewers. It states that the present condition of gang violence and the existence of underworld are due to the economic inequality prevailing in the city. The film banks upon the commonsensical idea of economic underdevelopment as the root cause for the increasing crime and violence in the city. But as the film progresses we see that this rhetoric of the welfare state inadequately explains the presence of the underworld in Mumbai. The expository mode addresses its argument of economic development to a viewer-as-citizen subject while remaining fully aware of the limitation of such an argument all along the opening sequence and the rest of the film. I would argue that the selection of an expository mode of documentary film form critiques the general tendency of finding easy solutions by equating any issue related to urban poverty to the class question. And *Satya* from the outset takes a very different stance. It consciously distances itself from the 'developmental aesthetics' of New Cinema and Middle Cinema as well as the mainstream Hindi films based on the state–community debate. *Satya* in its opening sequence does two things. First, it establishes a visual geography to represent the 'underworld' after the 1990s, which will be recreated or played upon in the later Hindi films, literature on Mumbai as well as media discourses and in the process will produce an audio-visual nomenclature for the underworld. In other words, it represents the process of a formation of an underworld culture. And second, the opening sequence ends with Satya coming out of the Victoria station. The commentary doesn't give any reference of Satya's past life before coming to Mumbai unlike *Parinda* (dir. Vidhu Vinod Chopra, 1989) or *Nayakan* (dir. Mani Ratnam, 1987), as we hardly recognize him in the crowd shown in long shot. It deliberately curtails any association of Victoria Station with the iconic shot of 'coming to the city' in Hindi cinema. At the same time, since the film robs

Satya of any subjectivity derived from his memory of the past, contrary to the protagonists in *Deewar* or *Parinda* or *Nayakan*, it allows interplay of signifiers from the past Hindi films without any signified whatsoever. Thus the anonymity of Satya makes him an 'empty signifier' being continuously reproduced in Bollywood.

Satya served as a trendsetter for later films about a vibrant Mumbai underclass culture after 1990. And more importantly *Satya* is conscious about its process of producing stereotypes. It poses the question of how far the new underworld films in Bollywood engage with the state–community debate which is of central concern in earlier Hindi gangster films. Or, is it to be understood as one of the processes of localization of Bombay cinema by Bollywood in the presence of multinational capital?

In the film *Satya,* the hero's entrance into the criminal world follows a set of motifs from the previous Hindi gangster movies. But the film gives new meanings to those motifs which I suggest has produced the standard narrative for representing organized crime in Mumbai after the 1990s. After coming to Mumbai Satya starts working in a beer bar. There he encounters a *bhai* (gangster in Mumbai is called *bhai*) for the first time. He gets involved in an argument with the gangster in the bar that ends in a fight where he is severely beaten by the gang members in front of a police officer who happens to be there for his routine bribe. Satya lands in the jail on a false charge for illegal trafficking of women (*bhrawagiri*). There he meets Bheeku Mhatre, another famous gangster. Mhatre arranges for the release of Satya from jail and Satya joins Bheeku Mhatre's gang. Lawyer Mule (Makrand Deshpande) better known as Uncle to the gang, takes him to Kallu Mama, the CEO of the Mhatre gang. We see a close-up shot from a low angle of a lane with low tin roofs of make-shift houses on either side as Satya and Mule enter the frame. They enter a house scarcely lit as a hand-held camera follows them. Uncle or Mule meets with the members as the camera holds them in tight close up. He is talking about his exploits the night before with Shabbo, a woman from the slums. The camera leaves Uncle and swiftly pans round the house with people moving here and there and some sitting on tables with overhead bulbs giving a yellowish tinge to the dark room. The camera moves from the noirish set without a single cut to a mid close-up of Kallu Mama talking to some one over the telephone about the utility of a peaceful way of extortion. The room in which Kallu Mama is sitting serves as the office from where business or *dhanda* is run. The set design here is starkly different from the set where the gang members are introduced. The room is brightly lit with locally made bamboo mats used to cover the walls, an old air-conditioner and a big office desk with telephones ringing all the time. This is neither the spacecraft-like chamber of the notorious criminal Lion (Ajit) in *Kalicharan* (dir. Subhash Ghai, 1976) nor the office of Davar (Iftikhar) from where Vijay (Amitabh Bachchan) steps into the world of crime in *Deewar*. It is not even like the place (though very similar in looks) from where Anna (Nana Patekar) conducts his business in *Parinda*. These films represent the nature of the Bombay/Mumbai underworld in the 1970s and 1980s which thrived primarily on gold smuggling and drugs apart from investment in films. The new phenomenon after 1990s is real estate. And the main business of Mumbai underworld post-1990s is extortion mainly from real estate developers, big corporate agencies and film financiers. In a scene set in the office of Kallu Mama, a builder named Ahuja enters soon after Satya arrives in the office with Uncle. Mama asks Ahuja about the delay in payment of the extortion fees charged by his gang. He gives the builder another 10 days to pay the money. The scene underlines the nature of the gang business in Mumbai after the 1990s, based on fear. Satya elsewhere in the film in a conversation with Bheeku says, 'Don't kill but always threaten to kill. This is the law of the *dhanda* in underworld.' *Satya* tells the story of a city where one is under constant threat from one or the other agencies whether a political party or a gang. The gang business is no longer conducted outside the general purview of law and morality. It is a part of the everyday, as much overboard as any other business, formal or informal, that runs in the commercial capital of India. The new gang business runs on the insecurity of the local people and their constant craving for personal safety, above all concerns. The film invites the viewer to be a part of the risky business of living in a metropolis. At the same time I would suggest that the neo-liberal world as a networked community where everyone everywhere is embedded in a web of trust and risk is played on a local level in the function of a gang community depicted in *Satya*.

The film touches upon but never explains the relationship of the real estate development and organized crime in Mumbai after 1990. Liza Weinstein in her essay, 'Mumbai Development Mafias: Globalization, Organized Crime and Land Development'[10] notes that the rise of Mumbai's organized criminal activities thriving on black market smuggling of gold and consumer electronics in the 1950s was due to India's macroeconomic policies of strict regulations on imports. Liberalization and deregulation in the early 1990s reduced the demand for smuggled consumer goods which diversified the gang business in the city. The closing of the cotton mills in the 1980s and opening of mill districts and port lands for real estate development, coupled with skyrocketing real estate prices in the 1990s with the coming of the service industries and direct foreign investments to the country's commercial hub, facilitated the organized crime syndicates' investment on property development. Weinstein argues that by 'an illicit nexus of politicians, bureaucrats and police, the mafia has emerged as a central figure in the Mumbai's land development politics'.[11]

In the late 1970s and early 1980s, some of the local gangs of Mumbai developed into organized crime syndicates. Varadarajan Mudaliar, popularly known as Varadhabhai was the first to run a powerful criminal organization way back in the 1960s based on illicit production and sale of alcohol in the squatter settlement of Dharavi, which today is Asia's largest slum. In the 1970s, Congress lost its single party dominance in the country and organized criminal groups having links with one or the other political party fortified their power with the new, predominantly ethnic political movements in the city. Meanwhile, due to police crackdowns in this period the largest gangs shifted their base of operation outside India. And in doing so Mumbai underworld expanded the geographic reach of its criminal activities and got linked to the global organized crime networks. It had access to new sources of power and new forms of capital.

Today Mumbai's two biggest gangs, D-company headed by Dawood Ibrahim, who was alleged to have planned the 1993 bomb blasts in the city, and his one time Hindu lieutenant Chota Rajan's gang, are carrying out their operations in Mumbai from Karachi and Kuala Lumpur respectively. The organized crime syndicates in Mumbai since the 1990s with the help of information technologies and global financial infrastructure have built an increasingly global organization. Scholars like S.P. Singh[12] and A.V. Papachristos[13] have pointed out that local gangs and criminal networks, like many organizations, are becoming increasingly transnational, as the institutions established to facilitate globalization of formal economy have been appropriated by the purveyors of the informal economy.

Underworld films since 1990 have changed in its depiction of the metropolis as the Mumbai underworld has emerged as a global criminal network. The cassette cover of Ram Gopal Verma's recent film, *Contract* (2007) gives useful insights about this shift in perspective, of the representation of crime and the city in underworld films. It describes the film, *Contract* along with two previous films by the director, *Satya* (1998) and *Company* (2002) as follows: *Satya* is an inside view of the underworld, *Company* is an overview of the underworld and *Contract* is a film where underworld meets international terrorism.

Interestingly the question of land development politics in Mumbai pivotal in understanding the city's underworld never featured in a big way in *Satya* accept a few passing references. The issues of land acquisition for real estate with underworld emerging as a huge economic force and as an indispensable part of the local governance along with the emergence of a plebian politics resulting in dividing the city on communal lines, are systematically silenced with the gradual Bollywoodization of the underworld films.

Bollywood owes a lot of its present success to its music industry which was initially based on the film songs and then diversified into various other forms of music during Bollywood's initial foothold in the world entertainment business. Today the music industry in spite of suffering heavy losses from rampant piracy is still a major player in selling Bollywood dreams. The new age Bollywood has moved a long way from its song and dance spectacle with colourful exhibition of an exotic Indian-ness. With expanding market it has to be in constant lookout for new products. This has resulted in constant localization of musical content with an incorporation of folk forms, specific singing styles like Sufi musical style, use of regional dialect in the lyrics and fusion music. The song 'goli maar bheje mein' from *Satya* can be seen as one of the earlier instances of this process of localization in Bollywood music. I have discussed elsewhere how this song, its musical arrangements and its representation have produced a new form of urban music in Bollywood. Here I will not go into that detail, instead I will look at how the song sequence, *goli maar bheje mein* reworks the previous notions of hero and couple formation in Hindi cinema in the context of the networkedness that runs Mumbai underworld. And I will try to illustrate how it gets disseminated within the Bollywood culture industry in the formation of the new brand *tapori*.

Ranjini Majumdar in the chapter, 'The Rebellious Tapori' notes that in post-1990s Bombay cinema the figure of *tapori* (vagabond) replaces the previous 'angry young man hero' of the 1970s personified by Vijay (Amitabh Bachchan) in *Deewar*. She describes a *tapori* as a person of the streets with performance and performative gestures key to his/her agency. She defines a *tapori* as 'lacking a home but longing for a family, a *tapori* occupies a middle space between the crisis of urban life and the simultaneous yearning for stability'.[14] She explains that *tapori* talking in a hybrid language called Bombayya of the multilingual and regionally diverse streets do away with the predominance of Hindusthani in Bombay cinema. She also notes that the figure of a *tapori* has changed the idea of a north Indian male as the ideal hero figure of Hindi cinema.

Bheeku was shown arrested by police earlier in the film for plotting the murder of a big movie producer. In the jail he met Satya. Hero's life changed in the prison—a recurrent motif in Hindi cinema. After a court room drama making fun of the legal apparatus, Bheeku is released of all charges in plotting the murder. He returns home to his gang. A party is organized in the building I mentioned before to celebrate his return. The song *goli maar bheje mein* comes in this party scene. To commemorate the return of the gangster Hindi film narrative traditionally breaks into a cabaret number, a filmy mujrah or kawali where the famous vamp or the revengeful heroine makes her appearance. But where does one place the celebration of a group of drunken men dancing to celebrate their boss Bheeku's return. The song sequence does not remind us of the archetypal scene in Hindi cinema of the gang-lord returning to his den from long exile. And Bheeku is no traditional villain of the past Hindi movies where there is a clear demarcation between crime and law. He is part of the large informal economy which is what Satya calls *dhanda* that functions in a grey zone between the legal and the illegal. The blurring boundaries of legality make possible the builder Ahuja going for protection to gangs and not to the police and Bheeku conducting his daily gang business from jail.

Satya borrows a lot from the Hollywood crime thrillers and gangster movies like the previous crime fictions in Hindi Cinema. But *Satya* has a fundamental difference with those films. It resists the formation of an individual subject. Genres like Gangster, Western and later Film Noir are principally talking about a male narrative where the presence of a woman is marginal or absent. The presence of the *femme fatale* (vamp as a weak parallel in Hindi films) with her new found subjectivity in her sexuality threatens the patriarchal constitution of the 'tough guy' hero or the cerebral detective. Nonetheless the films are about the individual hero's dilemma between law and justice or between moral and amoral. The films depict the quest of the hero for his masculine identity.[15] I mentioned earlier that Bheeku is not the traditional villain or anti-hero of Hindi cinema craving for individuality. He knows that he has no existence outside his gang and the larger community of the underworld. In a similar manner, there is no necessity for marginal characters like the vamp or the prostitute as the other to reinforce the self identity of the male protagonist.

The song *goli maar bheje mein* is a dialogue between the community and the individual or in other words a conversation between Satya and the Bheeku Mhatre gang. It can also be read as a narrative of the underworld after the 1990s. And Satya can not be given a place within this narrative grid and so he is a passive onlooker in the entire song sequence. Prasad reads the film as Satya's impossible search for 'normality'. Satya tries to find this 'impossible normality' in a romantic union with Vidya.[16] I would argue that a formation of a modern nuclear couple consisting of Satya and Vidya, premised upon the idea of a fully formed citizen subject, is impossible within the narrative economy of the film. Satya fails to find his cherished couple space in the film's diegetic world, because his idea of couple formation is not ingrained within the collective interest of a community life that sustains a gang like Bheeku Mahtre's. The film, *Satya* on the contrary, posits a new couple made of Bheeku and

Pyaari (Shefali Chaya) who have learned to live with the presence of gang culture in the underworld economy. The engagement of the family in constant negotiation with the modern state still continues to be a point of narrative tension in the post-1990s films though in a changed form due to a deeper penetration of capital into the community life. The song is staged like a theatre where the characters are playing out different aspects of life in the Mumbai gang-world. The camera is predominantly static unlike its high mobility in the rest of the film. It holds a group of gang members in crammed shots with only one onscreen light source, giving the shots a musty and tactile quality. The music uses ambiance sounds and unconventional sounds like gun shots and breaking of beer bottles and police siren with no effort to blend them with a traditional musical arrangement. They act as specific markers or narrative points in the song.

As I have already said, the song is addressed to Satya in the film. It is the inability of Satya to understand the world view of the gang community that eventually brought the gang's downfall. The song in a way serves a choric function commenting on the events that will follow towards the inevitable destruction of the Bheeku Mhatre gang. A similar narrative technique is followed to create the tragedy in *Maqbool* (dir. Vishal Bharadwaj, 2003). Both Satya and Maqbool are doomed because they are individual subjects who want to run the underworld on their own terms. But as the song suggests the underworld belongs to a different order of reality. Here every element is organically linked to the other, such that a disruption in one leads to the destruction of the whole structure. This does not mean that it is a weak structure but an extremely fluid structure which continuously reorganizes itself in the presence of new forces.

This is also the nature of the new virtual capital which does not produce commodities but concepts. I would argue that the song tells us about a new era of brand culture in Hindi film industry where the new tapori brand that it creates will reinvent itself 'as a cultural sponge, soaking up and morphing to its surrounding.'[17] The *tapori* brand has opened up a huge market for lifestyle merchandizing signifying the life in Mumbai. I will present two instances of the brand business regarding the tapori culture created by Hindi films in recent years. Coke used the tapori style to create its brand image in India. The indigenization of the Coca Cola began in India in a big way with Prasoon Joshi, the national creative director of McCann Erickson Add Agency. He made the word, *thanda* (cold drink) synonymous with Coke. And the first major add campaign of Coke with the catch line, *thanda matlab Coca Cola* (cold drinks/soft drinks means Coca Cola)featured Amir Khan as a tapori going to a downtown restaurant and ordering a *thanda*. The dumb waiter uncorks some other cola for him. Amir breaks into a tapori lingo only to drive home the point *thanda matlab Coca Cola*. *The Hindu* in an article on the film, *Munna Bhai M.B.B.S*(dir. Rajkumar Hirani, 2003) reported that during the India–Pakistan cricket match in Karachi, the Pakistani fans used different tapori words from the film to address the players. Quoting the film's scriptwriter, Abbas Tyrewalla it says:

> The quintessential Mumbai *tapori* or street slang used in the film has become a sort of style statement. It is amazing that the word *mamu* which is a typical Mumbai slang has become popular with even the NRIs in London! Now every other Bollywood film is trying to inject Mumbai slang to pep up the script.[18]

Let me again return to the song, *goli maar bheje mein* talking about living in Mumbai as a part of the gang community with another song of the city, '*yeh hai Bombay meri jaan*' (C.I.D, dir. Raj Khosla, 1956) discussed at length by Sudipta Kaviraj.[19] Both the songs are about a struggle for living in Mumbai which offers new problems and threats to its inmates every day. It is also a place of freedom. But what is this freedom that Kaviraj talks about? He reads the song as a narrative of the city which offers many possibilities and dreams. His Bombay is the city that attracts a huge migrant population which pours into the city every day. The freedom that he is talking about comes from the creation of a private space in an incessant flow of anonymous population. But the city that the song *goli maar bheje mein* in *Satya* describes is the city that is a network society where an ordinary couple can not find its niche. I would suggest that it's a city after the 1993 Bombay riots and then the serial bomb blasts. This is the city that has to be seen in the light of the broad event of mass scale violence and anarchy. Jim Masselos suggests that the riots brought a shock which cannot be understood solely through a politics of exclusion or communal polarization. He notes that the promise of the city of a livelihood and relative independence gets dismantled because the economic parameters are not that strong.[20] The song creates a film form that represents the facilitation of global consumer capitalism in appropriating aspects of the local with profit potential. It shows how they are repackaged into idealized and decontextualized forms and then promoted as disembedded ethnic motifs.

The history of xenophobia in the city that surfaced with the Bombay riots and the bomb blasts thereafter remain as an undercurrent in *Satya*. When Anurag Kashyap made a film on the bomb blasts, it is interesting to note that he followed a film form standardized in *Satya* to represent the city's underworld. And in the process he resorted to the stereotypes produced by *Satya*. *Black Friday* is a film on the serial bomb blasts that shook the city in 1992–93. It was believed to be triggered by the Muslim underworld as a reaction to the riots which saw systematic massacre of the Muslim population by the Hindu fundamentalist forces following the Babri mosque demolition in Ayodhya. *Slumdog* recreates an elaborate police chase of a riot suspect. What incites *Slumdog Millionaire* to recreate such a sequence? Is it the camera moving in the dingy lanes and by-lanes of a slum in Mumbai chasing a gangster-? Is such a chase sequence the reception of a film style created in *Satya* and mastered in *Black Friday*, which interests the Western viewer and more importantly, the jury of the Oscar award? I will try to look at how *Black Friday* unfolds the narrative of the blast and what is its point of convergence with other popular representations of the blast.

Black Friday posits at the outset that the criminal Muslim underclass might be the immediate force behind the blast. But more than the fundamentalist argument about the blast, the film suggests that the riots suddenly disrupt the structure of community life in Mumbai. Previously various communities interacted among themselves predominantly on the basis of an economic relationship. But after the riots the population is divided on communal lines. This makes impossible the constant negotiation of capital in a bourgeois democratic state which has small communities and interest groups within its domain. This also affected the economic base on which the underworld functions. The underworld's role in the blast is seen in the film as a reaction to this change in the social and economic life in Mumbai after the riot. As I have said before, the city after the riot and the blast thereafter, is a city in a transitional state where the previous forces that used to determine the community life and its relation with the nation state are no longer strong and the new fundamentalist ambitions are yet to take full force. *Black Friday* represents this tension in the cultural life of the city, through the 'underworld' or 'gang' culture.

Black Friday begins with a sequence of shots about the chance arrest of Gullu, a small time street thug giving the information of a bomb blast that is about to happen in Mumbai. Gradually all the characters are introduced in a series of shots and the plan of the blast slowly unfolds. The sequence goes on to the depiction of the event—the scene of the blast in the stock exchange building juxtaposed with television footage and news reports. Police detect the first evidence, a Maruti van near the Siemen's office in Worli and continue to the arrest of Asgar Muqadam (Nawazuddin), Tiger Memon's (Pavan Malhotra) secretary. From him we get to know the rest of the story about how the serial blasts took place. The opening sequence with fictional shots, newsreel photography with a mixture of documentary and fictional style of film-making sets the paradigm within which the narrative will proceed for the rest of the film. The style of the opening sequence in *Black Friday* reminds us of the expository mode in the opening sequence of *Satya*. Anurag Kashyap, director of *Black Friday,* is also the co-scriptwriter along with Saurabh Shukla of *Satya*.

Black Friday is based on the work of S. Hussain Zaidi. Let me now look at another novel on contemporary Mumbai, Suketu Mehta's *Maximum City* (2004) and how it organizes its narrative of the blast. The account of the blast begins as follows:

> The commissioner told Ajay' (very similar to the character, Rakesh Maria in *Black Friday* played by Kay Kay Menon) to take charge of the investigation….On the night of 14th March, Ajay called twenty of the best police detectives he knew in the city. They gathered in the command room in 11.30 p.m. and the process of putting information together began; five hours later, on the morning of 15th March, Ajay arrested the first suspect.[21]

Both the film and the novel tell the story of the blasts in episodic narrations of the police hunting down the accused one after the other. The narrative is organized by vivid empirical details from the exact time, date and place of each blast to the number of casualties in different parts of the city supporting each fictional element with official documents on the blast. This should not be seen solely as the text's search for detailing to produce an authentic account. It is also a deliberate underplay of the fictional possibilities in the text. The overt dependence on empirical data and documentary details in the form to produce an objective totalizing knowledge creates inherent contradictions in both the texts representing the events of mass scale violence like the Mumbai bomb blasts. Such a strategy always questions the rational idea of norm. The narrative unfolds like a detective thriller with evidence leading to an arrest. When we see the characters like Badshah Khan (Aditya Srivastava) running as a fugitive from one corner of India to another, hoping to flee to Dubai and be saved from arrest, we know that sooner or later he will end up in the police remand room.

The film can be seen as episodes of police interrogations. Let me again return to the novel and see how it gives an account of the police interrogations. Quoting Ajay the novel says:

> Fear of death is the most effective. During bomb blasts I just took a few suspects to the Borivali National Park and fired a few bullets past their ears. But with many of these suspects ordinary violence wouldn't work. There had to be special methods. Those who have no fear of death also have no fear of physical pain. For them we threaten their family. I tell them I will plant some evidence on their mother or their brother and arrest them. That usually works.[22]

If one looks at the scenes of the police interrogations in *Black Friday* from the chance arrest of Gulam Mohmmad to the first arrest of Asgar Muqadam made after the blast investigation started and the later arrests and interrogations that followed—the images show a strange resemblance to the description of police torture in *Maximum City*. Is it a mere coincidence that *Maximum City* and *Black Friday* are strikingly similar in their representation of the blasts? To add to the similarity in narration in the two texts I will also point out the texts' preoccupation with the character of a tough and cerebral cop and the appearance of underworld dons in the texts as they are supposed to be in real life. Rakesh Maria in *Black Friday* and Ajay Lal in the *Maximum City* are like hardboiled detective heroes tormented between the moral world and the modern institution of law. Both the cops are well aware of the limitation of the legal apparatus to crack down on the communitarian violence. They know that they have to resort to a host of coercive forces outside the legal ambit to bring the hostile communities under the rubric of the modern law. I will suggest that Rakesh and his gang of police officers remind respectively of Amod Shukla and Khandelkar (Aditya Srivastava) in *Satya*.

Both the texts seem to be in competition to talk about the exiled dons given celebrity status by popular media. The texts do not change the name of these celebrity gangsters and try hard to represent them as authentically as possible. The result is the appearance of Dawood Ibrahim in *Black Friday* in a checked court and dark glasses or the account of Mehta's candid interview with Chota Shakeel in *Maximum City*.[23] I would suggest that they are glaring instances of the brand underworld. I will give one example to support my point. In 1997 *Absolut* Vodka came up with an ingenious online advertisement of their product. In the website Absolut Kelly only the name of the site advertised the product; the rest was an illustrated excerpt from *Wired* magazine editor Kevin Kelly's book *Out of Control*. The brand not as add but as art. *Absolut* is still a major advertiser in *Wired,* but online, it is *Absolut* that is the host and *Wired* editor the supporting act.[24] Today the best known manufactures no longer produce products and advertise them but buy products and 'brand' them.[25] The appearance of real-life figures like Dawood Ibrahim and Tiger Memon in *Black Friday* or Chota Shakeel in *Maximum City* add on to the star value of the texts. Their association with the underworld gives them a relative obscurity in the public eye—a necessary precondition in the production of a star persona. Their image in the film and the novel remains true to their media avatars. These figures do not feature in the texts as illustrations to add to its glamour quotient but as an integral part of the narrative. This makes them serve a dual function of adding an authenticity to the content in the text on the one hand. On the other, it gives the text the status of a brand as experience, as lifestyle. The brand image that the texts bank upon is what I call 'brand underworld'. The new marketing opportunities (according to Rajadhyaksha)[26] that Bollywood after the 1990s presents in merchandising its products, I suggest, will centre on the underworld theme in future.

Rajadhyaksha proposed a model of the spectator in Indian films as a site of contestation between the official liberal discourses of democracy and its indigenization. In the case of Bollywood's use of the cultural repertoire of the underworld, this site can be best understood through the present corporatization of Indian cinema. The increasing share of multinational capital in Hindi film business is fast destroying a hierarchical film industry comprising big individual producers producing big budget films for foreign exports and domestic markets as opposed to another group of low budget films either hooked to a specialized urban class generally called Multiplex films or the B-grade films made mainly for the rural market. In the present Hindi film industry, the share of corporate finances is not restricted only to the production of films but also to their distribution and exhibition. The increasing corporatization of Hindi cinema with expanding market and competition will result in the growing demand for films which are much more localized in their content, allowing newer marketing opportunities for business in the Bollywood culture industry. This means that for profit maximization of a film through allied culture industries, producing 'feel good' versions of an Indian culture are no longer required. The 'underworld' today has emerged as the most important category in Bollywood. And I would suggest that *Satya* creates a comprehensive model for exploring the possibilities of this category. *Satya* imagines an urban spectator-subject who is at the same time a part of the global culture of consumptions as well as rooted to a much localized urban reality.

The 'inscribed viewer' (borrowing from Rajadhyaksha)[27] in the recent underworld films follows the model of *Satya*. This viewer is located in a complex matrix, negotiating with the narratives of democracy, globalization and different registers of nationalism, played upon by the images and stereotypes of organized global crime syndicates with their ground operations based in Mumbai. The new avatar of Bollywood indicates the fact that the present incarnation of the underworld represented in Bollywood does not involve the real criminal world but a world of images highly localized in content that are to be reproduced in new forms to cater to the need of a global consumer subject. Returning to where it all started, I think perhaps *Slumdog Millionaire* loaded with necessary glitters and acclaims is finally showing signs of Hollywood thinking the Bollywood way to make sense of a highly problematic Indian film spectatorship and working out a strategy to enter the domestic and diasporic markets of Indian cinema, a slippery terrain, restructured somewhat by Bollywood—a market which Hollywood could never quite fathom previously.

Notes and References

1. Amit Roy, 'Eye on England', *The Telegraph*, Calcutta, 19 April 2009.
2. Randeep Ramesh, 'Bollywood icon Amitabh Bachchan rubbishes Slumdog Millionaire'. Available online at http://www.guardian.co.uk/film/2009/jan/14/amitabh-bachchan-rubbishes-slumdog-millionaire (accessed on 17 June 2009).
3. Ravi Vasudevan, 'Meanings of 'Bollywood', *Journal of the Moving Image* 7 (December, 2008):149–54.
4. See Ashish Rajadhyaksha, 'Bollywoodization of Indian Cinema: Cultural Nationalism in Global Arena', in *City Flicks: Indian Cinema and The Urban Experience*, ed. Preben Kaarsholm (Calcutta: Seagull Books, 2004), p. 116.
5. Amitava Kumar, 'Slumdog Millionaire's Bollywood Ancestors'. Available online at http://www.vanityfair.com/online/oscars/2008/12/slumdog-millionaires-bollywood-ancestors.html (accessed on 5 July 2009).
6. Andrew Johnson, 'Britain Jumps on Bollywood Bandwagon'. Available at http://www.independent.co.uk/arts-entertainment/films/news/britain-jumps-on-bollywood-bandwagon-1682305.html (accessed on 7 July 2009).
7. Madhava Prasad, 'Realism and Fantasy in Representations of Metropolitan Life in Indian Cinema', in *City Flicks: Indian Cinema and The Urban Experience*, ed. Preben Kaarsholm (Calcutta: Seagull Books, 2004), pp. 86–87.
8. Judith Walkowitz, 'Urban Spectatorship', in *Urban Culture: Critical Concepts in Literary and Cultural Studies*, ed. Chris Jenks, vol. IV (London and New York: Routledge, 2004), p. 86.
9. The expository mode of documentary film uses 'voice-of-God' commentary directly addressing the viewer about the argument presented in the film. The film takes shape around the authorial commentary where the images come as illustrations or counterpoint to the voice. Editing in this mode generally serves to establish a rhetorical continuity rather than a spatial or temporal continuity. The expository mode emphasizes the impression of objectivity and of well-substantiated judgment. This mode is inclined towards a generalization since the all powerful voice-over can extrapolate from the particular instances offered in the image track. The viewer of documentaries in the expository

mode generally holds expectations that the commonsensical world will unfold in terms of the establishment of a logical cause/effect linkages between sequences and events. Finally, the viewer will typically expect the expository text to take shape around the solution to a problem or puzzle—in case of *Satya*, it is the problem of crime and gang violence that (as the commentary suggests) is on the rise in Bombay.

10. See Liza Weinstein, 'Mumbai Development Mafias: Globalization, Organized Crime and Land Development', *International Journal of Urban and Regional Research*, volume 32(March 2008).
11. Ibid., p. 22.
12. S.P. Singh, 'Transnational Organized Crime: The Indian Perspective', *Resource Material Series* No. 59 (2002).
13. A.V. Papachristos, 'Gang World', *Foreign Policy*, March/April 2005.
14. Ranjani Majumdar, *Bombay Cinema: An Archive of the City* (Ranikhet, India: Permanent Black, 2007), pp. 41–43.
15. See Frank Krutnik, *In a Lonely Street: Film Noir, Genre, Masculinity* (London, New York: Routledge, 1991), pp. 78–90.
16. Prasad, 'Realism and Fantasy in Representations of Metropolitan Life in Indian Cinema', p. 92.
17. Naomi Klein, *No Logo* (London: Flemingo, 2002), p.17.
18. *The Hindu*, 6 August 2004.
19. Sudipta Kaviraj, 'Reading a Song of the City—Images of the City in Literature and Films', in *City Flicks: Indian Cinema and The Urban Experience*, ed. Preben Kaarsholm (Calcutta: Seagull Books, 2004), pp. 68–73.
20. Jim Masselos, 'Postmodern Bombay: Fractured Discourses', in *Urban Culture: Critical Concepts in Literary and Cultural Studies*, vol. IV, ed. Chris Jenks (London & New York: Routledge, 2004), pp. 228–30.
21. Suketu Mehta, *Maximum City: Bombay Lost and Found* (India: Penguin Books, 2004), pp. 147.
22. Ibid., p. 143.
23. Ibid., p. 225.
24. Klein, *No Logo*, p. 43.
25. Ibid., p. 5.
26. Rajadhyaksha, 'Bollywoodization of Indian Cinema: Cultural Nationalism in Global Arena', pp. 122–23.
27. See Ashish Rajadhyaksha, 'Viewership and Democracy in the Cinema', in *Making Meaning in Indian Cinema*, ed. Ravi Vasudevan (New Delhi: Oxford University Press, 2002), pp. 267–96.

Chapter 6

Translating India Today
Local Cultures, Global Ambitions and Colonial Hangovers[*]

Sayantan Dasgupta

Introduction

Translation has always been a political act, the word 'political' used here in its broadest sense. The very act of translating a work from one language into another implies a consciousness of change and an awareness of the dynamics of intercultural interactions. Not simply the mode of translation, but even the very act of shortlisting or selecting the work that is to be translated is dependent on the historical conjuncture within which translation activity is located; so, too, is the choice of Source Language (SL) and Target Language (TL). Translation is thus, in both its spatial and temporal senses, a 'conjunctural' practice.

Translation activity may have behind it a number of different motives. One may consider translation an act of patriotism[1] and translate one's own literature into a foreign, perhaps more global, language with the objective of making visible to the world, the achievements of one's literary tradition. Again, translation has also doubled as an organic component of the colonial machinery; the colonizers found that their

* This chapter emerges out of a project on 'Translation as a Cultural Process' undertaken by the author under the aegis of the Studies in Cultural Processes as part of the activities of Jadavpur University under its University with Potential for Excellence scheme.

access to indigenous literatures and cultures (through translation) made it easier for them to 'map' and manage their colonies more efficiently.[2] That does not mean, of course, that all translation of Indian literature (to take an example) undertaken by foreigners was consciously meant to feed into the colonial project. Translation of Indian literature in the colonial period was, after all, also undertaken with the aim of enriching the TL (English or German, etc.) culture by enhancing its access to 'desirable' elements and thoughts identified in Indian literature but absent in European TL literature.

Translation in the context of a multilingual state like India, particularly in the 'post-colonial' era, has also had national integration and nation-building as factors motivating it—translation of Bangla literature into Malayalam, Tamil, Marathi, Punjabi, Hindi (and English) and vice versa were thought to have the potential of enhancing understanding between various language communities in independent India. India's diversity has always been an intriguing question for the Indian national imaginary and it has traditionally been sought to be 'managed' by invoking the very effective slogan of 'unity in diversity'. Poetry from various Indian languages, for example, has sought to reconcile the apparent conflict between the claims of diverse regional/linguistic/ethnic identities and the homogenizing claims of the nation state by positing this diversity not as a weakness but as a strength and by celebrating it.[3] The attempt to use translation as a tool for nation-building is part of a similar stimulus, one could argue. Again, translation may also be perceived as being motivated by the desire to build solidarities between communities united by shared histories (of colonialism, for instance) and separated by the monopoly of attention claimed by Western literature and culture.[4]

Translation of Indian *bhasha* literature into English in particular has always been a complicated area, and motivations fuelling the act of translating into English have been more ambiguous. The ambiguous location of the English language in India, incorporating at one level the status of a power language, and at another level, the baggage of its colonial inheritance,[5] as well as its global claims as an international language with a readership spread across several continents is largely responsible for this.

Translation of Indian literature on the part of Indians into English in the colonial era may have been substantially fuelled by the notion of translation as an act of patriotism, but what are the dynamics at work in the translation of Indian *bhasha* literature into English *today*? While translation into English has always been a complicated field of analysis, the processes of globalization that have been at work on Indian society in the 1980s and the 1990s and the enhanced visibility and 'branding' of Indian literature in the global market over the last three decades or so have brought in new questions for those interested in studying translation not merely as a linguistic exercise but as a process of cultural negotiation.[6]

This chapter attempts to understand the relationship of translation with the culture of nationalism and to attempt to understand translation as a site of contest where pressures of linguistic hegemony, decolonization, globalization and cultural imperialism are seen to negotiate among themselves. 'Indian Literature in English Translation' or the body of ILET texts published by various publishers from the 1990s onwards constitutes my primary objects of study. I focus primarily on English translations of Bangla SL texts, but also refer to translations of fiction from other Indian languages wherever appropriate. This chapter will try to investigate the motivations, dynamics and problems of translating Indian *bhasha* literature into English at the specific historical conjuncture discussed earlier, viz., the post-1990 Indian context.

The Immediate Context

The 1990s evidence a distinct 'boom' in the Indian Literature in Translation (ILET) industry.[7] It is around this time that a number of private publishers can be seen to take up ILET seriously. Katha, one of the more significant players in the ILET industry, is founded in 1988–89. Macmillan publishes its first 11-novel set of its Modern Indian Novels in Translation (MINIT) series in 1996. This is also when Orient Longman becomes more visible with its Literature in Translation (LIT) series. Even a basic study of the evolution of the ILET market in India in recent times suggests that it may be worthwhile probing the premise that translation in India may have gone from being a primarily state-sponsored activity aimed at constructing a 'national' culture to a more 'marketable' exercise—one in which private entrepreneurship has a stake—and to investigate the possible repercussions of this change. Since a full-scale history of the activities of organizations like the Sahitya Akademi and the National Book Trust or of the evolution of the private sector's involvement with ILET is neither feasible nor particularly relevant for this chapter, we shall refrain from venturing too far into those areas; we shall merely try to understand the agenda of state-sponsored translation and focus on ILET activities of private publishers in the period already mentioned earlier.

State-sponsored translation of Indian literature into English has been around for several decades; other publishers, too, have been publishing ILET even before the 1990s. Yet one finds a sudden efflorescence and visibility of ILET in the 1990s; private publishing houses, we see, seem to take up commissioning ILET not just in the form of one-off titles but in the form of series of titles in this decade. We need to ask here what factors are responsible for this visibility, whether the notion of the target (English-speaking) reader is different here from that implicit in ILET published earlier or by organizations like the Sahitya Akademi or NBT, and whether there is any difference in the agenda of translation itself. It is quite possible to think of the act of translating Indian literature into English even in the 1980s and 1990s as an act of patriotism, or more appropriately perhaps, of nationalism. It may be worth conjecturing if the 'boom' is not linked to the visibility Indian literature in general got in the 1980s in the international book and awards market. The award of the Booker to Salman Rushdie in 1981 marked the beginning of a renewed focus on 'Indian English literature' and posited Indian English as a global phenomenon; Indian (English) literature was now seen more than ever as the empire writing back[8] and it was (mis)construed as the public face of India. This essayist does not, of course, imply that the 'boom' in the ILET market was merely an offshoot of the sudden attention Indian English literature claimed after the 'arrival' of Rushdie; that would be far too simplistic an estimate. Rather, it would perhaps not be unfair to say that just as the enhanced international visibility of Indian English literature may have made certain publishers look on this as an opportunity to carve out a niche for ILET in the international market, so, too, perhaps the incommensurate attention commanded by

Indian English literature may have played a role in getting translators, writers and publishers alike to rethink the need for interrogating this monopoly of Indian English literature on the label, 'Indian literature' in the international market.[9]

Translation in the colonial Indian context was intimately linked with the mechanics of colonization itself and translation in the post-colonial era in India has been just as inextricably linked with the nation-building process. Translation was seen by the state as an activity through which a multicultural Indian society could be 'united'. Thus, the state involved itself in translation activity very early in the history of independent India. Early state-sponsored translation activity in independent India aimed, among other things, (*a*) to introduce literatures of various languages of India to other Indian language groups through translation from Indian languages to other Indian languages and to English, and (*b*) to make accessible and to showcase to the (English-speaking) world masterpieces of Indian literature from various Indian languages, both intimately related to the trope of translation as an act of patriotism.

The nation-building agenda was very clear in the setting up of institutions like the Sahitya Akademi (1954) and the National Book Trust (1957). The stated objective of the NBT was to promote the culture of the book in independent India and translation was seen as a part of that activity. Thus the NBT, since its very inception, has operated in a missionary mode, the mission in question being the spiritual and material upliftment of Indian citizens by introducing them to the culture of reading. That this mission is closely related with the imperatives of nation-building is very clear from the list of areas on which the NBT's Aadan Pradan translations series purports to focus—'the classical literature of India, outstanding works of Indian authors in Indian languages and their translation from one Indian language to another',[10] etc.

The missionary mode of the NBT is further evident from the assertion on the NBT website that the trust aims to pay attention 'to those genres of publishing which, despite their importance, have not been adequately covered in India'[11] and that 'the NBT was never visualized as just another publishing house, competing with other Indian publishers. Nevertheless, by undertaking the publication of some series of books of national significance, the Trust has played an important role in filling critical gaps…and…act(ed) as a catalyst to encourage publishers to enter hitherto unexplored areas of relevance and responsibility.'

Interestingly, this missionary stance of a body like the NBT, which, perhaps not incorrectly, seeks to highlight its non-commercial nature and its agenda of filling up certain 'gaps', seems to get appropriated in the 1990s by private publishers. Blurbs, prefaces and publicity material related to ILET titles frequently posit ILET as a missionary activity and this impression is replicated and magnified in reviews of such books. This location assigned to ILET is not, of course, at all unfounded; the hegemonic claims of Indian English literature have resulted in a relative marginalization of and a scuttling of the global ambitions of Indian *bhasha* literature. But the point is that perhaps for several private publishers venturing into ILET in the 1990s, ILET is a commercially viable venture and the missionary stance merely an inherited trope, which, dare one speculate, also happens to be a marketable stance.

The sampling of ILET titles published around the period considered reveals a few distinct patterns. There is, for instance, a sudden profusion, indeed, a line of titles, not always too well produced, perhaps pointing towards a rush to cash in on a phenomenon that has suddenly gained visibility. This seems at least partly applicable, to take only one example, to the poorly edited and proofread series published by Srishti, New Delhi. Srishti comes out with a fairly impressive array of ILET titles, at least in terms of numbers when one keeps in mind the size of the publication house. There is again a line of titles published to coincide with the release of cinematic versions of the SL texts. Nothing wrong with that, of course; conversion of book to screen affords a legitimate opportunity and occasion for trying for a re-dissemination of the text. The move, however, becomes questionable when the translations are seen to be either lacking in fidelity or readability or both, or to suffer from contradictions in terms of its position on the act of translation itself.[12] The sampling of ILET titles also reveals a disturbing inconsistency in one's approach to translation at the level of language use, translation of culture specificities and one's understanding of target readership. Instances of the same will be discussed in the next section; they are indicative, as we shall see, of the conflicts and contradictions implicit in the act of translating local cultures into an international language in a global world.

Sayantan Dasgupta

Local Cultures, Global Ambitions, Colonial Hangovers

This chapter posits the thesis that the location of translation activity in the last two decades or so is probably more complex than one might expect and that the relationship between recent ILET ventures by private publishers and state-sponsored ILET activities is more ambiguous than it may seem at first glance. For instance, the target readership envisaged by the NBT and the Sahitya Akademi is apparently an Indian one; yet the importance accorded by the NBT to international book fairs (during 2004–05, NBT participated in book fairs in Bologna, Tokyo, Budapest, Kuala Lumpur, Kathmandu, Seoul, Beijing, Frankfurt and Lahore.)[13] seems to make the NBT's concept of the target reader more ambiguous. Similarly, there is a not-insignificant body of ILET texts in which the mode of translation may give the impression that these translations are meant not for an international readership, but for an Indian one. Therefore, it would be incorrect to assume that state-sponsored translation in India caters solely to the demands of national integration and private publication houses cater solely to an international readership and have only got interested in ILET in the context of globalization in India.

The most important question for understanding the negotiation between the claims of the local and the global in the context of translation activity in India is, perhaps, that of target readership—who is the intended reader of ILET? Who are we translating for when we translate Indian literature into English? In theoretical terms after all, it is quite possible, thanks to the international circulation enjoyed by the English language, for an English-language translation of an Indian *bhasha* literary text to be read by readers in Kerala, West Bengal, Uttar Pradesh, Australia, Canada, the US, the UK and South Africa. But the location of these readers with respect to the SL culture is varied—the question that comes up here is would the needs of these readers be the same, and if not, then how could one possibly respond to the different needs of different readerships of ILET? More importantly, what kind of politics and what kind of positions are discernible in attempts of translators, editors and publishers to satisfy the varied demands of the very heterogenous

ILET readership in today's 'global-village' scenario; what kind of compromises does this process entail and what is the political significance of such compromises? ILET, thus, needs to be mapped in further detail to understand how translators engage with the concepts of 'equivalence' and 'function'[14] while translating Indian *bhasha* literature into English in contemporary times.

ILET can be seen to cater to broadly two different target readerships whose needs are substantially different. An Indian reader reading an English translation may not share the language code of the Source Language but would probably share much of the culture code embedded in the SL text. A non-Indian reader, on the other hand, would probably not share this culture code and might need explanations to culture-specific markers retained in the TL text and not explicated through parenthetical qualifiers. The mode of translation and the extent of foreignization and domestication[15] would offer clues regarding the location of the translator, her/his notion of the target reader, and her/his position on the politics of translation itself.

The ILET titles studied for this chapter display an ambiguous understanding of this problem; a substantial number of them seem to lack a clear understanding of the needs or even the identity of an intended reader. A study of the sample of ILET titles accessed for this chapter reveals several patterns. First, they generally point towards the lack of a well-defined and coherent translation policy and therefore to the lack of a well thought-out position on the politics of cultural interaction and reception in the context of post-colonial power equations and social realities. This is evident from the disturbingly frequent attempt to straddle both worlds and to satisfy the largest number of potential readers through a process of 'dumbing down' or simplification. This may make sense in terms of the reach of the translation, but it gives rise to various contradictions and renders the location of the translator suspect. While it is very important to translate Indian literature into English for a number of very pressing and legitimate reasons, speed cannot be privileged at the cost of a sense of location or at the cost of an awareness of the pressures of linguistic hegemony and cultural imperialism which form the backdrop to all translation activity in the post-colonial world. While the globalization-induced visibility of ILET may have spurred on a body of translations, it seems to have also unfortunately deterred many translators and publishers on many occasions from properly theorizing the act of translation itself. Second, the mode of translation seems to be often left entirely to the whims of individual translators in the absence of any style sheet or translation policy whatsoever. The essayist is not, here, of course, pleading for a mechanization of translation or of setting up a corpus of 'norms' that individual translators would have to abide by. Translation is a creative act and two different translators will translate the same text differently—this potential of plurality and multiplicity can only contribute to a more nuanced understanding of the text (the translator, in any case, is said to be the most intimate reader of the text);[16] it is a strength, not a weakness. But a near-complete lack of any stated position regarding target readership and mode of translation has meant that on many occasions, even the same series of translations brought out by the same publisher would have titles that embody a conflicting and contradictory approach to the politics of translation. Third, several titles are seen to go out of their way to explain culture specificities to a readership that, one supposes, is assumed to be global in scope. In cases where this is done consistently, one can at least argue that such translations have a distinct position vis-à-vis the notion of an intended reader and that it is trying its utmost to 'translate' in the literal sense, that is to 'carry across'. However, this position again seems politically suspect as it appears to embody a sense of colonial hangover that finds hospitable shelter in the neo-colonial context that masquerades as globalism. Surely, an Indian reader would have no need for a glossary of 'sari'! Why then should we go out of our way to explain such a word—the glossary can only sound trite for most readers in India! Is it because even in this 'global' world, many of our translators feel only too happy to have the 'West' sit up and take notice of our literature and therefore they feel prepared to go that extra mile to make things easier for such a readership. Again, I am not arguing that Indian literature should be translated for a solely Indian readership, nor am I carrying the brief for an extreme form of foreignization. My point is that where the functional value of a word like 'sari' is clear from the context of a literary work, any attempt to measure, map and define it further in terms of length, material, colour or texture can sound like an effort to exoticise, to suit the palate of a Western readership, and to whet the appetite for a further perpetuation of already existing stereotypes. Of course, this is not as widespread a practice as it could have been; many translators do not gloss such markers, nor do they even italicize them. Fourth, there is a substantial deployment of one-word glossaries, again leading to spectres of exoticization and superfluity. If a word in the SL can be explained away with one single TL equivalent, why retain the original in the text at all? Is it merely to bring in an element of 'local colour'? Fifth, there seems to be an occasional tendency for notes to culture-specific markers to reach the level of the prescriptive in several of the ILET titles studied. Words like 'sindoor', for instance are often retained, but explained and their relationship with social practice elaborated in such a way that it assumes the guise of a generalized prescription. Readers not sharing a dynamic, living relationship with the SL cultural space may well be led to the conclusion that *all* married Hindu women *must* wear sindoor in the Indian context. This approach again raises questions regarding the intended readership of the translations; perhaps the conscious attempt to showcase one's culture for a foreign or diasporic readership leads more easily to the temptation to create watertight sacred categories of immutable imperatives.

Let us now look at specific instances of how these patterns emerge from the texts themselves and examine how ILET has dealt with culture specificity and the notion of the intended reader. Moti Nandy's *Striker, Stopper* (1994) and MT Vasudevan Nair's *Kaalam* (1998) are both English translations published by Orient Longman. Mihir K. Das' 'Translator's Note' to the first envisages an Indian target reader—'In translating Moti Nandy's stories, I have had in mind lovers of football in India who do not read Bengali.'[17] Understandably, therefore, Das does not gloss or explain in any other way, words such as 'kachuris' and 'jelebis' which are almost pan-Indian in circulation. Yet, when he writes: 'In our days, we did two-fifty *donns*, five hundred *baithaks*...',[18] without glossing the words, his notion of target readership appears to get problematized. Here he seems to translate for a reader who has some access to Bangla but would rather read the text in English translation, a tribe whose membership seems destined to grow in an age of globalization where the hegemony of the English language threatens the survival of other languages.

Das also refrains from glossing any kinship terms; in fact, this translation carries no glossary. On the other hand, Gita Krishnankutty's translation of *Kaalam*, published under the same Disha imprint, has an extensive glossary plus a glossary of 'Kinship Terms',[19] plus a 'List of Malayalam months with approximate equivalents in the Gregorian calendar'.[20] This discrepancy seems to indicate that the series does not have a translation policy and that the mode of translation, notion of target reader and of the task of the translator seems to vary according to the perspectives of individual translators. There are other discrepancies as well—some texts in the series feel the need to gloss local flora and fauna while others do not. *Kaalam* explains that the 'kuvalam'[21] is a tree, while *Striker, Stopper* retains 'siuli',[22] signposting it through italics but not commenting on it in any other way. One is also struck by the glossary of *Kaalam*. Mythic and religious references like 'yakshi', 'brahmarakshasu' and 'anna prasanam' are explained in brief; again, this raises questions regarding the target readership of this translation. These words, beliefs and rituals are common to many Indian languages and glossing such markers seems aimed at non-Indian readers. I was also piqued to find that *Kaalam* retains the word 'deepam' and glosses it as simply 'lamp'[23] and glosses 'sastrams' as 'the scriptures'.[24] If the cultural nuances of an SL marker can be summed up in a single TL word, then why not use that word itself rather than retaining the original and glossing it? Are words like 'deepam' then retained merely to impart a flavour of the exotic for readers outside India who might be thought to constitute the target readership of this translation? These are some of the many contradictions that seem to characterize the recent translation of Indian literature into English—contradictions that underscore the complex cultural politics of trying to carry something across from an Indian language into a language like English in contemporary India.

Similar contradictions are also evident in Orient Longman's Literature in Translation titles. 'The Impostor' in Subodh Ghose's *Shock Therapy* (2001) translates 'payesh' as 'rice pudding'[25] while MT Vasudevan Nair's *Kuttiedathi and Other Stories* (2004) retains the Malayalam *payasam*.[26] Again, *Kuttiedathi* retains and glosses *sindooram*[27] while *Shock Therapy* condemns to erasure the Bangla *sindoor* by translating and transforming it into 'vermillion mark' in the text itself.[28] Moreover, *Shock Therapy* retains *alta*[29] even as it translates *sindoor*. *Shock Therapy*'s confusion regarding culture specificity is evident in the way it retains 'luchi'[30] and serves it up with 'fried aubergine slices',[31] retains 'darbesh',[32] 'rabri'[33] and 'sandesh',[34] but rounds off dessert with 'sweet curds'[35] and 'rice pudding'.[36] This kind of uncertainty characterizes many of the translations studied. *First Light* (Penguin, 2000), Aruna Chakravarty's translation of Sunil Gangopadhyay's *Prathom Alo*, for instance, retains *ilish, bori, bakul* and *baasar*, but translates *michhri* as 'palm candy crystals'! Surely, the latter contradicts the former's politics of translation.[37] Similarly, Rani Ray's translation of Saratchandra Chattopadhyay's 'The Unprotectable' uses 'paan' and 'betel-box' not just in the same story, but on the same page[38] and again retains the word 'balaposh' but uses the more domesticated 'cowdung cakes'.[39] Again, *At Sixes and Sevens*, Nupur Gupta's translation of Ashapurna Devi's *Noi-Chhoi*,[40] uses 'Thakuma' in direct speech[41] and 'grandmother' in indirect speech,[42] but retains 'didi'[43] and 'jamaibabu'[44] in both direct and indirect speech and uses 'sari' without apologizing for it with either italics or glossary. This trend reinforces the conviction that English translation of *bhasha* literature needs to be theorized further and the fear that we are perhaps missing the opportunity the current interest in ILET affords us to do so, and are perhaps indulging in a bout of frenzied translation often without sufficiently clarifying our stand on who we translate for, the dynamics of translation as a cross-cultural process, and the politics thereof. Moreover, the decision to transform *payesh* into 'rice pudding', *sindoor* into 'vermilion mark' and *michhri* into palm-candy crystals does seem a politically problematic one if one keeps in mind Tejaswini Niranjana's comments on 'homogenisation'.[45]

Even a relatively consistent and authentic translation such as *Four Chapters*, Rimli Bhattacharya's rendition of Rabindranath's *Char Adhyay* (Srishti, 2002) occasionally has '*ole, kotchu, ghent*'[46] co-existing with 'boiled peas to go with fried parched rice, with a dash of pepper'.[47] But, at least, Bhattacharya's translation retains many culture-specific markers that may have been tempting to erase and offers notes rather than a glossary, providing, for instance, detailed explanations of mythical references, useful not just to a non-Indian reader who does not know, but also useful for an Indian reader.

The Katha translations seem one of the few sustained efforts in the field that have consistently and clearly defined mode of translation and target reader. The beginnings of the Katha translations *were* rooted to a certain extent in the notion of 'translation as patriotism' ('the idea was to encourage, foster and applaud creative writing in the various Indian languages', writes Geeta Dharmarajan in her preface to *Katha Prize Stories Volume 1*),[48] but was at the same time, critical of the missionary stance that we have talked about. ('Our interest in the short story was not fuelled by some kind of misplaced sympathy to try and save a genre which has been an intrinsic part of a storyteller's repertoire in our country for many years.'[49]) The first volume itself defines the target reader as Indian. 'Translating Differences', Rimli Bhattacharya's note to *Katha Prize Stories 1*, makes this clear: 'We have thought...of the Indian reader or even the subcontinental reader who is familiar or at least half familiar with many of the almost untranslatable codes, beliefs and acts of our daily lives. Therefore there is no glossary. The various words from the original language we have chosen to retain in the translation seem capable of standing on their own.'[50] In the Katha volumes, thus, kinship terms are almost always retained, the weaving in of apologies through the use of italics and other signposting devices are almost totally absent. Katha translations also seem to generally privilege the regional variation to the 'standard' 'Indian' one. Thus, 'kumkum' is 'kumkum' in the English version of a Bangla story while it is 'kumkumam' in stories from South Indian languages. This is a very different response to the cultural dynamics of translation from the one we see in *Oriya Stories* (Srishti, 2000), for instance where *kali jugo* is glossed as *kalyug*.[51] The assumption here (in homogenizing *kalijugo* into *kaliyug*) seems to be that the transforming the 'regional' version into the 'standard' Hindi version is necessary for readers to understand the concept.

This researcher has also been looking at Mini Krishnan's Macmillan MINIT series, extremely successful in terms of the sheer number of very powerful texts it has made accessible as well as of readability. The series is funded by the MRAR Educational Society, Madras. Krishnan's series introduction states that the series targets both Indian and non-Indian readers.[52] It is in trying to cater to the needs of these two readerships that MINIT seems to slip up, perhaps. It ends up glossing not just kinship terms that are widely understood across India, but also words like mangalsutra, shehnai, mantra, antakshari, Sita and even sari. A case of the translator bending over backwards to satisfy the perceived demands of the non-Indian TL reader, perhaps?

At Heaven's Gates, Sanchayita Chatterjee's translation of Sunil Gangopadhyay's *Shorger Niche Manush* (Rupa, 2004), offers a curious trend in the ILET body. The translation explains 'Baitarini' in terms of its resemblance to the Styx;[53] it also writes: 'The trident or the trishul is a three-pronged long fork. It is the chosen weapon of Lord Shiva in Hindu mythology...also the weapon of Zeus and Poseidon [Roman mythology]'.[54] Not only does the translator here mistake Greek mythology for Roman, as a result of which, she uses a footnote that is not just inaccurate but a gross mistake, but she also indulges in an extreme form of domestication. It is the TL culture that is clearly prioritized and put at the centre; it is in relation to 'Western' mythology that Indian mythological references are to be explained and understood—non-Western cultures therefore remain on the peripheries, reduced as they are to being mere footnotes or addenda to more 'mainstream' Western or European traditions and cultures. The only way, it seems, Indian or other non-Western traditions and cultures can become the focus of the gaze is when they approximate to the Western traditions and cultures; their importance seems to lie only in terms of their similarities with the latter. It is the latter that is the index or the master text against which the non-Western SL text is to be read, judged, evaluated, understood, explained and accorded recognition and made visible.[55]

Nor is this one isolated example. One notes that the translator uses the same strategy in her translation of Sunil Gangopadhyay's Bangla novel, *Yubok Yubotira* (translated by her as *The Youth*). We note, for example, her explanation of the line, 'A lovely *ghaat* was built on the bank of the river...'[56]—'These *ghaats* are somewhat like the European strands.' Again, she uses the following explanatory sentence on the very next page: '...somewhat like the tradition of marching behind the coffin in a Christian funeral procession.'[57] She goes on to explain 'Boudi' as 'sister-in-law'[58], 'sadhu' as 'an Indian saint, ascetic',[59] 'babu' as 'similar to the respectful "Sir"',[60] 'Pishima' as 'father's sister',[61] 'baba' as 'father',[62] 'kochuris' as 'an Indian snack made by stuffing little balls of wheat with different vegetables or pulses and deep frying them',[63] 'zamindar' as 'rich landowner',[64] 'Holi' as 'the Indian festival of colours',[65] 'daroga' as 'police officer in charge of a county (!)',[66] 'dhoti' as 'a very traditional Indian dress for males',[67] annotates 'ghee' as something that is 'made by melting butter',[68] and feels the need to footnote words like 'yagna'[69] and 'Kashi'.[70] In what seems a rather desperate attempt to showcase India to the English-speaking US American world (one assumes this is her target audience as she explains 'Honours' elsewhere as 'Major'[71] and because she herself is based in the US), she goes out of her way to explain not just kinship terms and items of everyday consumption and practice in India, not just words, but also sounds, expletives and expressions—'Chi-chi' is thus explained as 'an expletive expressing shame'.[72] Her attempt to paraphrase India in made-easy terms leads this translator into two other pitfalls already discussed. First, that of plain inaccuracy—in her desperation to find equivalents between languages and cultures, Chatterjee footnotes *mairi* as 'A Bengali curse, somewhat like "F... man"'.[73] Etymologically, the word, *mairi* comes from swearing by Mary, and the association made by the translator with the sexual expletive, 'Fuck, man' seems unwarranted and inappropriate. Second, her glossaries and annotations also border on the prescriptive; we note, for instance, the generalization implicit in the following explanation: 'Brass utensils are common in Indian homes. And, everyone receives a set in his or her marriage.'[74]

Clearly Chatterjee's stance as a translator tends towards one extreme— she seems to privilege the perceived claims of the target reader, in her case, the English-language reader based in the US perhaps, and thereby seems to do a disservice to the SL culture, reducing it as it were, to the status of a footnote that can only be understood or be of any value in comparison with Western norms. It should come as no surprise then that Satyajit Ray, for the translator, can be understood best not in terms of his work or his contribution to Indian or even world cinema, but in terms of what recognition he has got from the Western world—he is footnoted as 'legendary Bengali film maker; he won the life-time achievement award at the Oscars.'[75]

Significantly, it is not only translations funded by the private sector which do this—*The Ancestor*, Arun Mohanty's translation of a Gopinath Mohanty Oriya novel (Sahitya Akademi, 1997) considers it the task of the translator to explain 'bhai' as 'brother',[76] 'mantra' as 'hymn',[77] 'puja' as 'prayer'[78] and even 'anchal' as 'fringe of a sari'.[79]

And, *The White Envelope*, Suchandra Chakraborty's translation of Moti Nandy's novel, goes even further, offering an explanation of the 'sari'[80] itself, as well as of 'salwar-kameez',[81] primary kinship terms, 'khadi',[82] 'samosas',[83] 'thana',[84] 'zamindar',[85] 'chapattis'[86] and 'gold balas'.[87] This is a curious trend and it evidences a stance that perhaps sees active collusion of both the processes of globalization and colonial hangover.

Let us now look at a few more ILET texts and examine their stance on translation as a cultural process. Rini and Pritish Nandy's translations of Premendra Mitra's short stories[88] try to take out an insurance against possible losses incurred during the process of translation by translating the titles of each story, but also giving, side by side with the translated title, the original title (for example 'Discovering Telenapota: *Telenapota Abishkar*'). Also notable is the fact that the translators seem to steer consciously away from linguistic explanations and focus on cultural explanations. Thus, 'sindoor' is explained not as 'vermilion mark' but as '…the vermilion mark traditionally applied to the parting of the hair by Hindu women as a sign of marriage. It has enormous resonance as a symbol of the very state of marriage. Every Hindu wife must wear it, widows must symbolically wipe it off. Hence Bhupathi's taunt about the importance of applying *sindoor*.'[89] There is thus an attempt here to capture the cultural resonances implicit in the SL in the translation as well and the translation does not quite effect a total surrender in the way Sanchayita Chatterjee's translations do though, of course, the attempt to paraphrase Indian culture could be unpalatable to some. Again, this translation is almost completely bare of single-word glossaries, a strategy which appears problematic, as we have discussed earlier.

The River Churning,[90] Enakshi Chatterjee's translation of *Epar Ganga Opar Ganga*, goes one step further. If Sanchayita Chatterjee's translations of Sunil Gangopadhyay had indulged in footnoting 'babu' as 'sir' and 'boudi' as 'sister-in-law', Enakshi Chatterjee's translation seems to steer purposefully away from that approach. It retains 'jamai-babu'[91] and uses it without signposting it with the apologetic use of italics or quotes, and goes on to consistently retain words such as 'kakima',[92] 'didi',[93] 'boudi',[94] 'mashi',[95] 'Amulya babu'[96] and 'Chhorda'[97] without footnoting them.

Selected Stories[98] by Manik Bandyopadhyay employs a strategy similar to the one used by Rina and Pritish Nandy. The titles are translated into English and the translated titles are followed by the original titles (for example 'The Right to Suicide: *Atmahatyar Adhikar*'). But the translator also inserts a two- to three-paragraph introduction to each story, discussing the nuances of the language used in the original and the translation itself. This serves as insurance against possible losses that may have taken place thanks to the steamrolling effect of the English language. Implicit in this approach is a respect for the claims of the specifics in the original text and a consciousness of the pitfalls of translation as well as an attempt to minimize the element of betrayal that translation carries with it, particularly true of translation of post-colonial literatures into English.

Another syndrome affecting ILET titles is to be found in Ashapurna Devi's *Snakebite, The Distant Widow: 2 Novels*, translated by Anima Bose.[99] Like several of the Srishti titles, this volume, too, suffers from a problem in trying to negotiate the claims of fidelity and readability and ends up with several sentences that not only jar but that are also grammatically and idiomatically incorrect. Sentences such as 'there are innumerable smaller mistakes galore of this type'[100] pepper the text. Likewise, there is a problem with the register of the English language used as well—the translation often uses sentences like 'Millie left just now',[101] which are common in Indian usage of English but which would not be deemed 'proper' English—'Millie has just left' would have been more widely accepted as 'proper English'. It is possible to think of deliberately using such a brand of English to challenge the hegemony of English as target language itself and to perhaps posit 'english'[102] as a possible alternative for translating Indian literature, but there is little to indicate any such consciousness in this translation—it is, rather, an inadvertent gaffe.

Conclusion

We have seen how translation activity is predicated upon a complex set of cultural processes that sees ideological equations relating to linguistic hegemony, decolonization, globalization and cultural imperialism formulate and reformulate themselves. The location of translation as a vector of these processes is particularly complex in the context of Indian literature because of the multilingual and multicultural canvas in India.

The situation is further complicated in the context of Indian literature in English translation because of the problematic and ambiguous status of the English language in India. On the one hand, the English language carries even today the stigma of its entente with colonialism in India (Macaulay et al.); on the other, it is a symbol of social status and upliftment even today in post-colonial India. On the one hand, the English language is acknowledged as having played the role of a lingua franca and held the nationalist struggle together; on the other, it represents the greatest threat that indigenous Indian languages and literatures face today. On the one hand, writing in or translating into English in India today can be read as the quest for an international audience; on the other, it could also be read simply as an attempt to reach out and carve out solidarities between various language communities in India itself. All these contradictions make the field of Indian literature in English translation most challenging to study.

In the Indian context, translation seems to have morphed from being (principally) an activity that was once actively encouraged by the state with the purported objective of forging national integration in a country that was seen to be extremely diverse, into a venture that is perhaps a little more visible and financially viable and therefore capable of attracting the involvement of a greater number of private publishers. Yet we find that it would be too simplistic, and indeed incorrect, to assume that state-sponsored translation in India is solely committed to forging national integration and private publication houses cater solely to an international readership; the nature of intended readership is far more complex and ambiguous in both the cases, as we have discussed.

As the Indian literature in translation market has witnessed a boom in the 1980s and the 1990s, it has become even more important to take a closer look at Indian translation activity in this period. Our study of 1990s' English translations of Bangla fiction reveals several disturbing trends.

Many of the translations studied are seen to be either lacking in fidelity or readability or both. There are enough examples of translations that appear to have been hurried through, where a proper bout of careful copyediting would have prevented the TL text from appearing to jar. Again, there are enough examples of translations that imagine the task of the translator to be that of the editor or censor. Also in evidence are innumerable contradictions in terms of positions regarding the act of translation itself. There are disturbing inconsistencies in the same translator's or publisher's approach to translation in terms of use of language, culture-specific markers and perceived target readership; these seem symptomatic, as we have seen, of the conflicts and contradictions implicit in the act of translating local cultures into an international language in a global world. What is evident in many of the texts studied is a curious and very dangerous collusion between globalization and colonial hangover; the English translations of several of the Bangla texts studied seem to double as hospitable spaces for the neo-colonial impulse.

The boom in the Indian literature in English translation market and the burgeoning interest in ILET in recent times offers us an opportunity to disseminate our literatures and to fight back against notions of a monolithic, monolingual global canon as well as to combat the hegemony of dominant literatures. Yet that opportunity comes with a certain responsibility. And that is a responsibility we are yet to take seriously, if the texts studied are anything to go by. Translate, we must; but we also need to theorize the act of translation even as we translate. Insensitivity towards the cultural processes and politics that influence the dynamics of translation activity can only lead translators towards political bankruptcy and rob translations of their inherent political charge.

Notes and References

1. See Sujit Mukherjee, 'Translation as Patriotism', in *Translation as Discovery* (Hyderabad: Orient Longman, 1994). Mukherjee writes:

   ...once they had acquired enough English, Indians seemed to have developed an uncontrollable urge to demonstrate to their rulers that their own literature had much more to offer than had been found by the British, and also to show that they were no less competent in translating such literature into English. (p.127)

   Mukherjee cites the example of Pratapchandra Roy:

   A typical cultural broker of the last century in Bengal was Pratapchandra Roy. According to a bibliographical note by P Lal, Pratapchandra migrated from his village to Calcutta and became a bookseller. 'By 1869 he had put by enough money to buy a small printing press and start a publishing concern.' After he had brought out a Bangla *Mahabharata* in 1876, 'a new idea fired him: the complete Mahabharata in English. His purpose was to unfold the richness of the Indian heritage to the British rulers and to foreigners in general.' He collected the necessary funds through donation, enlisted the collaboration of Kisari Mohan Ganguli as translator, and published the first complete and faithful translation of the *Mahabharata* in English in eleven volumes from 1888 to 1896—for free distribution (pp. 125–26).

2. Note Mini Krishnan's comments: 'For the first hundred years, translations of Indian texts into English were prepared by Englishmen in collaboration with Indians. Why did they undertake such translations? British scholars urged their government to discover, collect and translate information about the land the East India Company was controlling.' Mini Krishnan, 'Introduction', in *Short Fiction from South India* eds, Subashree Krishnaswami and K Srilata (Delhi: Oxford University Press, 2007), p. xxii.

  For another, if slightly stronger, analysis of the entente between colonialism and translation in this context, one may see Paul St-Pierre's excellent essay, 'Translating (into) the Language of the Colonizer'. St Pierre posits the act of colonialism in terms of the metaphor of translation and also explains the relationship between translation activity and colonial administrative practices in the essay. Please see Jatindra Kumar Nayak (ed.), *Fakir Mohan Senapati: Perspectives on His Fiction* (Jagatsinghpur: Prafulla Pathagar Publications, 2004), pp. 235–75.

  'Translating (into) the Language of the Colonizer' is, in fact, a very good essay for understanding several of the issues this essay deals with, in particular, the power equations between languages and how they shape the translation of culture-specific indices and fuel the attempt to assimilate 'alterity' into 'familiar' spaces—there is, of course, an irony in the way I use the words 'alterity' and 'familiar' here, for, it is exotropic translation that we are discussing, not endotropic translation, which is where this assimilation of alterity into familiar spaces is generally identified with. St-Pierre's essay takes up for comparison four different English-language translations of Fakir Mohan Senapati's 1897 Oriya novel, *Chha Mana Atha Guntha* (literally Six Acres and Thirty-two Decimals)—the way the title itself has been translated by the various translators offer enough clues vis-à-vis the translatorial stance: the translated titles are as follows: *Six Acres and a Half, Six Acres and a Third, A Plot of Land* and *The Stubble under the Cloven Hoof*!

3. See Rabindranath Tagore, 'Holy India', tr. Visvanath Chatterjee, in *Modern Indian Literature: An Anthology Volume I: Surveys and Poems*, (ed.) K.M. George,

(New Delhi: Sahitya Akademi, 1992), pp. 484–86. Another example is Haider Bux Jatoi, 'Nation's Independence', tr. D.K. Mansharamani, in *Modern Indian Literature: An Anthology Volume I: Surveys and Poems*, ed. K.M. George (New Delhi: Sahitya Akademi, 1992), pp. 1040–41.

4. Harish Trivedi, 'The Politics of Post-colonial Translation', in *Translation: Its Theory and Practice*, ed. A.K. Singh (New Delhi: Creative Books, 1996), pp. 45–56.

5. One notes the extremely depreciating tone in which Thomas Babington Macaulay talks of Indian civilization and culture even as he propounds the case for English education in India in his infamous 'Minutes'. See Thomas Babington Macaulay, 'Minute on Indian Education', reprinted in *A South Asian Nationalism Reader*, ed. Sayantan Dasgupta (Kolkata and New Delhi: Worldview, 2007), pp. 163–65.

6. One notes, in the context of this argument, the following comments:

> ...the act of translation always involves much more than language. Translations are always embedded in cultural and political systems, and in history. For too long translation was seen as purely an aesthetic act, and ideological problems were disregarded. Yet the strategies employed by translators reflect the context in which texts are produced.

Susan Bassnett and Harish Trivedi, 'Introduction: Of Colonies, Cannibals and Vernaculars', in *Post-colonial Translation: Theory and Practice*, eds Susan Bassnett and Harish Trivedi (London and New York: Routledge, 1999), p. 6.

7. Various scholars, publishers and translators have already commented on this phenomenon. See, for example, Subash Jeyan's comments in 'Translation as Reclamation', published in *The Hindu* (Literary Review), Sunday, 4 September 2005. Available online at http://www.hindu.com/lr/2005/09/04/ stories/2005090400310500.htm (accessed on 22 October 2009). One could also see 'For a Word's Worth' in *Outlook Magazine*, 25 February 2002, available at http://www.outlookindia.com/article.aspx?214681 (accessed on 22 October 2009).

8. I borrow this phrase from Bill Ashcroft, Gareth Griffiths and Helen Tiffin, *The Empire Writes Back: Theory and Practice in Post-colonial Literatures* (London and New York: Routledge, 1989). One of the most popular and visible works on post-colonial literatures.

9. It is not as if this trend does not have its problems; there are hegemonies within hegemonies, and, as Trivedi and Basnett warn, '...translations from the various Indian languages into English, whether done by foreigners or by Indians them-selves, have attained a hegemonic ascendancy. The widely shared post-colonial wisdom on the subject is that the Empire can translate back only into English, or into that lower or at least lower-case variety of it, English, according to some

pioneering and influential theorists of the subject.' Bassnett and Trivedi, 'Introduction', pp. 10–11.

10. Available at http://www.nbtindia.org.in (accessed on 12 July 2006).

11. Ibid.

12. This problem is perhaps not exclusively applicable to the present context; one remembers how Bibhutibhusan Bandyopadhyay's *Pather Panchali* was published in a mangled and abbreviated translation (T.W. Clark and Tarapada Mukherjee tr. *Song of the Road*. London: George Allen and Unwin, 1968) many years ago, a form that Tathagata Bandyopadhyay, who is currently working on a new translation of the same Bangla novel, feels was perhaps influenced by the success of Satyajit Ray's celluloid version. Bandyopadhyay had the following to say on the translation: 'Clark and Mukherjee's translation was more an annotated version of Ray's versions than a translation of the Bibhutibhusan novel...In fact, I am not sure if the novel would have been translated that early had it not been for Satyajit Ray's film' (quoted from a talk given at Worldview Bookstore, Jadavpur University, Kolkata, on 27 October 2009).

13. Available at http://www.nbtindia.org.in/fair.doc (accessed on 12 July 2006).

14. See Lawrence Venuti's comments:

> The history of translation theory can in fact be imagined as a set of changing relationships between the relative autonomy of the translated text, or the translator's actions, and two other concepts: equivalence and function. Equivalence has been understood as 'accuracy', 'adequacy', 'correctness', 'correspondence', 'fidelity', or 'identity'; it is a variable notion of how the translation is connected to the foreign text. Function has been understood as the potentiality of the translated text to release diverse effects, beginning with the communication of information and the production of a response comparable to the one produced by the foreign text in its own culture.

Venuti, Lawrence, 'Introduction', in *The Translation Studies Reader*, ed. Venuti Lawrence (London and New York: Routledge, 2000), p. 5.

15. See Friedrich Schleiermacher, 'On the Different Methods of Translation', in *German Romantic Criticism*, ed. A.L. Willson (New York). Also see Walter Benjamin, 'The Task of the Translator: An Introduction to the Translation of Baudelaire's Tableaux Parisiens', in *The Translation Studies Reader*, ed. Venice Lawrence (London and New York: Routledge, 2004).

16. Gayatri Chakravarti Spivak, *Outside in the Teaching Machine* (London: Routledge, 1993), p. 183.

17. Moti Nandy, *Striker, Stopper*, tr. Mihir K. Das (Hyderabad: Orient Longman [Disha], 1994), p. i.

18. Ibid., p. 9.
19. M.T. Vasudevan Nair, *Kaalam*, tr. Gita Krishnankutty (Hyderabad: Orient Longman [Disha], 1998), p. vi.
20. Ibid., p. 238.
21. Ibid., p. 237.
22. Nandy, *Striker, Stopper*, p. 5.
23. Nair, *Kaalam*, p. 236.
24. Ibid., p. 238.
25. Subodh Ghose, 'The Impostor', in *Shock Therapy* (Hyderabad: Orient Longman, 2001), p. 138.
26. M.T. Vasudevan Nair, *Kuttiedathi and Other Stories*, tr. V. Abdulla (Hyderabad: Orient Longman, 2004), p. 188.
27. Ibid., p.14.
28. Subodh Ghosh, 'The Harlot', in *Shock Therapy*, ed. Subodh Ghose (Hyderabad: Orient Longman, 2001), p. 41.
29. Ibid.
30. Ghose, 'The Imposter', p. 138.
31. Ibid.
32. Ibid.
33. Ibid.
34. Ibid.
35. Ibid.
36. Ibid.
37. See Sayantan Dasgupta, 'Vast Historical Saga', in *The Statesman* (Review), Calcutta, 15 April 2001.
38. Mridula Nath Chakraborty and Rani Ray, eds, *A Treasury of Bangla Stories* (New Delhi: Srishti), p. 36.
39. Ibid., p. 49.
40. Ashapurna Devi, *Noi-Chhoi: At Sixes and Sevens*, ed. Swapna Dutta (New Delhi: Srishti, 2002).
41. Ibid., p. 65.
42. Ibid.
43. Ibid., p. 39.
44. Ibid., p. 38.
45. Homogenisation or sanitization of a text is usually done in translation 'to simplify a text in a predictable direction, towards English and the Judeo-Christian tradition and away from the multiplicity of indigenous languages and religions, which have to be homogenized before they can be translated'. See Tejaswini Niranjana, *Siting Translation: History, Post-Structuralism and the Colonial Context* (Berkeley: University of California Press, 1992), p. 180. This critique is

probably more apt for the Rupa translations of the Sunil Gangopadhyay novels we talk about later on in this chapter.

46. Rabindranath Tagore, *Four Chapters*, tr. Rimli Bhattacharya (New Delhi: Srishti, 2002), p. 57.
47. Ibid., p. 89.
48. Rimli Bhattacharya and Geeta Dharmarajan (eds), *Katha Prize Stories Volume 1*, (New Delhi: Katha, 1991), p. 9.
49. Ibid.
50. Rimli Bhattacharya. 'Translator's Note' in *Katha Prize Stories Volume 1*, eds. Rimli Bhattacharya and Geeta Dharmarajan (New Delhi: Katha, 1991), p. 13.
51. Vidya Das (ed.), *Oriya Stories* (New Delhi: Srishti, 2000), p. 212.
52. Mini Krishnan, 'About this Series' in *Gone are the Rivers*, ed. Dilip Kaur Tiwana, tr. S.C. Narula and Bhupinder Singh (Chennai: Macmillan India, 1998), p. v.
53. Sunil Gangopadhyay, *At Heaven's Gates*, tr. Sanchayita Chatterjee (New Delhi: Rupa, 2004), p. 29. Surprisingly, Sumanta Banerjee and Rani Ray, compilers of *Homes in Emptiness*, do the same thing in their otherwise better thought-out anthology of Bangla stories in English translation—'Baitarini' is again glossed as 'River of Hades' here (see Sumanta Banerjee and Rani Ray comp., *Homes in Emptiness: Anthology of Bangla Stories* [New Delhi: Srishti, 2000]).
54. Sunil Gangopadhyay, *At Heaven's Gates*, p. 110.
55. Perhaps, then, Trivedi and Bassnett's comments on the (ab)use of translation in colonial contexts are not entirely out of place even in the context of post-colonial translation practices:

> Translation has been at the heart of the colonial encounter, and has been used in all kinds of ways to establish and perpetuate the superiority of some cultures over others. But now, with increasing awareness of the unequal power relations involved in the transfer of texts across cultures, we are in a position to rethink both the history of translation and its contemporary practice.

Bassnett and Trivedi, 'Introduction', p. 17.

56. Sunil Gangopadhyay, *The Youth*, tr. Sanchayita Chatterjee (New Delhi: Rupa & Co, 2003), p. 23.
57. Ibid., p. 24.
58. Ibid., p. 6.
59. Ibid., p. 23.
60. Ibid., p. 25.
61. Ibid., p. 46.
62. Ibid., p. 69.

63. Ibid., p. 102.
64. Ibid., p. 136.
65. Ibid., p. 156.
66. Ibid., p. 70.
67. Ibid., p. 98.
68. Ibid., p. 33.
69. Ibid., p. 4.
70. Ibid., p. 20.
71. Ibid., p. 84.
72. Ibid., p. 32.
73. Ibid., p. 2.
74. Ibid., p. 3.
75. Ibid., p. 138.
76. Gopinath Mohanty, *The Ancestor*, tr., Arun Mohanty (New Delhi: Sahitya Akademi, 1997).
77. Ibid.
78. Ibid.
79. Ibid.
80. Moti Nandy, *The White Envelope*, tr. Suchandra Chakraborty (New Delhi: Sahitya Akademi, 1997), p. 122.
81. Ibid.
82. Ibid., p. 121.
83. Ibid.
84. Ibid., p. 122.
85. Ibid.
86. Ibid., p. 121.
87. Ibid., p. 121.
88. Premendra Mitra, *Snake and Other Stories*, tr. Rina and Pritish Nandy (Calcutta: Seagull, 1990).
89. Ibid., p. 129.
90. Jyotirmoyee Devi, *The River Churning*, tr. Enakshi Chatterjee (New Delhi: Kali for Women, 1995).
91. Ibid., p. 6.
92. Ibid., p. 23.
93. Ibid., p. 31.
94. Ibid., p. 32.
95. Ibid., p. 45.
96. Ibid., p. 43.
97. Ibid., p. 44.
98. Manik Bandyopadhyay, *Selected Stories*, ed. Malini Bhattacharya (Calcutta: Thema, 1988).

99. Ashapurna Devi, *Snakebite, The Distant Widow: 2 Novels*, tr. Anima Bose (New Delhi: Prachi Prakashan, 1983).

100. Ibid., p. 41.

101. Ibid., p. 40.

102. See Bill Ashcroft, Gareth Griffiths and Helen Tiffin (eds), *The Empire Writes Back: Theory and Practice in Post-colonial Literatures* (London and New York: Routledge,1989).

Chapter 7

Kya Hum Pehle Kabhi Yahan Aye Hain

Re-turning to Look at the 'Indian' in Indian Cinema through Farah Khan's Om Shanti Om[*]

Ipshita Chanda

Thirty Years Ago...

In *Karan Arjun*, Shah Rukh Khan returns to his village with Johnny Lever in his second avatar and tells Lever, '*Kya hum pehle kabhi yahan aye hain?*'

In *Om Shanti Om* (hereafter *OSO*): once more Shah Rukh Khan returns to the burnt-down set on which, in his previous life, he died trying to save the most popular heroine of yesteryears. This time he returns as a star, in whom the spirit of the old Shah Rukh, the junior artiste who loved the heroine, has reincarnated itself. This time too, he turns to his secretary who is accompanying him and says, '*Kya hum pehle kabhi yahan aye hain ?*' That provides a cue for the secretary to retell the mishap that occurred on these very sets 30 years ago. They were destroyed in a fire and the picture stopped, the very night the heroine mysteriously disappeared. No one of course had any concern for Shah Rukh in his previous avatar—he was just a junior artiste, dreaming big dreams, besotted with the heroine and then finally giving up his life in

---

[*] This chapter is a gift for those who taught me to travel—it is the smallest possible expression of gratitude, because I hope, that *picture abhi baaki hai, mere dost.*

a futile attempt to save her. But not before his spirit entered the little form of a baby born to the most popular hero of those days, who accidentally knocked him down while he lay burnt and battered outside that inferno. The hero was taking his pregnant wife to hospital in his car when the accident occurred. Shah Rukh the elder was thus in the same building—the moment of his death and the moment of the birth of the new Shah Rukh coincided exactly, and in the belief system that characterizes Hindi films as a world, this is the moment when one soul leaves a body and enters into another. Farah Khan uses Shah Rukh as one myth and the sequence of events, a stock episode in Hindi films involving second comings, as the other. If we follow Roland Barthes' primer, *Mythologies*,[1] then we shall not have trouble remembering that there are two sign-systems here. The overarching sign-system of Hindi cinema, harbours both the 1970s and 1980s 'past' of Shah Rukh the elder as depicted in the first half of this film as well. The contemporary 2007 sign-system that produces both character and situations involving Shah Rukh the younger in the second half of the film is predicated on the earlier sign-system of the first half. The location seems similar in space. It is the same industry, but it is different in time: three decades have passed, and the 1970s are now memories, tropes, themselves cinematic signs. These sign-systems are related by location, both in its similarity and difference. The first constructs a receptional threshold, what Jauss has called a 'horizon of expectation' for the second. And the purpose of this chapter is to discern how that first sign-system is produced as well as how the second may be produced from the first: in other words, this is an exercise in understanding the process of change within and across specific temporal and spatial locations.

In sum, that is also what we may read as the message of Farah's film—that the reality of mass India (an entity that the civil society newly conscious of itself has never met, and the political society has claimed to represent but has actually milked) is embedded in the world created on celluloid by films made in the subcontinent in its undivided state, and vice versa. If one enters Indian reality, then one also enters the world of film, Hindi mainly, but also Tamil, representing perhaps two of the ancient ur-strains in Indian civilization, permeated in aesthetic representation and in cases, in aesthetic philosophy, by the other important elements in the leaven that produced this civilization: the Islamicate and 'Western' cultures.

Witness the narrative form that Farah uses, where she scores over another period film released just a few days after *OSO*: *Khoya Khoya Chand*, by Sudhir Mishra who is a master of *cinema verite* Indian style (or ishtyle, if you want to use the filmi idiom). In fact Mishra attempts to go beyond the milieu of the film world to the world of the artistes who established and enacted this representative mode with their lives. His movie is about the 1950s and 1960s, the time of the 'Muslim social' with its concentration on love-tropes borrowed from Sufi poetry reso-nating with its underlying philosophy. This era was also studded with talented heroines trapped within patriarchal social structures, yet free to hurl themselves into doomed love affairs: as if enacting in their lives what was then so popular on screen, the deep involvement of the real and the celluloid worlds, one powerfully inflecting the other. *OSO* is an object lesson in how this may be depicted on-screen. The idiom of Hindi cinema is unrealistic, cheesy (for want of a better word) and downright offensive sometimes. But this is the reality that forms a crucial part of our lives—Shah Rukh Khan, in the endless round of promos that he did before the release of the film, said that he felt sad and humbled when he thought of his fans—there were so many of them who, despite the fact that he did not know them, loved him sincerely and unconditionally. That is the constituency that Farah's film talks about by making Shah Rukh, the object of their desire, one of them, by making him enact their fantasies. This is a brilliantly orchestrated self-reflexive enactment where Shah Rukh Khan the fan, the man, the social being alive to the world he lives in and rules is humourously aware and critical of Shah Rukh Khan the persona, the star, the ruler of the hearts of millions, King Khan. Ironically, a number of Shah Rukh fans have recoiled from the movie (which means they have seen it once rather than 11 times)—and that is because this movie relentlessly satirizes the reality that it and they inhabit. Not all of us can laugh at ourselves, and it is now clear why Shah Rukh and Farah were so nervous before the film released and that explains the blitz of promotional slots they covered.

Both *Khoya Khoya Chand* and *OSO* thematize the history of Indian cinema—one in the realistic sense, the other using the entire gamut of cinematic resources developed, in 60 odd years, by the Hindi film as a broad genre. Sudhir Misra is not interested in making a popular film, a position he has vehemently stated.[2] He uses the resources used by Muzaffar Ali to make a biography of a person: *Umrao Jaan*. There, the world of Lucknowi culture and the persona of the heroine were all acutely filmi—they were exactly what Hindi films had been referring to in countless similar narratives. Even the woman who took the courtesan with a heart of gold persona to its apogee, Rekha herself, was used by Ali as a reference to herself in the film that underlined the genesis of the courtesan idiom and its nesting culture. *Umrao Jaan*'s very narrative itself, as well as in the aesthetic modes used to realize this narrative, the cinematic resources of Hindi film were deployed in such a way as to lead to an identification of the constructed 'real' world of the protagonist with the 'real' world of the film viewer, Hindi cinema itself being a crucial part of this 'real' world for the latter. In *Khoya Khoya Chand*, Mishra attempts to film an age in Hindi cinema through the biography of a single heroine: a tall order, undoubtedly. He has done it before, with 'real' life, rather than with cinema... But in the case of *Khoya Khoya Chand*, the reality is film itself, the biography of a film-era, film history is the text to be crafted out of the narration. One might, with apologies to the sensibilities of high culture enthusiasts, also say that this film narrativizes the culture of Indian film—in which case, the modes of representation have to adapt themselves to the medium which they claim to be representing. My argument is that *Khoya Khoya Chand* succeeds in doing this through the music, but not through the narrative structure of the film itself.

The point made earlier can be investigated by paying some attention to the songs. In both *Khoya Khoya Chand* and *OSO* such attention will reinforce what I have suggested about the idiom in which reality is represented being identifiably filmi. Each of the songs in the first film are beautifully crafted in themselves but are not set-piece picturizations as they are in the latter film. This is unfair to the film in general in these times of audio-visual media: to hear is not enough, seeing and hearing are both equally necessary, and *Khoya Khoya Chand*, by making the visual so intricately tied to the narrative that it cannot stand alone, has subtracted from it's own appeal. There are at least two genre songs in this film. First, *Yeh nigahein* a number that refers to the innumerable Salil Chowdhury compositions of the times which were based on jive-rhythms, and second, the title song that is identified with the quawali but also contains experiments with various forms of harmonization (another Salil Chowdhury element, peculiar to the era). Both are beautifully worded, using the repertoire of mystic Sufi symbols that came to form the basic idiom of love and longing in Hindi film music. But none of these songs can be found completely in the film. They appear as songs being picturized on the characters of the films being made by the hero/heroine/characters within the film. This realistic treatment of the songs translates into one reason less for the film being watched. Farah, in contrast is a choreographer by profession—song-picturization remains an area that she is adept at and in *OSO*, the songs are detachable items. They have been treated thus by the audio-visual media, but they are also part of the larger 'culture of Hindi film' that this film thematizes. We may treat this as an example of the same resources, located in a culturally shared space of memory, being used in different ways to produce two separate cultural artifacts. The rest of what follows will study the processes of production and reception that make this possible, with *Om Shanti Om* as the exemplar.

When the audience, whose horizon of expectation is produced by its familiarity with the idiom and language of popular film as a genre, is faced with a set of symbols or a loose configuration of elements, they are well able to connect these to the larger picture even if these elements have no direct connection to the film itself. In Farah's film, each song is a set sequence, but providing a dramatic turn to the story: the first glance from the beloved's eyes is a moment of celebration that is enshrined in Hindi film parlance, derived from the Islamicate culture that underlies the popular expression of love. One might even extrapolate from the medieval Hindavi romances, written in local languages, but combining the elements of Sufi philosophy of devotional love with the elements of Nathpanthi and Tantric body-disciplining practices current in central and western parts of India in the medieval period. The *razm-bazm-tilism-aiyyari* or elements of war-love-satire-trickery which characterized oral performances and kept them dynamic and popular have been borrowed by popular Hindi films, and celebrated in *OSO*. Every song sequence is a statement grafted onto the film because Hindi films always have had love songs, cabaret songs, patriotic songs and several such generic requirements. In contemporary films has been added the item number. In this film the item number displaying Shah Rukh's much publicized six pack is 'Dard-e-Disco', where the hero is the item rather than any of the minimally clad women he cavorts with. The very title 'Dard-e-Disco' fuses in one stroke the heterogenous multicultural reality that is Indian society. This number is its reflection in Indian film: *dard*, the anguish of unrequited love whose pangs are felt by the devotee and the lover who has surrendered all, joined expertly with disco, redolent of the often derided but irreversible and undeniable influence of the West, which has been enshrined in Hindi film as a genre through the Mithun Chakraborty 'disco' films. Both of these borrowings are actually indianized—I used the lower-case I for Indian, because I am proposing that it is an adjective with general validity at least in the subcontinent (and looking at the influence of Hindi film and Indian English worldwide, why only there?). One of the primary characteristics of this process is that it facilitates the existence of two such diverse strains of cultural discourse in coherence with each other, forming thus a version of the 'local' that assimilates and transforms the 'global' to its own requirements.

To return to the item song. This particular case is an item song in a film being made by Om in which the lead actor has almost no 'functioning body part' (a mean dig at Sanjay Leela Bhansali's *Black*). There is nothing to sell the man's movie unless he, as the hero, takes matters into his own hands (as Shah Rukh's nearest rival Aamir Khan is famed for doing). This introduces us to the situation in which the item song is born in this film: it combines the exigencies of the genre with references to the off-screen filmi culture that thanks to electronic media and page three, all self-respecting Hindi filmgoers are privy to. This makes space for the performer, the man before the camera rather than the director, the man wielding the megaphone, who finds a way out of a flop. Naturally, the extraneous 'item' introduced for commercial rather than artistic purposes, eventually results in the addition of a new element in the genre—a perfect case of the so-called base, in its complicated but inevitable form, influencing the superstructure, without the cast-iron notion of 'structure' in the gross sense. The difference is of course local, cast in the structure of feeling current in the Hindi film world. Aamir would have made the text more realistic in keeping with some idea of perfection within the genre, referenced from some artistic impulse, where perhaps the commercial would have been disguised. However, when Shah Rukh and Farah introduce the item, they reference it with current Hindi film reality but take care to thrust in a new element such that it remains a milestone to which everyone will refer—not only artistically, but commercially as well, quite visibly and without concealment. Shah Rukh's six-pack abs and the publicity that they have been accorded far outstrip anything recently perpetrated through the female body. The representation of the female body follows the various types of *nayika* enumerated in classical Sanskrit literature. But the sublimation of sensuous eroticism, whether through the influence of Vaishnava practices of *madhurya* and *bhakti*, or through the Islamicate influences recorded in the Hindavi *prem akhyan* genre, introduces to the history of the representation of the female body, the 'feminine' ideals of suppressed longing as well as *sharm-haya* most inadequately translated as shyness. Such representational tropes do not of course apply to the male body. In fact, the history of representation of the male body in Indian literary or visual art may be worth understanding, though this is not the place for such an endeavour. Suffice it to say here that Farah makes the most of the absence of any framing ideology of representation of the uncovered male body, and thus transforms her item number into a generic marker with a difference. The commercial viability of the generic marker is thus ensured: an uncovered female body sells, an uncovered male body, especially if it belongs to a particular male who has not yet 'taken off his shirt' (and Hindi film aficionados will understand the importance of this reluctance, and thus the value of this uncovering), sells better.

The most eloquent testimony to the indianization of the effects of the two cultures that entered India from outside at different times for different purposes, is borne by the lyrics of the song 'Dard-e-Disco' and its method of picturization. The backdrop for the song is constructed out of exotically artificial locales—film sets (remembering that Switzerland is used as a film set in the cinema of a tropical country like India), the toned multicoloured bodies in their perfectly colour-coordinated non-clothes, the heavily overt gestures which flaunt a plastic sexuality many worlds removed from the lyrics of the song itself, replete with tropes of concealment, thirst and the agony of unrequited love that the ethos of Sufi mysticism expresses. The suturing of these two worlds is done through everyday street humour that is aware of the incongruity of throwing both these together with a resounding clash. But this process too appears as a comfortable, self-reflexive weaving together, confident enough to laugh at itself even while doing it. After the high-flowing Urdu verse, describing the maddening effects of love that strike the hero speechless, when the truth is finally revealed—'*Futa jo khwab ka gubbara*'—then he is driven from pillar to post with agony. But in the twenty-first century, where we have no qualms about flaunting our liquidity (albeit in plastic), how is this emotion to be expressed so as to create identification and awe at the same time? Reply: '*firta hoon main London Paris New York LA San Francisco*'. This appears inevitable if the line must rhyme with '*Dil mein mere hai dard-e-disco*', metrically and culturally as well. This is an instance where the song reinforces the conventions of Hindi film, even while distancing these very conventions by staging them self-reflexively. One would agree with Madhava Prasad's observation[3] that Hindi film is a representation that gives itself to be seen. But one would take it further in the present when India is being pulled apart with the simultaneity of going forward and staying backward, stubbornly but resiliently. Thus we may further nuance his observation by trying to historicize and analyze the mechanics of being seen, attempting to explain the nature of this visibility by stressing that this is a purely orchestrated, extremely self conscious offering, knowing and acknowledging that we can see ourselves even while others are looking at us.

Bhago! A Brief Roadmap Away from Cultural Studies?

The way we have approached the text in this last section is an example of what may be called 'theory from below'.[4] This requires an initial self-effacement of the reader-with-a-viewpoint, in other words the critic, which that genre of human being is loath to accept. So let us just say that this film *OSO* is for those whose reality is reflexively inflected with the reality of celluloid, for those who are embedded in that reality by choice and compulsion, at once. This is the interpretive community that the film is obviously addressed to. But can that also be the position of the Indian Culture Studies critic, whose critical hardware comes from state-of-the-art Western academia? The reader might legitimately ask, what's wrong with using the latest technology? Let me humbly submit that the latest technology is not always the best for understanding responses that are culture-specific in ways that one has just begun to appreciate. The latest technology pretends to be general in hiding its own historical antecedents, trying to sound like a transcendental truth. Mostly, this due to the way in which these theories are popularized, rather than inherent flaws in the theories themselves. They could be, in their philosophical form, marked by the compulsions of the thinkers who worked them through; but those who learnt them as gospel did not share the insight into a particular conjuncture that they were the result of. Thus, those who dealt in theory without the attendant historicization and local specificities ended in generalizing them beyond their immediate locality. The positive input of Culture Studies is that, by putting all kinds of theories in all kinds of unlikely places, it has enabled us to wake up to the limitations of each theory as it confronts a reality that it has no roots in. The result is that it comes out sounding only like jargon. One way to neutralize the effects of that awakening is to deploy means of understanding that are culture-specific and hence rooted in one particular structure of feeling, in order to understand an application in a similar yet temporally or geographically distant location. In the case of the Hindi film, the genre itself is located in the space that we now know as India. This is the same space which pioneered theories of producing and receiving artistic texts in different media, as far back in time as the *Natya Shastra.* Hence it cannot be too much to ask whether this space has anything unique to offer by way of understanding what may be seen as cultural production located within this space itself ?[5]

This question is important to me as a comparatist, because I do not find anything proposed by the current formation that is labelled Culture Studies in India which the methodology of Comparative Literature has not already mapped out. Further, it appears that Comparative Literature might even make a few tentative methodological suggestions for Culture Studies scholars in India which might redirect them to the issue of an Indian approach to Culture Studies. The reader is by now aware of my agenda. I do not wish to engage with the debates that are ravaging Culture Studies the world over[6] because I'm unsure about their relevance to the Indian context. Rather than the methods of reading proposed by Western pundits of texts produced out of and received in the Indian context, I use my training as a student of Comparative Literature for such engagements. It is this training that underwrites my 'reading' of the cinematic text of *OSO*. My idiosyncratic question: is there, or can there be, an Indian Culture Studies whose method is rooted in something other than what is currently 'popular'? The framing of the question is consequent upon my reading of a film-text produced and received in the Indian context. So the representational aesthetics and modes used in Hindi film, act in this chapter as both question-frame, and the raw material with which to try and answer the question. The question, as I have stated earlier, is whether there exists an Indian Culture Studies. If it does not exist, should we have to invent it?

Let me get to the central point of this part of the chapter by making a couple of tall claims: what Comparative Literature has been doing theoretically is precisely what Culture Studies is claiming that it has been doing in the West since the late-1980s and in India since some literature departments found theory, as in finding god. As with every other thing that happens in the domain of single-literature departments in the world's most persistent and successful post-colony, this means that everyone from Eng lit to vernacs[7] will jump onto this band wagon. Discerning historians of the disciplinary politics within the humanities, especially if they have read Spivak's[8] indictment of the discipline in the US, will point out that Comparative Literature at one stage of its progress, offered the space to do newly minted Continental theory. Little wonder then that Spivak had to proclaim the death of that discipline. But let's not breast-beat about that right now. Rather, I shall endeavour to substantiate my claim that classical aesthetic theories are perfectly well able to address 'popular' cultural products and processes located in contemporary India. Whether the sceptic will grant that Comparative Literature is the pioneer in this area, is a different question: as a student of the discipline that seems to be living quite tenaciously despite the proclamations of mortality, let me at least not give up without a fight.

The products of the imagination that could be traced to an oppositional culture of the working class, the concentration on the popular or the privileging of heterogeneity arising from when Oxon folk came close to adult education, or even the need for adult education, are rather complex and intertwined in the society we are talking about. The informed reader will have identified each of these as foundational categories as shorthand for the different trajectories taken by Culture Studies as practice and discipline in the West. However, in contemporary Indian society to which Hindi films broadly appeal, these cannot serve as separate research questions with separate agendas. Therein lies the shortcoming of a single-strand approach that Culture Studies has been taking up in some of its guises. The idea of India, post-Independence, became a programme and a policy—the birth of India provided a geographical entity which served as context for the reality that films address and are made of. Film, in India, fulfilled a need that had existed in the composite scriptal and oral socius. It was characteristic of the many disconnected and independent or tributary societies that inhabited the subcontinent. The diversity travelled and metamorphosed, slowly amalgamating in an apparently single political unit that had necessarily to cling to the diversity because there was no other viable method of being together. Thus, the composite socius, in dynamic formation, sought a means of expression that included the diversity as an organic part of the whole, in language and idiom, generically and thematically. This is the logic of film as a form in India, a logic that *OSO* has foregrounded and which we may now consider.

That brings me to my second tall claim: I could say that *OSO* is the first Indian film that thematizes the self-conscious construction of its own discourse, and therefore may classically be called post-modern; except that such self-conscious narrative strategies existed in India at least from the time of Vishnu Sharma, the man credited with having written the *Panchatantra*. In one of the stories there, the famous one that we all know, of the donkey wanting to sing before he eats the cucumbers in the field, and being beaten up while all the cucumbers are eaten by the jackal, the donkey justifies his desire to sing by proving that he is a theoretically sound singer. He quotes from Bharata's *Natyashastra*. That he was an inept practitioner is something we do not need to be told. It was because he could not sing that the farmer whose field it was woke up and came out with a stick. Nothing less was expected from a donkey. Perhaps one of the multiple morals of this story is what the critic gleans from it—that between theory and practice, between pontification and performance comes many a slip. The writer of the *Panchatantra* is able to satirize or/and expose the mechanics of aesthetic fulfilment without actually executing/operationalizing the means themselves. This is how the oral world that is constantly self-conscious and self-reflexive enters the more settled, sedentary and organized world of writing. By doing this the narrator is able to include the constructed literary reality as part of the reality that the text inhabits or constructs. It took Cervantes 15 centuries after Christ to actually operationalize this in European literature. Let us not quibble about Vishnu Sharma's dates, or even his existence—the very existence of the text itself, is enough for us to rest our case. And the point I am trying to make here is that this is exactly what Farah Khan is able to do in the medium of Indian film—present a history of the genre by exposing its mechanical workings, thereby becoming completely self-referential. In that sense it is a reminder of the workings of an aesthetics that is unique to 'indian' as an adjective. Perhaps this signals the need for a method of studying it which is also rooted in Indian realities. I am offering Reception Studies, Contactual Relations and Influence methodology as a means of doing this. They have taught me engaged and located reading, a state of enjoyment that has been categorized in classical Sanskrit aesthetics as that of the *sahriday pathak*, rather than that of the critic, in the Western sense who seems by definition to have no cause and no use for enjoyment.

Picture Abhi Baaki Hai Mere Dost: 'Real' Cinema

But enough of the rhetoric—let us actually try to read the reality that Om Prakash Makhija, an obsessed fan of superstar Shantipriya inhabits in the first half of the film, a reality that is referred to, reiterated and used as a thematic and theoretical counter in the second half. The aspirations of Om Prakash Makhija the junior artiste are thwarted by just one thing—his name. Who could become a star with a name like Makhija? Think of all those who changed their names in order to catch the marquee lights of the garish world in which film posters used to be painted by the most powerful artiste that post-Independence India has produced? Think of Yusuf Khan (Dilip Kumar), Devdutt Anand (Dev Anand), Jatin Khanna (Rajesh Khanna). But think also of the only family that has never had to change its name because they were, nominally, exactly identifiable with the ethos represented by the Hindi film industry then: robust, cultured, from-across-the-border Punjabi Arya Samaji as opposed to the rustic this side-of-the-border Sikh Punjabi, that is. the Kapoors. In fact this is another entirely filmi joke shared by the entire nation that in the age of star-sons, first aggressively ushered in by Raj Kapoor for his sons and then followed with less panache by other film-maker, actor and director daddies, Shah Rukh was an outsider. He came from a non-filmi family, from a non-filmi place. How is anyone to make a mark in filmdom if they do not belong to the inner circle? In the very first moments of the movie one comes upon one such star–aspirant, whose story the film audience knows by now—the *Virar-ka-chokra* Govind Ahuja, who frequented the studios until he became a star. On-screen, 'thirty years ago' as the writing on the screen tells us in the very beginning of the film, what we see is his struggling pre-star self, plagued by the problem of an unfilmi name (not Kapoor or Kumar) and a suburban stamp. The fact that this latter was Govinda's selling proposition in the innumerable risqué movies he did, ironically with Karishma, a filmi princess from the 'royal' Kapoor family, the first generation of the Kapoor women to enter films, merits another Farah Khan film in itself. Here, intertextuality is immediate for the informed viewer, who has identified Govinda with his yellow pants (as the viewer will later identify Jeetendra with his white shoes, Rajesh Khanna with his trademark flicking back of an imaginary parrot-tuft of hair) and his place of origin (Virar) even before he says his name. The response from Om Prakash and his friend Pappu, both street-smart city slickers in the world of film studios, is immediate: Change your name to Govinda, they advise him. Of course, in 'real' life, the man did do so, and the rest is, as the audience knows, history. The intertextuality does not end there—in the mother of all celebrity song–dance sequences itself referenced from Amitabh Bachchan's waiter act 'John-Jani-Janardan' in *Naseeb*, Govinda appears as himself, and teaches the second Shah Rukh, playing a star-son and consequently, the current star in the movie, to dance like himself. So does another hero famed for his dancing ability and acceptance with the masses, Mithun Chakraborty. These men seem to be wanting to give a little of themselves to the ongoing non-stop performance that is Hindi cinema, the continuous process of reality formation that it is party to. In that same stroke, they are also being archived on celluloid in their own personae with what they will be remembered for by audiences.

Sometimes, this archiving is not quite complimentary: witness the representation of Manoj Kumar as an actor who always had his face covered by his hand while he emoted on-screen, a fact that the film uses to pass off the two junior artistes Omi and Pappu for him. That is how they gain entry into the premier of 'Dreamy Girl' (remember Hema Malini in and as *Dream Girl?*) in which Omi's heart-throb Shantipriya is starring. They present their credentials at the gate with their hands in front of their faces Manoj Kumar style, pretending to be him, and thus wile their way in. When security stops the real Manoj Kumar, he pulls out his driving license to prove his identity, and lo and behold, the photograph on the license is one in which the hand covers the face, with the name M. Kumar underneath. There was much to-do when Manoj Kumar professed himself insulted, and Shah Rukh had to apologize. But Abhishek Bachchan, playing himself, which means a spoilt arrogant self-centred star-son, or Akshay Kumar playing himself, which means a martial-arts expert who thrusts his pelvis in order to fire bullets from a gun held in a halter at his crotch (look ma no hands!) have also been thus archived, and apparently with great good humour on the part of the people who are the butt of the joke. The on-screen and off-screen personae of the stars, which are parts of reality for their dedicated fans, is the element that causes a congruence between Farah's film represen-tation and the reality which animates this representation. *OSO* func-tions as an active preserving agent for an era of Hindi films not only by referring to the individual traits, styles, generic markers and thematic nodes of those times, but by also using each of these traits, styles, generic markers and thematic nodules to generate its own story, its own plot-line and representational aesthetics. In that sense *OSO*, in the quintessential dramatic meaning of the term, performs Hindi film before the camera as a process: it is a documentation of the aesthetic and cultural history of Hindi film. Can these two be separated? That is a question that Culture Studies in India must admit and then perhaps attempt to answer—theoretically.

This history is one of a reality that is impossible to construct without the existence of Hindi films themselves. Farah carefully puts together this reality from the very beginning. Om Prakash Makhija the junior artiste loves the reigning diva of the day, Shantipriya. He communicates with her as if she is real—which, to him, she is, because the huge poster of her film 'Dreamy Girl' is mounted above an overhead pedestrian bridge form which the entire sprawl of the slum area in which Omi lives can be seen. In a sense, the huge garishly painted image of Shantipriya dominates the lives of those who live there: she is the girl in their dreams, someone whom they will never be able to meet in real life. But real life is dominated by her presence all the same, and she is as real to them as she is to any girl next door. It is just that the two orders of reality are different. One can almost hear the echoes of the ninth-century text of Anandavardhan in this statement. According to him, there is a *bhavauchityam* (the *auchitya* or aptness of *bhava* or emotion) and a *prakritauchityam* (an aptness with reference to nature, perhaps more aptly, pardon the pun, called naturalism); a difference between what is apt for a god, or the *divya* and what is apt for men, that is *manush*; sometimes the divine uses the human as a receptacle (*manusahsrayen divyasya*). Any deviation from the human in the case of ordinary human beings is *anuchit* and devoid of *rasa*. But think of the episode of Satvahana's descent into the world of serpents which we know from legend, *sruti*. We all know that this is not possible for a mere mortal—yet, think of the effect it has on common people who hear of it—so what is *anuchit* about it (*tadlokasamanya prabhavatishayvarnaney kimanauchityam*)? The rule of a particular *auchitya* for *kavya* and another for real life, what is permissible in *kavya* and what cannot happen in real life, and the easy distinction between the two is the basis for the creation of a film idiom that forms a whole order of reality. Further, the rule for *auchitya* directly creates a metaphoric presence, larger than the human for people who are legendary—like Satvahana, the Pandavas, and of course, successful film stars. *OSO* actually thematizes the creation of this reality; and the end of this creation is the production of *rasa*, the effect desired from the representation.

Thus Omi goes to speak to his beloved Shantipriya on the poster, adoring her as a film hoarding, a dream that is beyond his grasp unless there is some divine intervention. There is, of course, a divine intervention. It comes in the form of a holy thread, *taveez*, sacred to Shirdi Saibaba, one of the most popular and hence the most reviled godmen in India that Omi's mother ties to his wrist. Omi and Pappu are lining the road outside the auditorium where 'Dreamy Girl' will premiere, waiting for Shantipriya to arrive. She steps out—or rather in cinematic idiom she appears from under the earth, the camera catches her as she rises to her full height from underneath, framed by fainting crowds in the background—an interesting way to introduce a newcomer to the screen, reminding us of many first-sightings of later superstars in the past. Be that as it may, Shantipriya sets out to enter the studio, her diaphanous *dupatta* floating behind her (and where else would one get those most convenient items of clothing that trail after one in mid air, open to innumerable possibilities and a life of their own, like the versatile sari *pallu* and the *dupatta*, but in India?), and of course, it catches in the *taveez* that Omi wears on his wrist, forcing him to trail after the woman of his dreams in actual reality. Then she turns around and looks at him—echoes of the innumerable love at first scenarios reverberate in the background. Of course Omi has seen her, as has the world at large, thousands of times in the past. But this is the first time she sees him—or, as she tells him after he has jumped into a studio fire run out of control to save her when the hero chickens out, 'I have met many kinds of people before, but none who has jumped into the fire to save my life'—this is her first brush with the world of real people, in whose world she is a dream, though she too lives in the same world as them. The point made here is that the 'real' reality and cinematic 'reality' intersect totally, one fusing into another throughout this film, and from the very beginning these intersections are marked because they build up into the climax.

Let us quickly take a look at some of the other intersections of the real and the celluloid and the reciprocal construction of one by the other. When Omi talks to the poster-image of Shantipriya, she is real to him.

He has seen her laugh, cry, dance and sing in a darkened hall where she does all this with him and none other. In every song sequence, it is he who replaces the hero, he who dons the hero's clothes and the hero's make-up and mannerisms and romances her. And so, when he talks to her, despite the fact that she doesn't answer, he keeps saying 'I hope you aren't getting bored?' and when he hears her in his mind, saying no, he smiles and says, 'Thanks' with the proper Indian accent, which sounds like 'Thenks'. Such a friendship between heroine and junior artiste can only occur in the make-believe world of Hindi films, and in this case actually does occur only there. In the song sequence where he serenades her in reality, rather than in his dreams, it occurs on the sets, using every single accessory that is so crucial to the filming of the love-duet in the Hindi film, beginning from the snow machine (heroine typically bare-foot) to the stationary car with the moving scenery behind it. But each and every accessory is shown in almost Brechtian syle, defamiliarized by exposing to the gaze of the audience what is generally kept beyond the camera's gaze. At the end of the song, she asks him whether he is never unhappy. 'Never', he replies, 'and if I am ever sad, I go to see one of your films'. Reality inhabited by the Hindi film fan is never completely free of the presence of the world created by the film itself. There are thus spatial, temporal and affective locations traversed throughout the film: the 'real' world of the filmgoer, the 'real world' of the poor junior artiste, the 'filmi' world of the film itself and the 'filmi' world depicted within the film. It is through the intersections and negotiations between these that the cultural process of the production and the reception of *Om Shanti Om* unfold.

The relationship between the fan and the worshipped star is also inflected by the tropes through which love is represented on screen. This real-life dialogue with a screen beloved culminates in Omi's discovering that she is actually in love with the son of a famous producer who will be unable to marry her because he wants to cast her in the biggest film of all time. To recall one of the industry's favourite taboos of all time: who will pay money to see a married heroine? Also the producer's name is being linked with the daughter of a rich man who will finance the film; he has promised to marry this girl if her father provides the money for his dream project starring his girlfriend Shantipriya. When Omi discovers this he is shattered—not that Shanti has led him on in any way, but her easy friendship with him has led him to weave dreams around her. He knows now for sure that she will never be his. This entire episode may well have feminists rising to the bait. Unconditional love and self-effacement before the beloved/divine may have been sourced originally from the Bhakti and Sufi poets' unflinching pursuit of god-the-beloved who will not yield until the worshipper actually annihilates himself. He must destroy his ego in the throes of love, a condition known in Sufi terminology as *fanaa*, a stage that precedes the devotee's acquisition of/ union with god. In the popular conception, of course, it is a patriarchal trope. God is the beloved and the devotee the lover whose quest cannot be complete until total surrender of self has been achieved through pursuit that does not brook any barriers. But then if God is conceived of as male, then even the male devotee takes on the female gender: a reality in the practice of devotion among the Bhakt poets that we cannot consider here at any length. But we may point out that to be *diwanaa*, besotted, is the condition aspired to by all lovers who think of themselves as devotees, and Omi is both lover and devotee, Shanti goddess and beloved. That is the structure of feeling prevalent in the enactment of love on the screen in the time in which this story is set.

This is the structure of feeling that guides Omi's return to Shanti's poster on the bridge even after he knows that she has given her heart to another who may not be worthy of her. There the conversation that ensues with her is regarding happiness—he wants her to be happy with the man she has chosen, but should this man cause her any grief, he will have Omi to reckon with. Love, then, for him as for the Sufi devotee or Bhakt poet, is love-as-process—fulfilment may come in this life, but that is not the only goal of this process. Rather, it is incidental—love will be requited if the devotee is able to transcend one *maqam* after another to reach the final stage of the annihilation of the ego, the basis of the self, and make oneself worthy of receiving the beloved he is devoted to. This is common parlance for Hindi film representations, in lyric, in dramatic structure, in thematic deployment, and followed here faithfully. What is added by Farah's script is the fact that this is the trope used by fans of Hindi film personalities too—this rejection of 'getting' or 'possessing' the beloved, the utter disregard for the reciprocal of love, not possible when the hero or heroine is who he/she is and the fan is who he/ she is. At the most, like in the case of Omi, it is a momentary meeting, a dream come true. In truth it does not happen, unless it happens in a Hindi film: as Hrishikesh Mukherji's film *Guddi* pointed out in the mid-1970s.

This is a crucial thread in the arrangement of the plot that becomes the world of Hindi film permeated by the world of reality, hence allowing two of the locations contained within the film that we have referred to earlier to merge. The screen person is real and privately, exclusively, unconditionally realized for the fan/worshipper, whose real life is constructed around her/his screen idol. Unhappiness in the so-called real world is assuaged by a salve available in the world of cinema—the real world forms a part of the realm of cinema, as cinema itself cannot escape its roots in the real world. And the script creates a situation in which precisely this fact is articulated. When Om Kapoor, the baby into whom the spirit of Omi enters, grows up and becomes a star (his father is a star, remember, so this follows the norm of successful star-sons), he recalls his past. This brings us to the second part of the film, beginning with Om's discovery of the burnt set on which Shanti perished as a result of a fire started by her diabolical producer-lover who wanted to annihilate her because she was carrying his child from their secret marriage.

The set is one on which Om is shooting now, as Mohabbat-man, a super hero, which of course is a take-off on Hrithik Roshan's film *Krrish*. Be that as it may, the sets return Om to his former life, and the story comes full circle when he meets the producer Mukesh Mehra, responsible for Shanti's death. Om decides to re-enact the story of Shanti's murder and confront Mukesh Mehra with the performance of the events of that night when both Shanti and Omi perished in the fire, thus forcing him to confess. This, as the seasoned Hindi film enthusiast will remember, is the exact sequence of events that had occurred in Subhash Ghai's film *Karz*. There, the song 'Om Shanti Om' was the most popular of all in a film which elaborately stages a re-enactment of the murder of the hero's father by his diabolical mistress. In that sequence, which features a song telling that old story, the hero forces the murderess Kanchan (played by Simi Garewal) to confess to the murder by enacting scenes from the romance that Simi faked with his father in order to kill him and become heiress to his fortune. Rishi Kapoor plays the role of his dead father in the re-enactment song sequence, leading the fiendish Kanchan–Simi to mistake him for her real lover, come back from the dead to haunt her with her crime. The appearance of a person who seems exactly like the one she killed forces Kanchan–Simi to lose control and confess. The song sequence in the earlier film, *Karz*, was conceived, in picturization and lyrics, to be a catalyst for this confession. Farah has used this as reference for her film's title as well as its plot structure. The first episode of Farah's film, where the character of Omi is introduced, is the shooting of the song sequence 'Om Shanti Om' in Subhash Ghai's film. It is not difficult for the audience educated in the history of Hindi film to identify and hence understand the model of forced-confession through a song sequence in the climax, as coming from Ghai's film. This also fits into the horizon of expectation created for the audience by Hindi film reality itself. Thus, the second pair of locations that we have enumerated before also enters the process of the production and reception of the film *Om Shanti Om* as cultural artifact.

This may be the thematic climax of the film, but the generic climax is reached much before that occurs. It serves to construct the deep structure within which the thematic climax can be made to mean. In the second part of the film, where the story of confession unfolds, Om, the superstar who has the spirit of Omi within him, has selected a Shanti lookalike (this is the actress Deepika Padukone's second 'reincarnated' role) to play Shanti so that Mukesh is scared into thinking that this is Shanti come back from the dead to haunt him, as Kanchan had thought in *Karz*. Sandy–Deepika is a blind fan of Omi the superstar, and this fact inflects the plot as it proceeds in the second part of the film. She seems a parallel for Om who, in the first part, was shown as a blind fan of Shanti. And it is because of their uncompromising devotion to the object of their adoration that certain unreal things become eminently possible, as unflinching devotion has always, in the discourse of *bhakti* and *mohabbat*, been able to call forth the miraculous. It is this fact of fandom or devotion that also becomes the most crucial means for forging pathways of negotiation between the two sets of locations that we had outlined at the beginning. In the remainder of this chapter we will look at the ways in which an aesthetic is fashioned by these interactions. This aesthetic results from the text's being produced through travels between varied locations in time and space. These travels, in turn, take in within their scope interpretive communities located in an affective space and time, constructed partly by the 'real' world of viewership and partly by the 'mediatised' world of the Hindi film. How does this happen?

When Deepika, or Sandy as she is called in her reincarnation, is unable to imitate the grace, charm and histrionics of the original Shanti, Om says to her that she must believe in Omi's pain in order to understand Shanti's real character. He says he knows she cannot understand Shantipriya's fate and Omi's anguish because this story of reincarnations and ghosts is unreal, and no one will believe it in today's world. To this Sandy replies, 'I won't be able to believe it? But when you jump from fifty floors high and land on your feet, I believe it. When you beat up a hundred goondas single handedly, I believe it. When you fly in the air and walk on water, I believe it. I believe it all.' In one expert stroke, Farah has established the *raison d'être* of her film as well as of the world it inhabits. And that is the crux of the matter—the world of Hindi film is a world in which its fans dwell, it is a crucial part of their reality and their culture, influenced by it and influencing it in constant reciprocation. One is reminded of the *auchitya* theory and its explanation for '*satya*' in *kavya* as opposed to the mundane world. And this also brings us to an appreciation of the relationship between the world of the film and the world within which the Hindi film functions, both locations crucial to the cultural production of film as an artifact. *Om Shanti Om* is not merely a feat of self-referentiality or self-deprecating humour characterized by the irony that marks the post-modern chronotope in India. It is actually a representation of Indian reality, so deeply inflected by the multi-resonant film-world that it is both its product and part of the process of its becoming: another characteristic that marks the mediatized global world of 'Indian' urban reality. And that is the reality that this film inhabits.

And apart from the way in which the connection between film and reality is performed throughout the film, Farah uses a poster of the mother-of-all popular films, *Sholay*, to state the obvious—there is no single quote from this one blockbuster anywhere in *OSO*. A poster of *Sholay* flanks the poster of *Dreamy Girl* atop the bridge where Shah Rukh goes to talk with his beloved. The most popular film of the 1970s is actually taken as given—it exists as a poster only, as part of the materials which form the real world. Perhaps it can be seen as a sacred text that cannot be defiled by copying and consequently satirizing it. It seems to have Vedic status in the world of Hindi film made after the 1970s.

I am proposing that the methodology that we need to follow to understand a film text thus constructed, comprises the mechanics of reception, a processual understanding of genre and theme grounded in history, an appreciation of multiple media-systems and inter- and intra-systemic cultural relations that underlie the production of cultural artifact in any medium. This, in turn, must be placed within the ebb and flow of processes of intercultural translation, discernible through the dynamics of cultural contact and its consequences. Apart from this the variety of media must be taken into account, as the rich intertextual fabric of Indian life is shot through with the simultaneous operation of oral, scriptal and electronically mediated representative forms and models. Perhaps one might even say that the availability of all these forms, genres, themes and idioms, excepting those crafted specially for the electronic media, have existed for Indians at the very surface of their culture, in varying degrees and intensities depending upon their own positions in this multivalent society. *OSO* makes this exercise equivalent to watching the film—it is crafted by those who are educated in Hindi film as genre, and made for a similarly educated audience.

Nevertheless, we must remember the mode of quotation adopted in the movie—each and every one of the references are made within a variety of thresholds that can be identified as humorous. In each case, the person/event/element that is being referred to is satirized whether by exaggeration or by an ironical gaze or by exposure of the conditions that made it possible. This is the mode of operation everywhere except in one place where the audience educated in the reality-construction of Hindi film is expecting it to happen. One does not fault the audience for this expectation—it is a comment on the world of Hindi film itself that such an episode has been converted to a cliché. All the more reason to laud Farah's script that shows us the cliché and the world that constructed it in their true colours and quietly offers an alternative. Here the script works not through recognition or identification but their opposites—it offers what we, as educated Hindi film watchers, do not expect, and thereby forces us to realize the nature of what we have come to accept and even poke fun at as a result of our Hindi-film education.

I refer to an episode in the story where the script brings the filmi enterprise violently face to face with stark reality. It separates the two irrevocably by using words that have never been uttered in a Hindi film. A stock situation is offered, a stock cliché is available, but in this one instance, the script refuses to use the filmi idiom, thereby signaling that this is a real situation for which a filmi cliché would be inappropriate. This occurs when Shanti tells her lover Mukesh, 'I am pregnant.' In usual Hindi film parlance this would read, *Main tumhari bacche ki maa bannaywali hoon.* The inevitable reaction to this would be to set off sighs of déjà vu across the auditorium, for all heroines who have sacrificed their honour before wedlock are condemned to suffering and eventually death. No one has ever accused Farah of being a feminist film-maker or of making films with female subjects. Shanti here is a star, and she lives a filmi life—but her pain in not being acknowledged by her lover because he is scared that she will lose her standing as a star and hence jeopardize his film and his plans, is palpable: 'real' should we call it? But we also note that the film-maker, incidentally a woman, respects a woman enough to not turn a crucial moment in her life into a spectacle. Even on the huge public screen, this moment remains undramatized: almost touching 'reality'—the'reality' that art sometimes makes us conscious of. Her compulsions to keep her marriage to him a secret from the world (a truth that punctuated the lives of many starlets who had secret liaisons with top notch producers in real life) have to be shown respect by setting it apart from the idiom in which the rest of the film is spoken.

In a similar vein, one notices the careful underplaying of the reunion scene between an aged Pappu, and his old friend Omi whose spirit is lodged in a body 30 years younger. Kirron Kher, here playing Bela Makhija, Omi's mother, makes her first entry onto the screen with a long-drawn out typical '*Nahiiiin*' and is throughout characterized by her son and his friend as someone who overacts, and so remains a junior artiste. Yet she too rations her reactions carefully, exhibiting full control when she finally meets her dead son's spirit in a body with a face resembling him exactly. These are stock situations that mark the Hindi films of that period: and in a film that satirizes the period in any way feasible, restrains itself when certain emotions that are engaged in these so-called 'stock' situations are enacted on screen. As we have noted earlier, they almost touch the real.

From the structural point of view, these deviations from the typically filmi occur in the second half of the film because the filmi representational trope in the second half is instrumental to the central concern of the plot. The second half of *OSO* is no longer the world of Omi who lives in the tawdry splendour of the sets, but the world of Om who is using the reality of film to mete out justice and avenge the deaths of the body that harboured his own spirit and the wronged woman whom this spirit worshipped. A careful differentiation between extra-film reality and film-reality is the pivot upon which this part of the film functions. It is crucial to maintain the balance of reality and film-constructed reality in *OSO*, whose theme is precisely this balance that popular-film fanatics effect regularly in their daily lives. And because this distinction is maintained, the trickle of clues that lead up to the climax work—they are plans laid in real life, but go awry in filmi reality due to a filmi logic. Needless to say, the logic is by now familiar to the trained audience—it is the logic of another revenge film where another wronged woman who has been duped and supposedly murdered ....but should I reveal the climax? Surely the trained Culture Studies enthusiast, who is the target reader of this piece, knows which film I mean?

And the Batli Award Goes to....

Bhartrihari, an exponent of *vyakarana darsana* or the philosophy of grammar, identified the levels of speech as the *vaikhari* (manifested), *madhyama* (the middle) and *pasyanti* (the seeing) and the *paraa*. While the first three he articulated clearly enough, the final one he does not quite elucidate, though the commentary of Harivrisabha on *Vakyapaadiya*, Bhartrihari's text, does. Ashok Aklujkar analyses the vakyapadiya which contains the elucidation of the linguistic philosophy of Bhratrihari, explaining the final stage thus: 'Parapasyanti is beyond ordinary usage and experience. It is not covered by grammar, which can at the most be an instrument for reaching it.'[9] The *paraa* level has been variously identified with the absolute (Brahman) or being itself, and taken into the realm of Advaita Vedanta thereafter. Recent work in linguistics identifies the *paraa* level as discourse:

> (Bhartrihari's) well-known planes *vaikharii, madhyamaa, pashyantii,* and *paraa* mutually articulated on the most inclusive plane, the one known as *paraa*—the perspective within which the speaker and the hearer attain a shared understanding of the context of speech as well as the content.
>
> This take on language says that the perspective shared by speakers and hearers underwrites the discourse. The particular flows of what is said and understood, from *pashyantii* through *madhyamaa* to *vaikharii,* are the traffic, not the roadmap. To the extent that Bhartrihari's work fixes its bearings on the *paraa* plane, it cannot give formal primacy to the *vaakya*, which is just one of the units on the planes lower than *paraa*. No theory of perspective can afford to get fixated on the sentence. One cannot aim for anything less than the discourse.[10]

I have been arguing in this chapter that the shared understanding of the context of utterance must characterize the production of cultural texts and the Indian Culture Studies expert's reading of those texts. In other words, the *pasyanti* and *madhyama* that are encapsulated in each syntagmatic utterance or the *vaikhari*, will require for its 'study' on a very basic level, a shared understanding of those utterance-levels, and a familiarity with the *paraa* level, the paradigms within which the utterances can operate meaningfully. This is a vastly reduced version of the actual implication of Bhartrihari's insight for research into what we have been calling the human sciences. The only reason I refer to it here is to call attention to the fact that our own resources have existed unobtrusively for long enough. Perhaps it is time for us, as scholars of Indian culture (or is that Indian scholars of culture?) to begin looking in our own backyards. As for the methodology that we apply to this task, my primary tall claim, as the reader has already noticed, is that comparative literary studies in India, in its 50 years of existence, has developed the resources of studying contact, intersystemic transactions and generic and thematic processes that we have been deploying in the study of 'Indian' texts. The reader may also have noticed their utility in reading texts from other media—an exercise that I have attempted earlier. My effort in this chapter has been to demonstrate some of the varied possibilities of this method through reading the film text *Om Shanti Om*. *Om Shanti Om* is by no means the first fan film to be made in Hindi— that honour belongs to another 1970s film, *Guddi*, made by Hrishikesh Mukherji, wherein the school-girl heroine's love for Dharmendra leads her to weave dreams that obstruct the natural course of her life, that is marriage to a 'real' man who loves her. It is through the intervention of the 'real' Dharmendra and some family members that she returns to earth, grows up from Guddi the fan to a 'real' woman finally willing to treasure the love of a 'real' man. But what about the film world? In *Guddi,* there is a deep, moralistic divide between this world of celluloid, characterized as somewhat negative and based on a simple definition of 'real'. *OSO* takes the story much further by making the reality of the 'real' and the reality of film inflect each other, much as they do in 'real' life. And the world of the fan and its distance as well as proximity to the world of the adored object is staged at the 'batli award' ceremony in Farah's film. Just after his first in-the-flesh encounter with Shantipriya, Omi dreams of becoming a big star and finally winning an award for Best Actor. The speech Omi gives to his audience of failed junior artiste, Pappu, a gaggle of street children, a pavement dweller and some durwans who guard the houses of the rich stars, is repeated in the second half when the reincarnated Om Kapoor actually does get an award. The first ceremony, however, is the staged 'batli award ceremony, where the bottle emptied of liquor is given by Pappu to his fellow junior artiste Omi. Here, the longing to become part of the glittering world of Hindi film, the eternal hope of being rich and famous is quite directly articulated. Here the fans and the stars in their firmament are as far from one another as can be—and yet they have an effect upon one another that is difficult to explain but equally difficult to miss.

I submit that the tools offered by the methodology of comparative literary studies are amenable to reading the complex composite thickly (and even thinly) intertwined cultural reality that we as post-Independence Indians inhabit. It is crucial for us to begin to appreciate this reality as soon as practicable, because it is this, and only this we can leave behind as a legacy for the continued existence of 'Indian-ness'. This is what we will leave for the future, for all else will change. Even this complex intertwining will change, some strands getting thicker, some disappearing to return perhaps later or maybe never, some new influences appearing, in all a dynamic, multifarious reality, a world of light, colour, darkness and death, much like the Hindi film itself. As Omi assures his fellow proletarians at the batli award ceremony—if all has not come right in the end, then think that the picture has not yet finished: '*Kyunki picture abhi baaki hai mere dost.*'

Notes and References

1. Roland Barthes, 'Mythologies', in *Mythologies*, trans. Anne Lavers (London: Paladin, 1979).
2. *Outlook*, 30 May 2005.
3. M. Madhava Prasad, *Ideology of the Hindi Film: A Historical Construction* (Delhi: Oxford University Press, 1998).
4. Amiya Dev, 'Literary History From Below', in *Comparative Literature: Theory and Practice*, eds A. Dev and S.K. Das (Shimla: Indian Institute of Advanced Studies & Allied Publishers, 1989).
5. See, for instance, Lothar Lutze, 'From Bharata to Bombay: Change and Continuity in Hindi Film Aesthetics', in *The Hindi Film: Agent and Reagent of Cultural Change*, eds L. Lutze and B. Fleeiderer (Delhi: Manohar Publications, 1985); also P. Lugendorf, 'Is there an Indian Way of Film-making?', *Indian Journal of Hindu Studies* 10, no. 4 (2006).
6. See for instance, P. Bowman, *Interrogating Culture Studies:Theory, Politics and Practice* (London and Sterling, Virginia Pluto & Sterling, 1993).
7. This abbreviating of the word vernacular is a rendering used by a respondent to a survey on the lives of single women who live in the city of Kolkata alone, away from their families. Ipshita Chanda, *Selfing the City: The Single Woman Outsider in Kolkata and the Practices of Everyday Life* (Kolkata: Stree, forthcoming).
8. Gayatri Chakravorty Spivak, *Death of a Discipline* (New York: Columbia University Press).
9. Ashok Aklujkar, 'Brief Analysis', in *Encyclopedia of Indian Philosophies*, eds Harold G. Coward and K. Kunjnni (Delhi: Motilal Banarsidass, 1996), p. 197.
10. Probal Dasgupta, 'Knowledge and Language in Classical Indian Linguistics: Some Observations'. Unpublished MS, Indian Statistical Institute, Kolkata.

Chapter 8

Minority Rights in India
A View from the Regional Press

Partha Pratim Basu

Introduction

Ever since the resurgence of a *Hindu* nationalist movement in India spearheaded by the *Sangh parivar* in the 1980s, several scholarly attempts have been made to track the role of the press—both national and regional, English and vernacular—in shaping this phenomenon. The *Hindutva* wave, however, fed largely upon anti-minority—more precisely, anti-Muslim—hate campaign which propelled the present author to take up the problem at hand, that is the press' perceptions about the rights of the minorities in India which, it was felt, would be a fitting supplement to the research literature noted earlier. That apart, minority rights have emerged as a major debating point in political theory and practice in the current era of globalization which has given a mammoth push to mass migration across national boundaries with the result that even relatively homogeneous societies are fast assuming a multicultural character. In the Indian context, however, the debate on minority rights—given the enormous diversity and complexity of its social milieu—goes back to the early decades of the twentieth century. It was foregrounded once again in the last two decades not necessarily in connection with globalization but with the Hindu nationalist project mentioned before. The present chapter scans three momentous events of India's contemporary political history—the passage of the Muslim Women's Act (1986) following the controversial Shah Bano verdict of the Supreme Court of India; the countrywide riots sparked off by the demolition of the Babri Masjid (1992); and the anti-Muslim carnage in Gujarat in the wake of the Godhra train massacre (2002)—all of which had significant bearing on the Muslims of India, their physical survival, means of livelihood as well as their status and identity within India's social and political body.

Though firmly located in the arena of institutional politics, the issue of minority rights, needless to say, has pronounced popular cultural underpinnings. Popular (mis)perceptions of intercommunity relations, relations between the majority and the minorities, assume immense importance in upholding or undermining the notion of minority rights which in turn imparts salience to media representations shaping the relevant images and responses. The choice of the newspaper press rather than the more popular and ubiquitous television has been deliberate because the latter focuses on the 'immediate' and the 'momentary' while our object was to capture not simply the fleeting narratives, but arguments and analyses as well which still remain the print media's forte. The present study rests on an analysis of the content of two top-circulating Bengali vernacular newspapers published from West Bengal—the *Anandabazar Patrika* (ABP) and the *Bartaman* (BM)—which also calls for some explanation. While the English language papers were rightly depicted as the 'elite press' and apparently carried greater weight in relation to policy-making, the regional language press was much more influential in forming the perceptions and animating the emotions of ordinary folks, the import of which could scarcely be undervalued in connection with the events selected for our purpose. At the same time, the issues and events we have concentrated on were all of 'national' dimensions and the nature of their coverage by the 'regional' press pertaining to a State, that is West Bengal which could rightfully claim a centuries-old liberal and pluralistic heritage formed another axis of interest.

The chapter has three sections: the first briefly reviews the theoretical debate regarding minority rights with special reference to India; this is followed by an examination of press coverage of the three events in terms of the way of framing, the kinds of stereotypes deployed (or demolished), the voices through which minority viewpoints were captured, the factors identified as responsible for the minorities' predicament and the remedies suggested; and the final section seeks to reconstruct, on the basis of this analysis, the press' position concerning minority rights in India.

Minority Rights: The Indian Debate

'Minority rights' emerged as a major concern of political theorists since the multiculturalist turn in liberal political theory in the 1980s. In the first half of the twentieth century, liberal theoretical focus generally rested on preservation of individual autonomy via a legal framework which was group-neutral and uniformly applicable to all. This position met with a challenge from communitarian theorists who argued that individuals were embedded in definite systems of meanings which were derived from their cultural communities; therefore, constitutions should allow rights not only to individuals but also to their constitutive cultural communities. This formed the backdrop to the rise of multiculturalism which contended that any given society was composed of many cultures each of which was important to their members; therefore, these cultures should be granted recognition and valued for and of themselves. A stronger view further asserted that cultures which were vulnerable simply because they were in a minority needed supportive social and political environs and had to be protected through special legal-constitutional measures and shielded through 'group-differentiated citizenship rights'.

For India, the debate was hardly new as its constitution as early as in 1947 recognized rights of all minority groups to their own culture and religion. It was indeed tempting to read back the contemporary multiculturalist thesis into Articles 25 through 30 of the Indian Constitution containing a whole range of protections accorded to religious groups and argue that the authors of this document anticipated the Western theoretical world in the matter of differentiated citizenship. But this reading may not be wholly correct for grant of cultural rights to communities in India to reproduce the conditions of their own existence was the product of a certain historical conjuncture. The genesis of the idea in the Indian constitutional context could be traced back to the Motilal Nehru report (the memorandum produced in1928 outlining a new dominion constitution for India) which acknowledged the rights of minority communities to their religion and culture partly to allay the fears of religious minorities that they would be swamped in a majoritarian India, partly to neutralize the demand for separate electorates by Muslim leaders and also to devise a principle that could regulate intergroup relationships

175

within the Congress party and create conditions conducive to a mass struggle. Later, to clarify the Indian Constitution's approach to the question of minority rights, it was stated in the Constituent Assembly in May, 1949 that '…the state should be so run that they (minorities) should stop feeling oppressed by the mere fact that they are minorities and that…they should feel that they have as honourable a part to play in the national life as any other section of the community.'[1]

The debate, however, was reignited in India roughly during the same time as multiculturalism and minority rights had the intellectual capitals of West under their spell when multicultural nationhood of post-Independence India suffered an unprecedented onslaught of cultural nationalism which was not only exclusive but excessively dismissive of rights of religious minorities to live on terms of equality in the Indian polity. This thesis was propagated by the rightist *Hindutva* lobby consisting of the Rashtriya Swayamsevak Sangh (RSS) and its protégés, the Bharatiya Janata Party (BJP) and the Viswa Hindu Parishad (VHP) (together often called the *Sangh Parivar* or *Sangh* family). The 'nation' was defined in 'Hindu' terms, which was to be a homogeneous entity that disallowed or subsumed other ways of life. The minority communities were systematically and insistently denigrated; Muslims' 'clamour for being treated as a privileged minority' was disparaged; the Hindu–Muslim question was projected as a conflict between liberalism and obscurantism; and the Muslims were advised to learn to accept and respect symbols of national culture, predictably Hindu or associated with various reformist cults arising out of Hinduism.[2] This generated precisely a three-cornered debate—among the proponents of *Hindutva*, votaries of secularism as incorporated in the Indian Constitution (which included the notion of collective minority rights) and the critics of the secularists—a brief review of which appeared essential for situating our subsequent analysis.

Secularism, Smith[3] maintained in his path-breaking *India as a Secular State*, involved three distinct but interrelated relations concerning state, religion and individual: individuals were free to choose their religion (or to remain atheist) without any coercive interference by the state (the 'libertarian' component); all individuals were entitled to the same citizenship rights irrespective of religious beliefs held by them (the 'egalitarian' ingredient); finally, just as political power was beyond the scope of religion's legitimate objectives, equally it was not for the states to promote, regulate, direct or interfere in religion (the 'wall of separation' argument). Viewed from this perspective, the notion of secularism as incorporated in the Constitution of India implied two significant 'deviations' viz. (*a*) group rights in addition to individual rights were granted only to religious minorities (Art 30); and (*b*) the state was required to interfere in—primarily Hindu—religious affairs in the interest of social reform (for example removal of untouchability) that necessitated a departure from the principle of the state observing strict neutrality or equidistance vis-à-vis religion (Art 25 [2]).

While defending this 'Indian' version of secularism, Bhargava[4] pointed out that grant of these group rights had to be understood in the context of India's phenomenal diversity of religious communities: such diversity might coexist harmoniously, but could also generate conflicts—most importantly, conflict over values. Under the circumstances, a uniform charter of rights was not considered absolutely essential in policy matters of cultural import; separate rights were granted to minority religious communities to enable them to live with dignity; integration was not seen as coterminous with assimilation. Moreover, Bhargava continued, many religiously sanctioned social practices were oppressive by virtue of their illiberal and inegalitarian character which denied individuals a life of dignity and self-respect and, therefore, desperately needed to be reformed. Equal citizenship rights easily challenged hierarchical relations within communities which were particularly insensitive to the vital interests of those members at the bottom of the sanctioned order. Therefore, to ensure equal treatment and uphold the value of equal citizenship as well as secularism, the state must interfere in hierarchically organized relations. These arguments, he maintained, were all the more applicable to Hinduism for the absence here of an organized Church which meant that impetus for reform could not come exclusively from within and could hardly be initiated without help from some powerful external institution such as the state. Hence, he suggested, the 'wall of separation' thesis was replaced in the Indian Constitution by what he termed the 'principled distance' norm, that is whether or not the state would intervene in religious sphere or refrain from action depended on what, in its judgement, really strengthened religious liberty and equality. In this interpretation, a secular state neither mindlessly excluded all religions nor was blindly neutral towards them; it rather interfered in one religion more than in others, in keeping with the historical and social conditions of the relevant religions.

Continuing this line of defence Chandhoke[5] contended that in the context of the anti-Muslim tirade launched by the *Sangh Parivar*, the vision of secularism propagated by the 'Founding fathers' of the Constitution needed to be buttressed with reference to contemporary theories of multiculturalism and minority rights. Cultures and communities, she argued, were a good for the individual and access to this good was of such overriding importance that they should secure this access through the grant of a right. *Minority* rights were specially stressed because cases of unequal placement (of the minority in this case vis-à-vis majority) had to be treated unequally only to equalize access to distribution of this good. Finally, minority communities that were profoundly vulnerable could not secure their own existence and reproduction if wider social and political processes threatened them either through deliberate destruction or benevolent neglect. In such cases, she asserted, the state would have to intervene in order to secure a supportive social-political environment for the minority group. Moreover, if a minority community was subjected to perverse and demeaning stereotypes or ethnic targeting, this compromised the individual's self-esteem in the first case and right to life in latter. Thus the *individual's* right to life, dignity and culture was predicated on the antecedent right of cultural community to exist, to reproduce its practices and to be respected; and group rights were thus conceptualized as conditional for individual rights.

Mahajan,[6] however, drew attention to the problematic character of the community rights as conceded in the Indian Constitution not in the least because attaching priority to community cultural norms left the issue of *intra-group equality* completely unattended: community practices were protected even when they were in conflict with rights of individuals as citizens and the ideal of gender equality remained the worst casualty. Second, in a society where the hegemony of the religious domain over social life in general had not been dismantled (as in the West), sanctity accorded to religious and cultural community practices reaffirmed the special status of religious leaders within the community and the rest of society thereby restricting the possibilities of review and reassessment of the ongoing community practices. Last, the state in India was perceived by the minorities in a dual light, that is as a potential ally (for as a vulnerable community they were dependent on the state for protection of their life and property) and as a prospective threat (they firmly resisted the homogenizing impulse of the state especially pertaining to the socio-cultural life), which propelled the politicians to indulge in unhealthy 'vote bank' politics.

These perceived shortcomings of the variant of secularism embodied in India's constitutional norms and political practices generated a clamour for its abandonment in favour of either of two suggested alternatives. One emanated from the Hindu right who branded this given notion of secularism as 'pseudo-secularism' and charged the Indian state for practicing 'minority appeasement' throughout these post-Independence years. Ironically, at least at the theoretical level, they called for a revival of the 'Western' vision of secularism with a strict wall of separation between the state and religious communities. A second and more intriguing response came from scholars such as Nandy and Chatterjee[7] who based their propositions on a thorough critique of the secular ideal. For Nandy, true religions of South Asia were religions of *faith*, each representing a way of life, whereas both the modern state and the Hindu nationalists dealt with religion as *ideology*, with populations contesting for or protecting non-religious—usually political or socio-economic—interests, which was a perversion of the true nature and function of religion. He suggested that the safety and security of the minorities in India be best left to the custody of inherent tolerance of South Asian religions which were inherently open, heterodox and syncretic. Chatterjee too was opposed to the idea that the state should impose a framework for cultural rights of the minorities from outside and pleaded instead for a 'strategic politics of demanding toleration' which involved a twofold struggle: resisting homogenization from outside and pushing for democratization inside. Further, he insisted that an effective defence of minority cultural rights had to take its cue from a 'politics of difference' that empowered the minorities to say 'we will not give reasons for not being like you'.

> Given the inapplicability of the neutrality principle...it becomes necessary to find a criterion by which state involvement, when it occurs

in the domain of religion, can appear to the members of a religious group as both legitimate and fair. Toleration…can, it seems to me, supply us with this criterion…What this will mean in institutional terms are processes through which each religious group will publicly seek and obtain from its members consent for its practices in so far as those practices have regulative powers over their members.[8]

With this brief outline of the minority rights debate in the Indian context in view, a detailed analysis of the portrayal of the three events identified earlier in the two Bengali newspapers, ABP and BM, have been undertaken, from which the press' perceptions regarding the issue of minority rights would be sought to be culled out in the final section of the chapter.

Press Coverage I: The Muslim Women's Bill

Muslim Women (Protection of Rights on Divorce) Act 1986 had its proximate origin in the contentious Shah Bano judgement of 1985 delivered by the Supreme Court of India but its core concern, that is maintenance to divorced Muslim women, had a long and turbulent history involving two sets of legal systems. Under Muslim Personal Law which had its genesis among the trading communities of Arabia, marriage was viewed as a dissoluble contract with women accorded a right to remarriage. Consequently, while a sum of *mehr* was fixed at the time of marriage as a future security, the wife was not entitled to any further relief as maintenance after the dissolution of the marriage. The debate on the Dissolution of Muslim Marriages Act (1939) in pre-Independence India pivoted around the absence of women's right to divorce but the issue of economic rights of divorced women was left untouched. In 1973, during Indira Gandhi's premiership, Sec. 125 of the Code of Criminal Procedure (popularly known as CrPC) which granted the deserted or destitute wife the right to claim a maximum amount of ₹ 500 as maintenance from her husband was extended to a divorced wife. But in the face of protests raised by Muslim leaders, the government included a clause that if a woman had received the customary settlement (for example *mehr*), the amount of maintenance due to her would be set off against the amount she had already received. Matters, however, came to a head with the Shah Bano verdict which not only affirmed the right of a divorced Muslim woman but also interpreted Muslim Personal Law and called for a Uniform Civil Code (UCC). This provoked a severe communal backlash which prompted the Rajiv Gandhi government to introduce the Muslim Women (Protection of Rights on Divorce) Bill to exclude the divorced Muslim women from the purview of Sec. 125 of CrPC. This move placated the conservative Muslim leadership but generated vociferous opposition from women's organizations and progressive sections of the society.

To come to press coverage, the proposed law, it was argued, sought to remove the divorced Muslim women from the ambit of the CrPC (Sec.125) and institute a 'separate arrangement' for their maintenance which, instead of placing the responsibility squarely on the husband, laid it on the relatives of the estranged wife who would inherit her property or, in their absence, the State Waqf Board. This new law which was professedly in conformity with the *Shariat* or Muslim Personal Law had a transparent link with the case of Shah Bano, the lady who claimed and secured maintenance from her husband under the CrPC which the Muslim Personal Law Board (MPLB) and other Muslim organizations felt violated the *Shariat*. The new law (reminiscent, according to BM, of the regime of Ayatollah Khomeini of Iran), incontrovertibly signified a retrogressive step on the part of Rajiv Gandhi, tantamount to meek capitulation to the forces of conservatism, and betrayal of those Muslims who had set out to move towards the twenty-first century under his young and dynamic leadership.[9]

More precisely, the criticism levelled against the law was threefold. First,[10] the orthodox Muslim leadership was assailed for its opportunism and double standards. It was recalled that since the British days the *Shariat* in India applied only to the civil/personal sphere while all criminal cases including divorce suits were settled under the CrPC. If the latter was found un-Islamic, would *all criminal cases,* it was asked, be henceforth decided under *Shariati* law involving punishments such as mutilation of limbs and stoning to death? Otherwise, bringing only the cases of divorced Muslim women under the *Shariat* doubtless amounted to interference with their religious freedom—seemingly a pretext for relegating them to second class citizenship within the society and the family—and exposed the patriarchal and gendered character of the legislation which brought us to the second aspect of press' critique.[11] At one level, a commentator pointed out in ABP that though under Muslim Personal Law women did inherit property, this remained more a matter of theory than practice. In any case, those women who did own property need not depend on the financial support of relatives thereby rendering the law superfluous to that extent. In other instances, the dire financial shape the State Waqf Boards were in or the kind of corruption that afflicted them were enough to discourage the needy women to approach these bodies. At another level, a BM editorial contended that the underlying premise of the law was that Muslim marriage was a contract which was terminated by divorce; but contracts happened between 'equals', and when mere mouthing of three *talaqs* by the husband forced the wife together with the children out into the street, it would be a mockery to call it a contract.

Finally, the union government was lambasted for having subscribed to the demands of religious bigots bent on using the *Shariat* to demolish the wider claims of humanity in the interest of their own narrow ends and putting a seal of sanction on the fundamentalists' way of treating women as property rather than resource. By the same token, it was accused of having nullified the achievements of reform movements led by progressive Muslims, a point sought to be established with reference to the instance of Goa, Daman and Diu. The civil code prevalent in these areas when these remained Portuguese colonies equally covered Hindus, Muslims and Christians so that Muslim males were not allowed to engage in bigamy or issue *talaqs* to wives at the drop of a hat and progressive Muslims there had long fought hard with the fundamentalists for ensuring continuation of these arrangements; but now thanks to the hasty and indiscreet act of the Rajiv Gandhi administration, Goa's Muslim women's rights too would be endangered. Thus, the Prime Minister was indicted for his failure to perceive these women as *Indian* women rather than *Muslim* women per se and denying them the rights enjoyed by Hindu or Christian women simply by virtue of being Indian citizens and it was concluded that the possibilities opened up by the Shah Bano judgement were crushed by the Muslim Women's Bill.[12]

Once the bill was floated, the press sought to capture the gathering resistance and widespread protest against it in various quarters inside and outside the Parliament.[13] While the opposition—primarily left—parties slammed the bill as violating the secular ideal and contradictory to the constitutional provisions relating to equality and promotion of a UCC, simmering dissent within the ruling Congress party was highlighted too. The persistent opposition to the bill put up by Arif Mohammad Khan, a Muslim member of Rajiv Gandhi's cabinet who resigned after it was tabled in the legislature, was played up as were the congratulatory messages sent to him by political leaders of all hues including some Congress leaders. Eminent Muslim politicians belonging to the left parties of West Bengal such as the Speaker of the State Assembly Hasim Abdul Halim and Law Minister Mansur Habibullah were quoted as branding the bill 'anti-*Shariat*' because 'nowhere does the *Shariat* ordain that divorced women be sustained by their relatives or the Waqf Board'. The depth of resentment was underlined through photographs of Muslim women in chains demonstrating in front of the Parliament as the ruling party issued a whip to ensure the safe passage of the bill. Voices from the civil society,[14] especially Muslim organizations, were also duly recorded: thus the Committee for the Protection of the Rights of Muslim Women's spirited resistance to any change in S.125 of the CrPC and assertion that the *maulavi*s and others who spoke in support of the *Shariat* on the floor of the Parliament were not the only representatives of the Indian Muslim community received prominent coverage; the plea made to the government by the Muslim Satyashodhak Mandal for sponsoring a UCC based on the ideals of justice and equality in order to promote a modern, democratic and egalitarian society as well as greater participation and integration of the Muslims in national life too was impressed upon the readers' attention. True, the statements of conservative Muslim groups such as the Shariat Tehfuz Committee formed to defend the bill were covered too but these quite perceptibly fell beyond the main frame of the narrative as woven by the press.

To turn to the stereotypes used to develop the narratives, a hiatus between the *progressive* and *orthodox* sections of Indian Muslims was bound to attract notice. Thus, for example, the Janata Party leader Syed Shahabuddin who was also one of the leading lights of the Babri Masjid

Action Committee was projected as an arch conservative[15] when he was quoted as saying in a seminar organized by the West Bengal Action Committee of the All India Muslim Personal Law Board that he was indeed a *fundamentalist* for, he explained, a good Muslim always reposed faith in some fundamental tenets which constituted his fundamentalism. The message of the statement was sought to be amplified through the supplementary information in the report that no women were to be seen in the seminar—some reportedly were present but preferred to remain behind a glass partition—discussing, ironically, the fate of Muslim women which attested to the fact of marginalization of women within Muslim conservative circles. The counterpoint[16] was provided by enlightened and educated Muslim figures well-placed in the social arena, for example noted thespian Shabana Azmi who avowed that the Shah Bano verdict was not contradictory to the *Shariat* because the latter did not specify what kind of maintenance divorced Muslim women would be entitled to, or former Indian cricket captain Mansur Ali Khan (Pataudi) who candidly stated that while he respected those Muslim politicians who were clamouring for the new bill, they only remained leaders of particular segments and could not be regarded as representatives of the community as a whole.

A third stereotype[17] that emerged out of the coverage was that of the *opportunist politician* which applied primarily to a section of the ruling party leadership, but members of the opposition parties too fitted into this mould. Thus, the Prime Minister was reported to have reneged on his assurances extended to the Committee for the Protection of the Rights of Muslim Women that no change would be effected in the CrPC without discussing the issue with all concerned parties. While his compromise with Muslim communalism 'unprecedented in the 100-year history of the Congress' was sought to be interpreted in the light of the imminent State assembly elections in Kerala where his party banked on an alliance with the Muslim League, throwing the Muslim women to the 'fundamentalist wolves' for this narrow partisan gain was branded as both politically unjust and morally repugnant. The leaders of the Janata Party, the most important component of the then opposition, fared no better either as they were censured for their failure to muster the courage shown by lesser parties such as the Asom Gana Parishad and Telugu

Desam in unequivocally opposing the bill evidently not to alienate the conservative Muslim leadership.

Finally, the deleterious impact the bill was bound to produce on the Indian body politic and national solidarity was captured vividly and from several different angles.[18] On one hand, with the endorsement and institutionalization of the subordinate status of Muslim women leaving them at the mercy of the orthodox leadership, the Muslim community in India was being rendered perpetually maimed. If destitute women and children, argued, BM, proliferated within this community, and swelled the beggars' population, then eventually the whole nation would become crippled. On the other hand, the provision for a separate law for one community, reminiscent of the infamous 'two nation theory' propagated by Jinnah's Muslim League culminating in India's Partition, seemed to put the future of secularism in India at serious risk. ABP expressed the misgivings that if the fundamentalists could force an amendment in the CrPC on the pretext of saving their religion, they could in future very well demand and get Art. 44 removed from the Indian Constitution with which the prospects for crafting a UCC for secular India would be crushed once and for all. Indeed, the parallel between the 'two nation theory' and Rajiv Gandhi's defence of the bill was further underscored as BM pointed out that when the Muslim League had lost its relevance in both Pakistan and Bangladesh, it was scandalous that the Indian Prime Minister moved a bill at the behest of the chief of the Indian Muslim League which robbed millions of women of their religiously sanctioned rights. ABP too bitterly observed that when an enlightened Muslim opinion was taking shape around the Shah Bano verdict, Rajiv Gandhi, by drafting the bill in consultation with the leaders of the Muslim League, MPLB and Ittehadul Muslimeen—all communal entities subscribing to the 'two nation theory'—and acknowledging them as 'Muslim leaders' only gave the pernicious doctrine a fresh lease of life. Baharul Islam, a Member of Parliament and a former judge was quoted approvingly as saying that this heinous act would bring the country on the throes of another partition.

To sum up, the papers felt that the Muslim Women's Bill which instituted a separate arrangement outside the CrPC and professedly in consonance with the *Shariat* for addressing the problem of maintenance for divorced Muslim women in India, perpetrated a grave injustice upon the women of this community. A product of the unholy alliance between the self-serving 'Muslim leadership' and crafty politicians, the bill made a mockery of Indian secularism and killed the progressive possibilities inherent in the Shah Bano judgement pronounced by the Supreme Court of India. Passed in defiance of staunch protest from progressive Muslims irrespective of political affiliations, the bill not only weakened the Muslim community but dealt a bad blow to national solidarity as well.

Press Coverage II: The Post-Babri Mosque Demolition Riots

The demolition of the Babri Masjid and the nationwide turbulence and conflagration unleashed in its wake arguably constituted the most sinister communal flashpoint of independent India. Local history had it that the sixteenth-century mosque built in the reign of Mughal emperor Babur in Ayodhya stood on a location where there had previously been a temple to Lord Ram, the hero of the epic poem the *Ramayana,* on the site of his mythical birth. The mosque was locked up immediately after Independence following communal troubles, but in 1983, the VHP and the BJP revived the old demand that the mosque be handed over to the Hindus. Matters were further aggravated when in 1986 the District Judge, probably at the prompting of the Congress Chief Minister of the then Uttar Pradesh, reopened the mosque, gave Hindu priests its possession and permitted Hindus to worship there. This ignited communal passions, sparked off riots all over the country and the Babri Masjid Action Committee (BMAC) was formed to combat the VHP demand for construction of a Ram temple at the mosque site. As the 'secular' parties failed to intervene effectively, the initiative was seized by the Hindu communalists determined to exploit the sensitive issue to mobilize the Hindus and boost the electoral fortunes of the BJP. In 1989, the VHP issued a call for collection of bricks sanctified by the water of the holy river Ganga for all corners of the country to be taken to Ayodhya for construction of the Ram temple. The following year, the BJP president

L.K. Advani undertook an all-India *rath-yatra* to popularize the objective of temple construction which was followed by outbreak of communal riots at several places. In the Lok Sabha elections held in 1991, the BJP's tally shot up to 119 (from 4 in 1984 before the beginning of the *Ramjanambhumi* [liberation of Ram's birthplace] movement) and to further consolidate the political gains, the BJP-VHP leaders organized a huge rally of over 2,00,000 *kar sevak*s *(*volunteers) at the site of the mosque on 6 December 1992. In spite of explicit assurances to the contrary given by the BJP on the floor of Parliament and the BJP-led Uttar Pradesh administration to the Supreme Court, the Babri Masjid was pulled down by the *kar sevak*s in a matter of hours before the full gaze of the top BJP leadership who feigned helplessness. This traumatic incident set the country ablaze with the worst and the most widespread communal riots, the worst hit being Bombay, Calcutta and Bhopal, and Hindus who were in a minority in neighbouring Bangladesh and Pakistan were also exposed to retaliation by Muslims.

Press coverage of two aspects of the issue, that is the demolition of the mosque and the riots that followed in Calcutta would be analyzed separately and in this case ABP and BM seemed to diverge in certain significant ways. In early December, 1992, both the papers sought to bring out the sense of uncertainty and insecurity that had gripped the Muslim community, especially in and around Ayodhya. As a moving piece on the local Muslim flower vendors—who conventionally supplied flowers for the worship of *Ram Lalla* (Lord Ram)—the threat emanating from the anticipated disturbances was as much to their physical security as to their livelihood. Following the demolition, the frenzied attack by the *kar sevak*s on the medieval structure was captured in its dreadful detail; the dismal failure of the Central Police Force to prevent the incident was highlighted, and ABP stressed that the BJP Chief Minister of Uttar Pradesh resigned not in remorse but only to escape the responsibility of opening fire on the marauders which clearly revealed the inaction of the Union government and collusion of the State administration. A graphic account of the magnitude of the calamity suffered by the Muslims of Ayodhya—as already envisaged—in the wake of this incident was presented quoting the Officer-in-charge of the Ramjanambhumi Police Station who reported that the houses of 905 local Muslims were gutted;

none of the local mosques remained intact and some 4,000 Muslims were rendered homeless. The papers seemed to agree with those who called a *Bharat Bandh* that desecration and demolition of the mosque flouting the orders of the Supreme Court amounted to violation of the constitution.[19]

The Muslim 'voices' finding expression through the newspapers in connection with the event belonged to three identifiable categories.[20] First, of course, there were the predictable ventilations of deep anguish culminating into demands for the resignation of the Prime Minister, the Home Minister and the government of Uttar Pradesh for their collective failure to save the Babri Masjid. But almost equally visible were the series of appeals issued by prominent Muslim leaders—religious, political and intellectual—for maintaining patience and peace and desist from engaging in reckless acts of retaliation in the hour of crisis. But thirdly, and most importantly from the standpoint of this chapter, the reports clearly brought out the crisis of confidence the conventional leadership of the community clearly suffered from. Thus, youth organizations such as the Students' Union of the Aligarh Muslim University questioned the credibility of the organizations like BMAC in the aftermath of the flattening of the Babri Masjid, or the Indian Muslim Youth Conference condemned the Shahi Imam of Jama Masjid Syed Abdullah Bukhari for encouraging the radical Muslim organizations of Bangladesh to undertake a Dhaka–Ayodhya long march and inciting the Muslims of the neighbouring countries to launch an anti-India *jihad*. The credentials of the established Muslim leadership were also challenged by an eminent and highly respected Muslim scholar Maulana Wahiduddin Khan who was especially pained by the attempt of certain Muslim leaders who posed as the 'saviour' of the Babri Masjid, because that role belonged only to the Almighty. He, on one hand, urged on the Muslim leaders to refrain from converting the reconstruction of the mosque into a battle of prestige, and on the other hand, appealed to the ordinary Muslim citizens to consider this leadership with the required dose of scepticism. The confusion within the leadership was also exposed over the BMAC's call to 'all secular Muslims' for boycotting government functions on the Republic Day which was vociferously objected to by the MPLB and other sections of Indian Muslims. Nonetheless, the appeals for peace and calm iterated by the Muslim leadership and the visible cracks in the leadership itself contributed towards weakening, if not really dismantling, popular stereotypes of Muslims as a volatile and monolithic community.

However, differences between ABP and BM seemed to surface once one considered the way the responsibility for the tragedy was sought to be fixed by them. In an early editorial titled '*Ei Barbatratar Khshama Nei* (Such barbarity could not be pardoned)'[21] ABP strongly denounced the 'priests of darkness' who sought to take India back to the medieval age and called for banning, if necessary, all militant religious organizations—Hindu as well as Muslim—such as VHP, RSS and BMAC. But subsequently, the blame was laid primarily on the *Hindutva* lobby; VHP and BJP were indicted for jeopardizing the Indian heritage and lowering its prestige before the comity of nations, and all secular parties and organizations were urged to sink their differences and join forces to combat the communal forces head on. BM, however, from the outset sounded somewhat dissimilar[22] as an editorial on the eve of the tragedy advised 'all concerned parties' to reach a decision through discussion for while the old mosque structure remained a sensitive issue for the Muslims which needed to be duly respected, it was undeniable that *kar seva* in Ayodhya was inextricably connected with *Hindu* emotions and therefore could not be ignored by any government. Two things called for our attention here: first, the term *Hindu* was used as a monolithic category as if *all Hindus* of the country shared these emotions equally strongly; and second, no distinction was made between the sentiment behind the uncivil and anachronistic demand pressed by the *Hindutva* organizations and the sense of hurt felt by the aggrieved Muslims in consequence, both bringing the paper closer to the stand of the *Sangh Parivar*. After the mosque was pulled down, it agreed with ABP that the liability for this catastrophe rested squarely with the VHP and the BJP but added almost in the same breath that if the BJP had acted irresponsibly, similar irresponsibility was being shown by others as well—with reference obviously to the reaction of the Muslim leaders—whom it reminded that any retaliatory move would adversely affect the interests of the nation as well as *of their own community* which almost sounded like a grim warning. In a later editorial, the rise of 'Hindu communalism' in

India so many years after the Partition was traced to 'political opportunism' practiced by the so-called secular parties (smacking of the *Parivar*'s periodic outbursts against 'pseudo-secularists') such as the Communist Party of India (CPI-M), heading the Left Front government of West Bengal. The latter was held largely responsible for stoking the fire of communalism through its dubious, one-sided policies (presumably of turning a blind eye to the activities of Muslim communalists), and the ban imposed by the Front administration on meetings and processions by the BJP in the wake of the demolition was deplored as a 'fascist decision'. True, the importance of these factors in understanding the nature of communal politics in post-Independence India could hardly be underestimated, but using them in its effort to explain away (if not exonerate) the surge of Hindu fundamentalism at times made BM appear almost like a *Parivar* apologist. ABP, comparatively speaking, too demanded proscription of *both* Hindu and Muslim communal organizations; yet in laying the blame first and foremost on the forces of *Hindutva*—given the gravity of their misdemeanor and the consequent damage perpetrated upon the Muslim psyche—its stance appeared to be more balanced and carried greater conviction.

The same difference was writ large in the respective commentaries on the BMAC's call for boycotting the Republic Day. BM castigated[23] the *Muslim* leadership, heavily influenced by the *ulamas* (clerics), for raising this 'communal' demand which aimed at weaning the Muslims away from the Indian Republic; moreover, asking all Muslim MPs and MLAs to unite, it pointed out, was a sure recipe for throttling Indian secularism; and it warned that if this leadership instead of mitigating communal tensions continued to fuel them, it was bound to have its fallout inside the Hindu community. In other words, the paper treated the call as issued by the 'Muslim leadership' without mentioning that it attracted censure from Muslims themselves (reported by the paper itself); the effort to project Hindu communalism as 'an equal and opposite' reaction to instigation from its Muslim counterpart also remained plainly visible. ABP, contrary to BM, began by putting the demand in the perspective of the stunning blow suffered by the Muslim minority psyche which, it acknowledged, was enough to undermine their confidence in the Indian state; it also referred to the division and absence of coordination within the Muslim leadership that came into the open in connection with the call; at the same time it judiciously maintained that the boycott call instead of bringing the community any closer to the solution of the problem would only strengthen the case of their detractors. It also took this opportunity—when BM played up the prospective 'Hindu reaction'—to divest Hindu minds of such negative stereotypes regarding Muslims as are prevalent even within the educated sections in India (for example their 'alien-ness', practice of bigamy or lack of interest in family planning) further rubbed in by motivated campaigning by the *Parivar* and issued dire warnings as to the divisive impact such 'separatist politics' (engaged in by the champions of *Hindutva*) was sure to have for the future unity and integrity of the country. In sum, when BM sounded more and more like a mouthpiece of the majority, ABP undoubtedly displayed greater capability towards empathizing with the minority viewpoint.

To turn next to the riots in Calcutta, these were projected more as a law and order issue rather than a communal problem and their spread and scale was blamed primarily on the administration's ineptitude. It was reported by the ordinary people of the riot-affected areas that troubles were created primarily by 'outsiders', that is hoodlums enjoying political patronage who, for understandable reasons, remained 'absconders' in police records. The major purpose behind fomenting disorder, according to the reports, was either to loot houses and shops or to settle political scores, and people of both the communities were victimized in the process. An interesting report in BM tried to find out why the districts remained relatively peaceful when Calcutta suffered the pangs of 'communal riots' and argued that the Bengali Muslims in the districts, though distressed and aggrieved, did not take to the streets and the same was true for non-Bengali members of the minority community long settled in Calcutta. The attacks, on the other hand, were carried out chiefly by the infiltrators from Bangladesh popularly known as the 'Bihari Muslims' apart from the local hooligans of the city with distinct party allegiances seeking to expand their 'areas of influence' at the cost of their rivals behind the guise of 'communal' strife.[24]

The administration had to bear the brunt of press' criticism on several counts beginning with the police's failure to bring the riots under control (a charge which was reportedly partly acknowledged even by the Police Commissioner) and it was only the army's intervention that brought succour to the victims. Similarly, in the post-riot phase, the administration's incompetence in organizing relief and rehabilitation of the displaced—especially in contrast to the commendable work done by several private charities—also drew flak from the papers. But two other charges appeared still graver, first, the nexus between the politicians, police and criminals and second, the alleged communal tendencies exhibited by sections of the administration. Thus, an ABP investigative report (penned by the veteran columnist Gour Kishore Ghosh)[25] quoted popular complaints that the police 'joined hands with the goons belonging to both the communities to harass ordinary people'. After the riots too the papers repeatedly brought the police to task for their 'reluctance' to arrest the miscreants allegedly with high political connections who roamed about freely, and the explanation touted by the law-keepers— that their arrest was being delayed in anticipation of law and order problems—seemed to carry little conviction with the press. No less serious was the charge of 'communal' behaviour attributed to the administration as BM, immediately after the riots in Calcutta had broken out, chided the police for their reluctance to deal firmly with the 'frenzied and reckless behaviour of the youth belonging to *one community*' which was held responsible for the escalation of violence, and observed that for them all variants of communalism should be equally contemptible; branding one communalism as menacing and considering another as spontaneous manifestation of resentment was not conducive to restoration of peace. ABP also called attention to an incident that betrayed the communal leanings of a section of the police but, curiously enough, of a different shade when it reported that some 150 Muslims arrested in connection with the riots were forced in the jail to chant *Jai Shri Ram* (Hail *Shri Ram*) and sarcastically advised to leave India for Pakistan or Bangladesh thus making a mockery of West Bengal's tradition of communal harmony. However, in the interest of fairness it may be added that while the ABP report referred to a stray incident which could not be taken for an overall commentary on the State's police force, BM's editorial observations could have been somewhat coloured by its adverse evaluation of the brand of secularism practiced by the Left Front (as noted earlier), and in any case the two contrary strands of communalism reportedly found in the forces to an extent seemed to cancel out each other.

Simultaneous to censuring the police and the administration, the reports also focused the laudable efforts of private charitable organizations run by missionaries in bringing relief and comfort to the riot-hit people irrespective of their religious identities.[26] The signal contributions of the sisters of the Loreto Convent—associated with Mother Teressa's 'Missionaries of Charity'—which was located in the hub of the riot-torn East Calcutta, came up repeatedly. Its role in upholding the kernel of the religion of humanity in the midst of looting and killing in the name of religion was poignantly portrayed in a report titled *'Dharmandhoder shikaar ora, bechechhe dharmeri ashraye* (Targeted by religious fanatics, they found shelter under the umbrella of religion)'. Side by side, locally based popular initiatives, cutting across the communal divide, organizing relief and rehabilitation and restoring peace and normalcy were especially accentuated.[27] As Hindu families found refuge in mosques and Muslim mothers along with their children were put up in Hindu households, it was the ring of neighbourly care and protection that reportedly provided the victims greater succour and comfort than the presence of the police and the military forces could do. A Muslim meatseller who maintained that 'the onus of restoring peace in *our own homes* rested on ourselves; the leaders, police or other outsiders hardly had any role here' seemed to have the last word in this regard. A Muslim housewife who attached priority to arrival of relief material, rehabilitation measures and guarantee of future security *rather than retaliation by others on their behalf* also revealed the subterranean fraternal bonds that held the ordinary people across communities together.

To summarize, the plight of ordinary Muslims on the eve of the call for *kar seva* at Babri Masjid as well as after the mosque had been pulled down was captured by the press in vivid detail and attention was rightly drawn to the vandalism indulged in by the VHP supporters and connived at by the BJP leadership. The coverage of Muslim 'voices' consisted of expressions of intense resentment together with fervent and sincere appeals for maintaining peace by the Muslim leadership—thus throwing a different light on a 'volatile' community—though the shaken faith in this leadership within the community too was duly noted. While apportioning the blame for this outrageous act, however, ABP pointed primarily to the irresponsible and provocative words and acts of the forces of *Hindutva*, but for BM, the Muslim 'communal' leadership encouraged by the pseudo-secular posture of some political parties (such as the CPI-M) could not escape responsibility either. As to the riots in Calcutta following the demolition act, they were projected more as law and order problem— the handiwork of gangsters often enjoying political connections and protection—rather than as product of communal cleavages. The administration was taken to task for its maladroit handling of the riot situation as well as the relief and rehabilitation process; charges of communal bias (of contradictory kinds, interestingly) and linkages with shadowy politicians and criminal elements were also brought against the police forces. Simultaneously, private efforts at restoring normalcy often reflecting deep fellow-feeling across communities, and healing touch provided by missionary services which the victims found more comforting and reassuring compared to the administrative measures (or lack thereof) were especially highlighted.

Press Coverage III: Post–'Godhra' Gujarat Riots

On 27 February 2002, India was shocked into disbelief by the news that 58 passengers, including several women and children, of the Ahmedabad-bound Sabarmati Express had been burnt alive by a Muslim mob reportedly following an altercation between the *kar sevak*s who were returning from Ayodhya and a number of Muslim tea vendors at Godhra. The immediate backdrop was furnished by yet another call by the VHP for starting the construction of the Ram temple in Ayodhya by 15 March 2002, paying scant respect to the strictures of the Supreme Court, which occasioned regular congregation of *Ram bhakt*s (the devotees of Lord Ram) in the city. This heinous and repugnant event sparked off a retaliatory binge and the Muslims—their lives, property, religious places and cultural symbols—needless to say, had to bear the brunt of this macabre campaign. Indeed what initially appeared a natural backlash later turned out to be a concerted and premeditated communal pogrom masterminded and clinically executed by the *Sangh Parivar* trio BJP, VHP and Bajrang Dal. Officially the death toll was put at around 800 but unofficial figures overshot 2,000; hundreds were injured or declared missing; and the number of people taking shelter in refugee camps at one time crossed the 100,000 mark. And while the bloodletting continued for months together, the state machinery played out, to say the least, a dubious role: the police at times allegedly acted as active accomplices of the assaulters and the BJP-led Narendra Modi government long remained busy playing down the gravity of the gruesome developments positing them as 'natural outpouring over the Godhra massacre'. To be sure, Hindus were also at the receiving end of violence as in due course the one-sided annihilation of the minority community turned into full scale communal rioting, but this could by no means alter the fact that what was witnessed in Gujarat during those months was primarily a systematic and brutal targeting of a specific segment of the population: the Muslims.

The press reports graphically corroborated the stark reality that all over Gujarat the minorities were subjected to rampant assaults, arson and destruction of property and BM, in particular, brought out certain murkier aspects of these developments. Thus, it drew attention to the grisly fact that Muslims were being identified and targeted by professional killers with the help of the electoral roll—which unveiled the kind of blood-curdling calculation that went into the systematic butchery unleashed in the State—as violence spread in areas which had never in the past experienced communal discord. It also reported the tragic flight of Muslims leaving their hearth and home from Gujarat as well as of migrant labourers eking out their livelihood by working in small factories, most of which were devastated during the bloodbath, in search of an uncertain future. But most touching was perhaps the plight of Muslim Indian Police Service (IPS) officers many of whom, given the high degree of communalization of the State's armed constabulary (comparable only with its counterpart in Uttar Pradesh), had to go into hiding and actively seek transfer to places where 'we would be regarded as police personnel irrespective of our religious identity'.[28] The voices—ranging from the Shahi Imam and Syed Shahbuddin right down to the hapless inmates of the refugee camps—through which the grievances of the community were captured, seemed quite predictably to speak in unison which revealed the sense of trauma and indignation the Gujarat events etched upon the collective minority psyche.[29]

However, when it came to tracing the roots of the turmoil and apportioning responsibility, the divergence between the analyses of the two papers became clearly perceptible from the very titles of the first editorials each published on the issue: for ABP, it was '*Bishbriksher Bhayabaho Phal* (Poison Tree's Pernicious Fruit)' as against BM's '*Gujarate Daanga: Sarkar o Policer Shochoniyo Byarthata* (Riots in Gujarat: Miserable Failure of the Government and Police)'.[30] ABP, much in keeping with its position during the Calcutta riots, laid the blame for the tragic and barbaric turn of events ultimately on the '*Hindutva* brigade' when it described the Godhra tragedy as fateful and yet not quite unexpected in view of the way the VHP had been allowed to muddy the water over the temple construction issue for quite some time. BM, on the other hand, instead of directly accusing the *Sangh Parivar*, trained its guns on the administration of the BJP-ruled State headed by Narendra Modi for its despicable lack of preparedness for tackling the violence in spite of the warnings issued by the Union government immediately after the Godhra episode. The culpability of the Modi government, it felt, was confirmed and needed probing because it was simply unimaginable that the BJP-dominated Union government would have refused to extend the required aid and assistance for dealing with the riot situation had it been duly approached. True, the paper added that the Vajpayee government at the Centre should have been more vigilant about the VHP leaders and anticipated some such untoward incident happening in the wake of the assemblage of thousands of *kar sevak*s in Ayodhya from all over India but it was certainly in no mood to condemn the rabble-rousing tactics indulged in by the VHP. The latter, as was previously noted, was taken to be a 'natural' expression of the sentiment of the majority and it was the obligation of the *government* to rein in the organization or contain whatever damage its sensational campaign might have caused.

That the Godhra carnage was an act of sabotage, indeed terrorism, resulting from a diabolic conspiracy hatched by the ISI, Pakistan's notorious intelligence agency, was also explored following government suggestions immediately after the incident had taken place. Thus, ABP editorially commented that those who had set fire to the train compartment at Godhra could not simply be dubbed as mad men and excused; but however provocative the *kar sevak*'s behaviour might have been, it could not have instigated ordinary members of the minority community to retaliate in such a manner and urged on the government to find out the real culprits.[31] But what was notable though not unpredictable was that BM pursued the Pakistan angle with greater fervour compared to ABP through regularly published reports, some signed by its correspondents and others derived from news agencies. Thus, one piece was titled *'Sandeher tir* mulato *ISI r dike* (The Needle of suspicion *primarily* points to the ISI [Our italics])'; a second self-explanatory title was *'Godhrai bosei train e aguner chhak korechhilo 5 Pak jongi* (5 Pak militants schemed to burn train in Godhra itself)'; a third report highlighted the arrest of a top leader of the banned Students Islamic Movement of India (SIMI) in connection with the Godhra happening; a fourth account quoted Narendra Modi as saying that what happened at Godhra was not communal violence but a terrorist act.[32] Most interestingly, a report bearing the enticing title *'Godhrai train e hamlar songe Karachir jog* (Karachi connection in Godhra train attack)' rather blandly informed readers that a locality of Karachi was named 'Godhra Colony' and most of its residents had their relatives in Gujarat's Godhra.[33] This series of news items in BM (not appearing in ABP) which sought to put a definite frame upon the Godhra occurrence could arguably be viewed as a singular instance of the paper's editorial stance influencing the contents of its reports.

To return to the issue of the Modi government's response, it may be recalled that in case of the Calcutta riots following the demolition of the Babri Masjid too the administration was severely taken to task for its ineptitude in containing violence or bungling in managing relief and rehabilitation work. Some reports also suggested the existence of a police-politician-criminal nexus and questioned the 'impartiality' of the government as between the two communities involved (though with reference to its acts of omission rather than commission as was reflected in BM's reservations regarding the kind of 'secularism' practiced by the CPI-M). But in this instance, the Modi government was indicted for its *indifference* to the riots, *turning a blind eye* to the tormentors of the minorities and its *reluctance* to firmly bring the situation under control.[34] Indeed, the way the police remained inactive and in some cases joined the rioting mob in heckling the Muslims appeared to confirm that the Gujarat government *let it happen* as if to teach a lesson to the minorities. The National Human Rights Commission's virtual rejection of the primary report submitted by the State administration on the riot scenario for being 'insincere and uninformative' and the Commission chief holding the government's passivity and incompetence responsible for the devastations was prominently reported. The extent of the loss of credibility suffered by the government was evident when an ABP editorial titled '*Nutan botoley purano Modi*' (Old Modi in New Bottle) wondered if the abundant promises of the Chief Minister, presumably made in response to ever-growing domestic and international pressure, for rebuilding mosques and overhauling the relief mechanism were anything more than pure gimmicks. The same lack of trust was brought out through reports that in spite of profuse government assurances for providing security, Muslim students remained unconvinced and reluctant to take their Board examinations.[35]

The Gujarat riots stood out from the Calcutta riots in another crucial respect: when the administration faltered in its responsibility to arrange adequate relief and rehabilitation measures, the victims of Calcutta found comfort in the neighbourhood support system.[36] But what caused concern in the Gujarat case was the collapse of the neighbourhood bonds: mistrust and hostility pervaded not only the relationship between the government and the minority community; it spoiled the social ties as well. On one hand, there were the disquieting reports that the *Harijans* (untouchables) who occupied the lowliest status in the Hindu social ladder and the *Bhil* tribals who remained outside the Hindu society altogether were mobilized by the *Parivar's* vicious propaganda into maiming and killing the Muslim 'enemies'. A second worrying trend revealed by press reports was that even the social workers had to operate clandestinely as they were threatened by the 'goons' not to carry relief to the minorities (in sharp contrast with the remarkable services rendered by the missionary charities), a condition that was so unbelievably different, lamented the relief suppliers, from the post-earthquake scenario barely a year back. But most appalling was perhaps the plight of those Muslims who left the relief camps—themselves in so dire straits of mismanagement thanks to the government's callous attitude—to return and resettle in their homes only to find that they were no longer welcome in their neighbourhood and were pushed back into the camps once again.

In sum, the riots in Gujarat were portrayed primarily as a planned cleansing operation complete with the participation of professional killers against the Muslims. ABP quite characteristically attributed this pogrom to the cynical politics of the *Sangh Parivar*, BM did not ignore the nuisance potential of the VHP (though it paid decisively greater attention than ABP to the possible Pak complicity behind the tragedy partly at least to play down the domestic sources of the mischief) but on top of it, it framed the tragedy as a consequence of administrative failure. During the Calcutta riots too the State administration had to bear the brunt of press' attack for its incompetence in controlling violence and bungling in reaching relief to the sufferers which was partly blamed on communal prejudice and partisan loyalty, and for which the private charities and local community-based initiatives seemed to largely compensate, the Gujarat situation seemed different in two alarming respects. First, the allegation of the administration's communal allegiance and complicity in the riots appeared more forthright and convincing; second, grassroots-level intercommunity fraternity—-which was saving grace in riot-torn Calcutta—seemed to have reached its nadir which was not a little responsible for the ghoulish character the Gujarat carnage assumed.

Press on Minority Rights in India

Minority rights in India, as outlined in a previous section, remained partly a historical legacy, and partly a response to its phenomenal cultural diversity which often produced intercommunity conflict especially over divergent value systems. Under such circumstances, it has been argued, minorities were often found subjected to institutional inequalities as social arrangements, for example language policies, customary practices or state rituals which might make it impossible for them to survive on their own terms. Thus the individuals' rights to physical and economic security seemed to lose currency in situations as those witnessed during communal riots where people were in danger of being attacked because they belong to a particular community that has been targeted. Under such circumstances, the protagonists of minority rights would maintain, conferring collective rights on these vulnerable communities was a prerequisite for leading a dignified existence which explained the admission of cultural rights as part of the fundamental constitutional entitlements of the minorities in India. For the same reason, they would contend, the Indian Constitution which allowed the state to interfere in religious affairs to promote social reform seemed to have made an exception for the minority religious communities and left it to the discretion of the rulers to decide the nature and timing of intervention when it pertained to the affairs of the minorities. The provisions, nevertheless, remained controversial from the very outset, and once the debate was reopened in the backdrop of the aggressive propagation of a *Hindu* nationalism since the 1980s, the votaries of minority rights sought to back up the original conception with multiculturalist arguments which focused on celebration of social pluralism. Pluralism was valued, they would argue, because it was good for a society to be exposed to different ways of life which widened social horizons as people learned from each other different ways of negotiating the world. Moreover, secure membership of cultural communities was beneficial for individuals too as they acquired the evaluative capacities that helped them map out and assess the world from these community cultures; without access to these cultures, individuals experienced a sense of loss or diminishment. Indeed, given this supreme importance of the community for the individual, strong defenders of pluralism would call upon the state to support and maintain the distinctive existence of these communities.

Armed with this understanding, if we approach the press' position on the issue of minority rights as revealed through our earlier analysis, it would appear that the argument concerning pluralism was by and large accepted. The papers seemed committed to toleration of manifold diverse and inconsistent ways of life which constituted the best guarantee to prevent societies turning inwards upon themselves from becoming chauvinistic and narrow-minded. But they did not seem to be amenable to the logic of state 'support' for survival of minority/susceptible communities when support was interpreted by community leaders as entitlement to not only distinctive but separate existence as was implied by the demand for letting the Muslim (women) to be covered by religiously sanctioned Personal Law of the community instead of the national Criminal Procedure Code, a demand that was acceded to by the government under the Muslim Women's Bill. This was seen as a blatant infringement of the Constitutional Directive to the State

(Article 44) to gradually to bring the whole body of the citizens within the ambit of a UCC (though in some instances, the papers showed inadequate understanding of the fact that the Indian Constitution while granting equal citizenship rights to all had made some special provisions for the minorities especially in the cultural sphere as noted earlier). Indeed, the notion of minority rights in this sense was viewed as a potential *threat*—on one hand to the individuals within these communities and on the other to national solidarity—which was effectuated by the self-styled leaders of the (in this case Muslim) community as well as the devious politicians.

To begin with, the law as it proposed to shift the onus of maintenance of the divorced Muslim women from the husband to the relatives of the wife or the State Waqf Board—both unsustainable propositions especially for the financially weaker sections—was seen to further undermine the already fragile position of the women within the Muslim community, a travesty of gender justice. The press perceived the new 'Shariat-compatible' law as a pretext for confirming their inferior status and subordination to menfolk within the community, an image that was corroborated by the near absence of women in a seminar organized by the votaries of the bill deliberating, ironically, on the *Muslim Women's Bill*. Second, the bill was also regarded as an assault on the ethos of secularism and rationality in so far as it signified surrender on the part of the Indian state to the demand for acknowledging the authority of a legal discourse which was born in a radically different time and context and seemed hopelessly out of touch with the liberal notion of individual liberty. To substantiate the point, the bill was portrayed as reminiscent of the fundamentalist excesses of the Khomeini regime, negating the modern and progressive spirit of the Shah Bano judgement delivered by the Supreme Court of India and also completely ignoring the debates and churning generated in its wake within the progressive sections of the Indian Muslims. The menacing potential of the bill was further revealed through the contemplation—indeed institutionalization—of a 'separate' arrangement for the Muslims within the Indian legal-constitutional framework which provoked the papers to arraign the government for its refusal to consider Muslim women as *Indian* citizens and deny them rights available to women belonging to other communities in India simply by virtue of their religious identity. The press found in this move a throwback to the infamous 'two-nation' theory which threatened to push the country in the direction of another partition.

Two categories of people were seen as instrumental to the reduction of the notion of minority rights to the perilous proportions noted earlier, that is the orthodox, often obscurantist, Muslim leaders who fancied themselves to be the self-appointed custodians of the interests of the community; and the unscrupulous politicians perennially in search of petty electoral gain even at the cost of pandering to suspect and retrogressive political elements. The opportunistic character of the Muslim leadership was sought to be exposed who chose to *selectively* embrace the *Shariat* in criminal matters (that is bringing the Muslim women under its purview as far as divorce suits were concerned without espousing the harsh and inhuman penalties endorsed by the *Shariat* in certain kinds of offences). It was also difficult to follow, the papers maintained quoting eminent Muslim personalities, how the bill was attuned to the *Shariat* because the latter never laid down that divorced women should fall back on their relatives or State Waqf Boards. But no less hideous was the role of the wily politicians especially those belonging to the ruling party who, by accrediting a group of arch conservative Muslim leaders as the spokespersons of the community, played a complicit part in undercutting the demand for change stemming from within the community. Prime Minister Rajiv Gandhi was singled out for having betrayed his own promise of taking India into the twenty-first century who, instead of casting his lot with the progressive elements among Indian Muslims, was found hobnobbing with the dubious characters purely out of self-serving motives. Indeed, the proposition could be extended to argue that his act made a mockery of the celebrated stance adopted by his grandfather Pandit Nehru who believed that alterations in Muslim Personal Law should be effected only if the demand arose from the community itself, while his grandson not only chose to ignore such voices for change but also enacted a law which had virtually undone the gains gradually achieved through the painstaking struggles of the champions of reform within India's Muslim community.

Though the press appeared to have strong reservations as to the use of the provision for minority rights by 'Muslim leaders' for upholding a 'questionable' vision of 'community identity' which was clearly discernible during the controversy over the Muslim Women's Bill, there was ample acknowledgement of the multiple threats the members of the minorities were exposed to during aberrant circumstances as revealed during the post–Babri Masjid demolition riots and the Gujarat bloodbath. These threats included, first and foremost, physical assaults as the horrific details of the damages and desolation suffered by the Muslims in Ayodhya in the wake of the demolition and its aftermath or the moving imagery of Muslim citizens being targeted by professional hatchet men using electoral rolls were meticulously portrayed. The press also covered the way communal confrontation imperilled people's sources of living as reflected in the premonitions expressed by the flower-peddlers of Ayodhya or the bleak future that befell the migrant factory workers of Gujarat. No less poignant was the predicament of senior IPS officers in Gujarat who had to cope with a battered self-esteem. The voices of protest and expressions of angst originating in the community too were captured with great compassion and understanding.

The proximate source of these threats was located in the incapacity of the state and its administration in meeting the basic and crucial obligation of providing protection to its citizens, in this case belonging to a minority community. This failure on the part of the state machinery came up time and again in press reports and commentaries, for example when the Babri Masjid was razed to dust in defiance of the assurances given before the national parliament and judiciary—the most sacred of democratic institutions conceivable—or Muslims fell victim to a xenophobic offensive in Gujarat let loose by the sister organizations of the very party in power with the police pleading helplessness. The way the administration was incriminated for active collusion in the Babri Masjid tragedy (of the Kalyan Singh regime) or the Gujarat carnage (of the Modi government) or for overt or covert communal predispositions or unholy alliance with shadowy operators (a charge that did not spare the Left-led government of West Bengal either) only magnified this failure. Moreover, the political parties of both the rightist and leftist varieties were indicted for contributing to the insecurity of the minorities—the BJP through its persistent and spiteful anti-Muslim campaign as well as its motivated caricature of *Hindutva* (as repeatedly stressed by the ABP) and the Left parties by subscribing to a blinkered vision of secularism overly indulgent towards the minorities (as reiterated by BM) thereby trampling upon the

'Hindu' sentiment. But on top of it all, Muslims themselves were held by BM as no less responsible for the tight spot they found themselves in: its conservative leadership's excessive sensitiveness to and extreme obsession with the question of maintaining a 'distinct and separate identity', a mind-set which gave rise to the demand for the Muslim Women's Bill which challenged the liberal and secular ethos of the Indian Constitution and caused avoidable discomfiture in the majority community, contributed substantively towards their predicament.

But, if the papers diverged somewhat in diagnosing the roots of these maladies, they seemed in perfect agreement that none of these causative factors could be eradicated through the grant of collective rights to the minorities; if anything, the concept of minority rights and its practice in the Indian context constituted part of the problem itself. The threats identified earlier had to be principally addressed through strengthening and streamlining of the administrative apparatus, and the rest had to be left to the social mechanisms, that is toleration inherent in our civilization (reminding one of Nandy's position), grassroots-level communal harmony and private social support initiatives (which arguably helped keep the devastations during the Calcutta riots within tolerable proportions compared to the atrocities in Gujarat). On the other hand, if the administration failed largely in securing the entitlement of the *individuals* belonging to the minority community to the basic human goods such as physical and economic security, it was difficult to see how *collective* minority rights could be expected to have a different fate.

To conclude then, the press seemed to view the whole notion of minority rights with suspicion which, however, did not imply any inherently anti-minority or anti-Muslim stance for it was seen that the 'just' grievances of the minorities (in its perception) were treated and ventilated with sympathy and understanding, and negative stereotypes popular about Muslims which often vitiated intercommunity relations were sought to be busted. A distinction between 'minority rights' and 'rights of the minorities' might help clarify the position: the former represented *group* rights which, particularly when used to defend the separate Muslim identity and consciousnesses, were found loathsome and unacceptable by the press. The latter consisted of *individual* rights, rights which in its view every Muslim citizen of the Indian state was entitled to enjoy as much as their counterparts belonging to the majority community.

Indeed when ABP blasted the RSS for the outrageous suggestion to make the rights of the minorities conditional upon their 'good conduct', it was actually defending the rights of the Muslim *individuals* and not of the *community*. Its understanding of rights, therefore, coincided with its classical liberal conception which endorsed only one uniform set of rights charter for the whole body of citizenry: any exception made for the minorities—especially religious minorities—was liable to be seen as an infringement of secularism and antithetical to national integration. On the other hand, the state, it was insisted, had to strictly ensure that these essential rights, for example benefits of physical security, economic well-being and a degree of privacy, were available to all citizens irrespective of religious affiliation and that government agencies and the system of law did not work in favour of any religious group, minority or majority. However, rather curiously, while remaining wedded to classical liberal and secular positions, the papers seemed to appreciate—in principle at least—the role assigned to the state under the Indian Constitution to intervene in the religious affairs of communities in the interest of social reform as was evident in the exaltation of the progressive potential of the Shah Bano judgement. Their sympathy and support for the voices of reform and mounting resistance to the established orthodox leadership within the Muslim community was fully explicit, and the objection once again was raised against the *special concession* the Muslim leadership secured from the top brass of the ruling party culminating in the Muslim Women's Bill. But by the same token, they were sure to regard with a dollop of salt Bhargava's notion of 'principled distance' on the part of the state which called for a degree of statesmanship, sense of history and capacity for informed and refined judgement that seemed regrettably lacking in contemporary political leadership (as revealed through the press reportage of the selected cases) with whom rested the responsibility to furnish direction to the state machinery.

Notes and References

1. Neera Chandhoke, 'Individual and Group Rights: A View from India', in *India's Living Constitution: Ideas, Practices and Controversies*, eds Zoya Hasan, Eswaran Sridharan, R. Sudarshan (Delhi: Permanent Black, 2004), pp. 210–14.
2. Ibid., pp. 217–20.

3. Donald Eugene Smith, *India as a Secular State* (Princeton and Oxford: Princeton University Press, 1963): 20–21.
4. Rajeev Bhargava, 'India's Secular Constitution', in *India's Living Constitution: Ideas, Practices and Controversies*, eds Zoya Hasan, Eswaran Sridharan and R. Sudarshan (Delhi: Permanent Black, 2004), pp. 124.
5. Chandhoke, 'Individual and Group Rights', pp. 222–28.
6. Gurpreet Mahajan, *Identities and Rights* (Delhi: Oxford University Press, 1998), pp. 9–13.
7. Ashis Nandy quoted in Stuart Corrbridge and John Harriss (eds), *Reinventing India*, (Delhi: Oxford University Press, 2003), pp. 194–95; Partha Chatterjee, 'Secularism and Toleration', in *A Possible World: Essays in Political Criticism*, ed. P. Chatterjee (Delhi: Oxford University Press, 1997).
8. Chatterjee, 'Secularism and Toleration', p. 258.
9. Shyamal K. Chakraborty, '*Talak prapto mahilader prasange: muslimder jonno natun aain hochchhe*' (In relation to divorced women: new law on anvil for Muslims), *ABP*, 16 February 1986; Shyamal K. Chakraborty, '*Aagami soptahe shariat mene muslim mahila bill*' (Shariat-compatible Muslim Women's Bill next week), *ABP*, 21 February; '*Rajiver chintadhara jeno Khomeinir pothe cholechhe*' (Rajiv seems to emulate Khomeini), *BM*, 1 March.
10. '*tmasamarpaner udyog*' (Preparations for surrender), editorial, *ABP*, 24 February 1986.
11. Sunit Ghosh, '*Bhoter jonyo moulabader kaachhe rajiver atmasamarpane bohu muslim o bibroto*' (Rajiv's surrender before fundamentalists for electoral gain embarrasses many Muslims too) special article, *ABP*, 8 March 1986; '*Rajiver whip jaatir pithe kete bosechhe*' (The nation lacerates under Rajiv's whip), editorial, *BM*, 10 May 1986.
12. '*Kahar adhikar raksha?*' (Protecting whose rights?), editorial, *ABP*, 7 May 1986; '*Rajiver whip...; Muslim noi, bharatiya naari*' (Not Muslim but Indian women), editorial, *ABP*, 25 April 1986.
13. '*Prabal prativad upekshito, Muslim naari bill pesh*' (Huge protests ignored, Muslim Women's Bill presented), *ABP*, 26 February 1986, p. 1; '*Bill er prativade Arif er padatyag*' (Arif resigns in protest against bill), *ABP*, 27 February, 1986, p. 1; '*Prabal bitarko, teebro prativad, walkout, lok sabhai mahila bill pesh*' (Massive controversy, intense protests, walkout, Women's Bill placed in Lok Sabha), *BM*, 6 May 1986, p. 1; Ashis Ghosh, '*Muslim bill er aanch e rajyeo*' (This State too feels the heat of Muslim Bill), *ABP*, 12 March 1986.
14. '*Rajiv pratishruti rakhenni: Muslim mahila samstha*' (Rajiv hasn't kept his word: Muslim women's organization), *ABP*, 25 February 1986, p. 5; '*Poddhotigato trutite Muslim mahila bill uthlona, birodhi paksha-o dwidhabibhakta*' (Muslim Women's Bill not tabled due to technical flaw, opposition divided too), *ABP*, 22 February

1986, p. 4); '*Muslim naari bill er samarthane Janata*, BJP sadasyara' (Janata, BJP members in support of Muslim Women's Bill), *ABP*, 20 March 1986.

15. '*Ami moulabadi*' (I am a fundamentalist), *ABP*, 30 March 1986, p. 1.

16. '*Shah Bano mamlar raike samarthan korlen Shabana*' (Shabana supports Shah Bano verdict), *BM*, 21 March, 1986 p. 5; '*Muslimra nirapottar abhav bodh koren*' (Muslims feel insecure), *ABP*, 7 April 1986, p. 1.

17. '*Rajiv protishruti rakhenni*' (*n. 14*); '*Bhoter jonyo…*' (*n. 11*); 'Rajiver chintad-hara…'(n 9); '*Gachher o khai, tolar o kurai*' (Having the best of both worlds), editorial, *ABP*, 19 March 1986.

18. '*Dwijaati tatwer bhut*' (The ghost of two nation theory), editorial, *ABP*, 28 February 1986; 'Bhoter jonyo…' (n. 11); '*Rajiver whip…*' (n. 11); '*Kalankito ain*' (scandalous law), editorial, *BM*, 10 May 1986.

19. Debdut Ghosh Thakur, '*Raagi jubader niye Ayodhyai shanka*' (Fear in Ayodhya regarding the angry young men), *ABP*, 4 December 1992; '*Karsevakder un-matto akramone masjid dhulisat*' (Mosque flattened by the karsevaks' frenzied assault) and '*Lajja glanite noi, Kalyaner istofa guli chalanor dai erate*' (Not in anguish but Kalyan resigned only to escape the responsibility of opening fire), *ABP*, 7 December 1992; '*Lakshadhik karsevakke saranoi ekhon mul samasya*' (Real problem now is to shift the million *karsevaks*), *ABP*, 8 December 1992.

20. '*Pradhanmantrir istofa chailen Muslim netara*' (Muslim leaders demanded PM's resignation), *ABP*, 7 December 1992; '*Dhairya dhorbar ahvan janalen Imam*' (Imam called for patience), *BM*, 7 December 1992; '*Mile gelo dui Babri sangathan*' (Merger of the two Babri organizations), *ABP*, 27 December 1992; '*Ayodhyay ispater bera sesh hobar mukhe, darshan abyahata*' (Ayodhya steel fencing about to finish, *darshan* unhindered), *ABP*, 6 January 1993; '*Ayodhya issue niye ajatha barabai kora hochchhe*' (Ayodhya issue being unnecessarily played up), *BM*, 2 January 1993.

21. ABP, 8 December, 1992; '*Jatir astitva jokhon bipanno*' (When the nation's existence is at stake), *ABP*, 9 December 1992; '*Viswa Hindu Parishad o Viswa*' (World Hindu Council and the World), *ABP*, 10 December 1992; '*Prayajan oikyabaddha ladai*' (United struggle needed), *ABP*, 14 December 1992.

22. '*Ayodhya niye sangharsha*' (Clash over Ayodhya), *BM*, 3 December 1992; 'Ayodhyai tandav' (Vandalism at Ayodhya), *BM*, 7 December 1992; '*Chai shan-tirakshay sakoler chesta o kartripaksher drhirata*' (United effort and government firmness needed to uphold peace), *BM*, 7 December 1992; '*Baalir bandh sampro-dayikata rodh korte parbena*' (Sand embankments could not stem the communal tide), *BM*, 17 December 1992; '*Bamfront sarkarer fascistsulabh siddhanta*' (Left Front government's fascist like decision), *BM*, 18 December 1992.

23. '*Muslimra prajatantra divas boycott korbe?*' (Muslims to boycott Republic Day?), *BM*, 12 January 1993; '*Boycott noi, istafao noi*' (No boycott or resignation),

ABP, 17 January 1993; '*Prajatantra divas*, 1993' ('Republic Day, 1993'), ABP, 26 January 1993.

24. '*Upadruta elakai netader anupasthiti bismaykar*' (Absence of leaders in riot-affected areas astonishing), *ABP*, 12 December 1992; '*Durgatader ghare pherar pala suru*' (The affected start returning home), *ABP*, 15 December 1992; '*Metiaburuje Hindu Musalmaner ek i kotha: amra noi, hamla kore gechhe obangali mastanera*' (Hindus and Muslims of Metiaburuj assert that troubles were perpetrated not by us but by non-Bengali hoodlums), *BM*, 14 December 1992; '*Kolkatai jokhon eto gandogol jelaguli tokhon shanto chhilo keno?*' (When Kolkata had so much trouble, how could the districts remain quiet?), *BM*, 15 December 1992.

25. '*Danga-kabalito purbanchal*' (East Kolkata in the grips of riots), *ABP*, 12 December 1992; '*Lajja policer, prashashanero*' (Police and administration should be ashamed), editorial, *ABP*, 1 January 1993; '*Chai nirapeksha prashashanik kathorata ebong swabhabik jibonjatrar prabaha*' (Wanted administrative neutrality and firmness and restoration of normal life flow), *BM*, 9 December 1992.

26. '*anga-kabalito purbanchal; Dharmandhader sikar onra...*' *ABP*, 15 December 1992.

27. '*Traan milchhe, milchhena swasti*' (Relief received, not comfort), *ABP*, 16 December 1992; '*Danga-kabalito purbanchal II*', *ABP*, 13 December 1992.

28. '*Bhitemati chhere chole jachchhen bohu manush*' (Many leaving their hearth and home), *BM*, 5 March 2002; '*Gujrat e voter talika dekhe dekhe bechhe bechhe manush khun*' (People targeted and killed in Gujarat with voters' lists), *BM*, 8 March 2002; '*Gujrat er biponno sankhaloghu police kartara chaichhen bodli*' (Insecure minority police officers of Gujarat want transfer), *BM*, 10 March 2002.

29. '*Gujrat e himsa abyahato, policer gulite nihato 6*' (violence unabated in Gujarat, 6 killed in police firing), *BM*, 24 April 2002; '*Tran shibirer obostha shochoniyo*' (Relief camps in appalling state), *ABP*, 13 May 2002.

30. '*Bishbriksher Bhayabaho Phal*' (Poison Tree's Pernicious Fruit), editorial, *ABP*, 1 March 2002; '*Gujarate Daanga: Sarkar o Policer Shochoniyo Byarthata*' (Riots in Gujarat: Miserable Failure of the Government and Police), *BM*, 2 March 2002.

31. 'Bishbriksher...' (n. 30).

32. 28 February 2002; 2 March 2002; '*Sabarmati: atak SIMIr neta?*' (SIMI leader arrested at Sabarmati?), 2 March 2002; '*Gujarat kromei swabhabik*' (Gujarat gradually normal), 6 March 2002.

33. '*Godhrai train e hamlar songe karachir jog*' (Katrachi link found to Godhra train attack), *BM*, 7 March 2002.

34. '*Apadartho rajya, apadartho kendro*' (Worthless State, worthless Centre), *ABP*, 2 April 2002; '*Modike bidai kora dorkar*' (Modi should be sacked), *ABP*, 5 March 2002; '*Daangar jonno bhartshito modi*' (Modi chided for riots), *ABP*, 25 April 2002.

35. 5 May 2002; '*Nirapattar ashwas, tobu Gujrat e porikshay boste bhoy pachchhe Muslim chhattra chhattri ra*' (Muslim students afraid to take exams despite assurances of security), *ABP*, 21 April 2002.

36. '*Ushkanir phole adivasirao hinsra, cholchhe "shotru" nidhan*' (Tribals provoked into turning ferocious, slaughter of 'the enemy' continues), *ABP*, 7 April 2002; '*Tran niye berote parchhen na samajsebirao*' (Social workers deterred from supplying relief), *BM*, 3 March 2002; '*Ahmedabad e notun kore himsai nihato 7*' (7 die in fresh violence in Ahmedabad), *ABP*, 25 April 2002.

Chapter 9

Medical Advertisement
An Embodiment of Culture

Dalia Chakraborty

Introduction

Advertising has emerged as the central cultural form of commodity capitalism.[1] Richards[2] calls it a 'spectacle' because advertising translates *things* into a fantasy visual display of *signs* and *symbols*. Today, even medicines have become consumer products for mass consumption. Expenditure on health and medical care are growing faster in India than the overall rate of consumption spending. This has become possible due to the development of a new form of commodity culture: the spectacle of the consumer's body.[3] This chapter intends to examine the advertisements of health-enhancing tonic (*salsa*s in *ayurvedic* terminology), health food and drinks between the closing years of nineteenth century to the present days. 'Medicalization of life' is not at all a contemporary phenomenon. It was very much visible in the nineteenth century England.[4] India being a colony of British empire could not escape the influence. This justifies the choice of time frame for this work. Advertisements are nothing but representations, signifying specific cultural forms, carrying particular cultural meanings. To trace its changing meanings over time I have drawn from the analytic framework that emerged in the 1970s as central to critical media studies' approach to advertising.[5] To deconstruct the advertising message I have followed Saussure's semiological approach based on the distinction between denotation and connotation. Reading advertisements always draws upon the common experience of the social milieu. That experience is definitely mediated by the dominant practices and ideas. Thus reading of advertisements often reproduces them.[6] In this chapter the focus is on the way the written as well as the visual texts are designed by the advertisers to act as a specific discourse upon the individual, subjecting him, without necessarily winning him over his head. The construction of physical space in a picture and the positioning of the viewer in it are very crucial. Viewers are there either to watch the image advertised or read the text or they imaginatively get into action. Viewers' recognition of their position in the advertisement depends on their ability to read the picture—an ability, I repeat, which draws on their everyday experience of space.

Data and Method

I have collected advertisements from various sources ranging from daily newspapers and magazines (general as well as specialized) to *panjikas*, from church notices for general public to advertisements printed on matchboxes. Recent advertisements are taken from sources like newspapers, magazines, hand-bills, bill boards, advertisements pasted on the walls of railway stations, on traffic signals and on road signs. I have used qualitative method, which is 'multi-method in focus, involving an interpretive, naturalistic approach to its subject matter'.[7] To study the images in advertisements I have used visual method, which unlike the scientific, realist, observational approach to visual research, focuses on the constructedness of visual forms. Following Chaplin this work has not considered visual as mere data for verbal analysis but rather as knowledge and critical text by its own right.[8] To understand the text attached with the visual, content analysis proves useful. Social historical method has to be applied to trace the evolution of medical advertisements. Actually, triangulation of methods goes well with the spirit of qualitative research. I accept the role of researcher as bricoleur, that is jack of all trades— ready to use any strategy, method or data.

Advertising as a Social Practice

Advertising, following the definition given by the Definitions Committee of the American Marketing Association is 'any paid form of non-personal presentation of idea, goods or service by an identified sponsor'.

A very early definition is found in the issue of the *Advertising Age* dated 28 July 1932. Here, advertising is defined as 'the dissemination of information concerning an idea, service or product to compel action in accordance with the intent of the advertiser.[9] In this work I borrow Mazzarella's understanding that the practice of advertising is a kind of public cultural production, centred on a distinctive form of commodity production, that is the production of commodity images.[10] And this production is highly ideological in nature as it constantly intervenes in a wider public cultural field. Since advertisers want to reach the public in order to sell their products, it is argued that they naturally support the media, which are popular with the public.[11] Despite the presence of TV, newspapers continued to be regarded by many advertisers as a superior medium to television for advertisements with high information content. In case of magazines, not merely specific articles, but the entire content of such magazines is often designed to induce a responsive frame of mind to consumer advertising—the propaganda of capitalism.[12] In the world of brands, advertising remains the most powerful and persuasive tool of brand building. With the corporate brand at its core, every advertising strategy becomes a powerful tool of market growth.[13] In India advertising is a post-Independence phenomenon, though it traced its origins to a clutch of international agencies that were set up in the 1920s and 1930s. Till 1960s Calcutta was the advertising capital of the country, which later shifted to Mumbai. The fact that the advertiser is in a position to advertise at all testifies to a certain level of corporate strength. The consumers might, other things being equal, feel this to be reassuring, at least about the minimum quality-level to be expected from the product.[14]

To understand the impact of consumer advertising on the realm on health care we may recall Ivan Illich. He points out that by the turn of the century in the West the doctors had already perfected what he calls diagnostic imperialism, a method of examination built around the minute and detailed scrutiny of the patient's body by the doctor.[15] The closer the doctor looks, the more diseases there are to be found. The quacks pioneered a complementary medical technique that proved useful in snaring customers who as yet showed no sign of sickness. This technique can be called therapeutic imperialism, for it colonizes the body, not with diseases, but with remedies, which are invariably commodities. Therapeutic imperialism is concerned with the daily maintenance of the healthy body, and it relies on regimen. The advertising supplements are full of tonics, diets, methods, measures, regimes, exercises and other forms of what is called health 'culture'. Here culture is no longer the product of human work and thought characteristic of a given society; it has become a euphemism for the therapeutic powers of the commodity. Underlying assumptions behind all these advertisements are that all diseases or weakness can be cured; that cures will be technical in nature; that disease is not to be blamed on circumstance, or more precisely, on the capitalist system; that symptoms of disease are generally manifestations of individuality; that experts know best; and that the body's needs can best be met by consuming various kinds of therapeutic commodities.[16] Nowhere does one find the remotest suggestion that society at large is to blame for the social reality of sickness.

Advertisements as Social Portrayals

Since the closing years of nineteenth century till today in Bengal, if we closely follow the advertisements of tonics and health drinks which are primarily meant for general health, strength and vitality, we can identify a few regularities as well as some emerging patterns. Both the visual and the verbal texts are found in most of these advertisements. Distinction between literal or direct signification, that is denotation and implied or indirect signification, that is connotation is useful in this case. In advertisements it is usually the connotation rather than the denotation of a signifying element that is important. However, the denotation is not irrelevant. Indeed, it is a condition of the connotation. The distinction between denotation and connotation opens up and accounts for a distinction between the manifest content of a text and its latent content. For example, in the advertisement of 'Baidyanath Shankhapushpi—the memory enhancer', an image of a serious-looking boy reading attentively, with heaps of books on the table is found. Behind the boy, on the wall of that room there is a picture of Swami Vivekananda facing the viewer.[17] Vivekananda's picture denotes nothing but a sober decoration of the study room. But the connotation is very intriguing. It implies that this tonic will help the child to develop his mental abilities following the footsteps of Swami Vivekananda, who is admired for his inner strength and quiet resolve. This also reveals how advertisement intervenes in the visual and discursive articulation of national cultural identity.

Primarily the advertisements of tonics are positive portrayals of well being. To borrow John Hegarty's (UK's creative guru) expression... 'information goes in through the heart'. When people feel good about a brand's advertising, they feel good about the brand. If the advertising makes them smile, if it offers an escape or captures a spirit that simply feels good, people feel a kinship with the feeling—and through it with the product. They begin to want it just because they like it. This is advertising as goodwill ambassador. It opens the door to a relationship by engaging the consumer's attention and extending an invitation hand.[18] For example, in the advertisement of *Ayer's Sarsaparilla* (Figure 9.1) in the background of a rising sun the word 'hope' is written. Here sun constitutes the decorative periphery substantiating the rational core, that is justification of taking medicine. In some advertisements two contrasting pictures of a very sick and tired and a very healthy man with robust physique are used to signify the effect of the medicine. Advertisements of *Manna's Cooperative Salsa* (late nineteenth century), *Suraballi Kashay,*[19] and *Bovril* (Figure 9.2) can be cited as evidences. In the very recent advertisement of *Baidyanath Chyawanprash Special*, there is a picture of a confident adolescent holding triumphantly the prize for, as suggested by the written text, excelling both in sports and examinations.[20] This connotes the positive contribution of Chyawanprash for all-round development of children.

There are a few negative portrayals as well suggesting pain and exhaustion. In the advertisement of *Philco's Compound* (*JogiSakha* 1959, 5th year, 12th issue) we find a fragile-looking *sari*-clad lady, sitting on the floor, stretching her legs in desperation, while resting her face on her right palm, with the food (seems untouched) served in front of her on a plate and water in a glass (again full, signifying the same). This picture reflects exhaustion, and a loss of appetite, which can, as if, be remedied by taking the advertised medicine. Another evidence is the advertisement of Glaxose D, where a tired middle-aged man is about to take his shirt

Figure 9.1 Ayer's Sarsaparilla

AYER'S SARSAPARILLA.

For Purifying the Blood.

Impurity of the blood, whether inherited, or the result of exposure, uncleanliness, or a wrong manner of living, produces a decline of vitality and a great variety of scrofulous diseases and disorders such as Ulcerations of the Liver, Stomach, Kidneys, Lungs, Eruptions and Eruptive Diseases of the skin, St. Anthony's Fire, Rose or Erysipelas, Pimples, Pustules ; Blotches, Boils, Tumors, Tetter and Salt Rheum, Scald Head, Ringworm, Ulcers and Sores, Rheumatism ; Neuralgia, Pain in the Bones, Side and Head, Female Weakness, Sterility, Leucorrhœa arising from internal ulceration and uterine disease, Dropsy, Dyspepsia, Emaciation and General Debility, Syphilis, and Mercurial Disease, are the most dangerous sources of scrofulous infection.

FOR ALL THE FORMS of scrofulous, mercurial, and blood disorders, the best remedy is AYER's COMPOUND CONCENTRATED EXTRACT OF SARSAPARILLA ; composed of Sarsaparilla-root combined with Stillingia, Yellow Dock, and Mandrake, all of which are held in high repute for their alterative and curative properties. The active medicinal principles of these roots, extracted by a process peculiarly our own, are chemically united in AYER'S SARSAPARILLA with the Iodides of Potassium and Iron, forming by far the most health-restoring and reliable blood-purifying medicine that can be used. Prepared by Dr. J.C. AYER & Co. Lowell, Mass., U. S. A.

GENERAL AGENTS,

BALLANTINE & CO.,

Apply to *Manager*, .
Depot, No. 10, Radha Bazar, Calcutta.   G

6.5 cm × 9.8 cm, July, 1885

Source: *The Statesman*, July 1885.

off, may be after coming back home after a hard days work in office. But in the same frame there are some positive elements too like a packet of Glaxose D, a spoon full of it (though the holder is not visible), and a clock

Figure 9.2 Bovril

IF WEAKLY
TAKE
BOVRIL
DAILY

4 OCTOBER 1932

Source: The Times of India, 4 October 1932.

signifying that the subject is about to take it and that within minutes he will regain his energy (*The Times of India*, 19 October 1975).

Functional Specifications

Obviously, the tonics or health drinks are advertised for consumption. Naturally the consumers must be able to locate enough justification for the act of buying it. Hence almost all advertisements categorically mention the uses. Interestingly, advertising arms consumers with information and options. This often frustrates some doctors. Advertising 'encroaches a bit on the patient-physician relationship', said Carey Kimmelstiel, director of clinical cardiology at Tufts New England Medical Center. Over the years in Bengal purification of blood appears to be the most frequently used effect cited by the advertisers (for example, advertisement of Dr Ayer's Sarsaparilla, July 1885, *The Statesman;* B.N. Dutt's *Amrita Bindu Salsa* (Figure 9.3); *Mahashakti Tonic,* 1981, *Bishudha Siddhanta Panjika*).

With the growing specialization of medical knowledge, initial projection of tonics as universal remedies for all known diseases (typical of a period between late nineteenth and mid-twentieth century) has been replaced by a pointed specification of its limited functions. As instances of cure-all medicines we may refer to Sarsaparilla, which is described as having positive effect on liver, stomach, kidneys, lungs, and various diseases ranging from eruptions and pimples to rheumatism, even sterility. The advertisement of Water of Life or Neurotic Catholicon projects it as 'universal sovereign remedy for all the various and complicated ailments to which the nervous system is liable in consequence of

Figure 9.3 Amrit Bindu Salsa

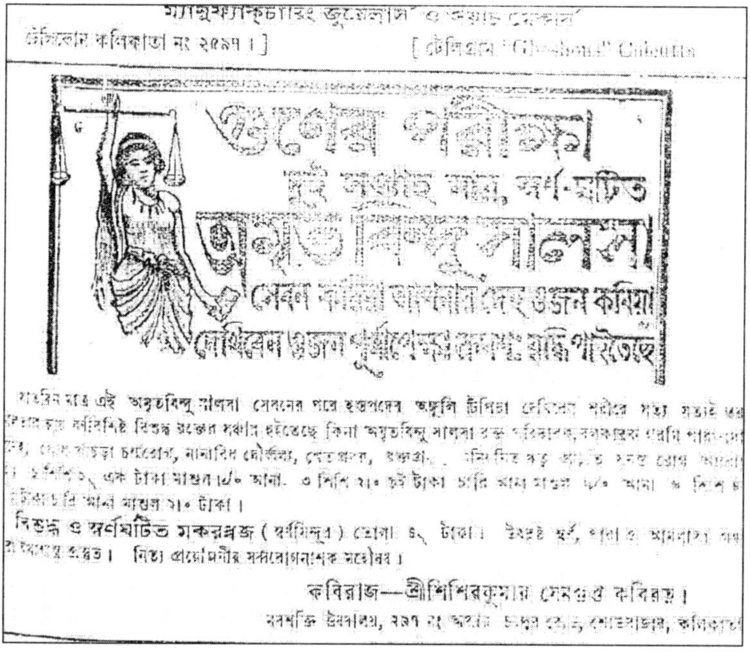

Source: *Probasi* 1905.

217

the innumerable causes natural to humanity'.[21] It, the advertiser claims, radically cures nervous, muscular and general disability; infuses youthful health, strength and energy; corrects morbidness of intellect and of sensibility; assists concentration of thought and capacity for work; removes the most obstinate lumbago, sciatica and diabetes; enhances functional power of sight, hearing and digestion; corrects cerebral, abdominal and liver torpidity, etc. Advertisement of Dr James Tonic Pills[22] assures physical strength, youthfulness, remedy of nervous exhaustion, malaria, cold and cough, even plague. It claims to solve the problem of mental depression as well. Though there is a decline in the number of diseases, claimed to be cured by a single medicine, still we come across advertisements like that of Mahashakti Tonic (Bisudhha Siddhanta Panjika, 1981), which reportedly can cure skin disease to anaemia, acidity to allergy, piles to rheumatism. The eventual narrowing down of the claimed range of tonics' function is visible in the advertisement of *Chyawanprash Special* (2005), which focuses on bones, brain functions and cold and cough, or that of *Baidyanath Kesari Kalp Royal Chyawanprash* (*The Statesman*, 18 January 2006) focusing only on rejuvenation, stimulation for nervous system, and energy and vitality.

Specifying Consumers

Not only the functions of medicines, even how to take it, and who can take it are important issues for the users. The intention to expand its market is clearly in sight in the declarations in most of the advertisements regarding the absence of any lifestyle restriction (for example advertisement of *Amrita Bindu Salsa*), or any bar on age for its use (for example advertisement of *Mahashakti Tonic*). Often it specifies the target consumers. The growth of market research and the growing marketing sophistication that accompanies its development give rise to more precise definitions of the intended audiences for advertising campaigns. The new approach is based, as a leading pioneer succinctly put it, on 'thinking about the market rather than simply about the product'.[23] This tends to reduce the size of the audiences actively sought in advertising campaigns: vague generalizations like 'the mass market' are superseded by a more narrowly defined 'target markets'. The advertisement of Graefenberg Vegetable Pills claims that the residents of hot climate would find them indispensable and no family should do without them. The focus on hot climate and family as consumption unit reflects the urgency to make it appear India-specific in nature. Again the very frequent use of the word 'pure' in the advertisements of foreign (mostly British during colonial times) tonics signifies attempts to win over the Indian consumers on the basis of a stereotypical image of Indians or more specifically the Hindus. Hindus are perceived as preoccupied with the idea of purity and pollution as these constitute the very foundation of Indian caste system. For an example we may refer to the advertisement of Invalid's Port in the fourth January issue of *The Times of India*. Here just beneath the name of the tonic in very bold letters the caption 'Analysed Pure' was printed with equal emphasis.

Specifying Manufacturing Details

All advertisements mention the composition of the medicine. This probably is one way of establishing its value in the eyes of potential buyers. Various herbs and minerals (both names and numbers specified) are the common ingredients. Of late, vitamins are added to the list, for example Philco's Compound, Complan. Even the guidelines for making medicines have become items to advertise. Ancient Indian scriptures (for example *Mahashakti Tonic*) on one hand, and modern science (for example Dr James's Tonic pills) on the other, bestow prestige to the tonics manufactured following either of the two principles. Advertisement of *Baidyanath Kesari Kalp Royal Chyawanprash* (2006) proudly announces the achievements of Baidyanath Research Foundation. *Cooperative Salsa* is presented as a great nineteenth century discovery, while Dr James's Tonic Pills as that of the twentieth century. The very manufacturing process is also crucial. With the growing public concern about food and drink adulteration, many advertisers stressed the purity of their wares, sometimes publishing complex reports of chemical analyses. Advertisement of Eno's Fruit Salt (Figure 9.4), foremost among the common aids to health recognized in India since 1878, contains the following statement: 'Untouched by hand during manufacture'.

Figure 9.4 Eno's Fruit Salt

Source: The Statesman, December 1925.

Advertisement Gimmicks and Marketing Strategies

Dazzling advertisement campaigns are launched by various brands of health-care facilities, fighting to retain their monopolies over the highly lucrative at the same time fiercely competitive medical market. Testimonials by high-ranking beneficiaries or attractive offers for the buyers are mentioned to invoke the trust and to draw the attention of the target people. Testimonials are the regular items in early advertisements. *Manna's Cooperative Salsa* (late nineteenth-century) establishes its worth by pointing out that it is appreciated by cross section of people, that is doctors, *kabirajs*, as well as the laymen. In the *Phosferine* advertisement (Figure 9.5) image of an aristocratic English lady (signified by her flowing gown, gracious standing posture, and her frilled umbrella) is followed by a caption that 'a charming lady acknowledges our help'. Here Englishness and its association with 'quality' are built into the advertisement. In the same advertisement, to add more weight to the testimony to its excellent quality, a part of a letter appreciating this medicine and mentioning its possible uses, particularly in the context of modern times, written by one Countess de Fleury has been published. Even that does not seem sufficient. The names of royal families of various European countries like Russia, Greece, etc., are mentioned as the regular customers. While considering the position of both the subject and the products in the *Phosferine* advertisement the viewers will definitely perceive them as upper class.

Another early practice of establishing worth and authenticity is to inform the public that it is registered following the rules of the government. Actually, thereby the advertisers utilize government's credential to win over the public trust. Advertisement of *Cooperative Salsa*, even mentioned the year (1893) and date (2 February) of registration. The recent advertisement[24] of *Baidyanath Shankhapushpi* claims to get an approval of Central Drug Research Institute. Some advertisements use images of famous personalities in their ad to entice their clients. For example, in the advertisement of Branolia, wearing the full costume of a magician, P.C. Sarkar Jr, the famous magician, is smiling towards the viewers, holding a bottle of Branolia in one hand, and making a gesture in the other suggesting the magical power of the tonic (photograph taken by N. Mukherjee, 2007).

Figure 9.5 Phosferine

Source: The Times of India, 23 April 1906.

Similarly *Dabur Chyawanprash* uses the images of film stars like Vivek Oberoi and Amitabh Bachchan. The text reveals how Vivek Oberoi recommends it for its capacity to enhance positive energy and its power to maintain physical and mental stability of its users. Striking is the use of a very young upcoming star more prominently than the very senior respectable one. The advertiser's intention to catch the younger generation's attention is one possible explanation. Obviously Vivek's posture reveals his age and energy level. Contrastingly, a giant bottle of Chyawanprash is almost giving support to the senior star who, it seems, in recognition to the product's contribution to his health and mind points a finger towards the bottle (*Anandabazar Patrika,* 31 December 2005).

Another form of advertisement gimmick is the words of caution written in the text of advertisement for the common 'innocent' people to make them aware of fraudulent advertisements, as if, to protect them from buying counterfeit products. In case of Dusart's Syrup (Figure 9.6) the last line of the written text is 'Beware of imitations'. The advertisement of Cafiaspirin[25] ends with a note: 'Be sure of legitimate product—check the sign.' Rather than rousing doubt about the quality of the product in the mind of consumers the contemporary market strategy is to advertise various attractive offers for the buyers. Twenty-five per cent of the product is given free to the customers of Glucon D (*Sukhi Grihokon* June 2005). Honey comes free with every packet of *Baidyanath Chyawanprash.* Complan advertises it in three different 'delicious flavours'.

Now in India the control over the misleading advertisements of Drugs and Magic Remedies is exercised by the State Governments under the Drugs and Magic Remedies (Objectionable Advertisements) Act, 1954, under which it is prohibited to take part in publication of misleading advertisements relating to drugs or magic remedies for treatment of certain diseases and disorders. Cosmetics, Devices and Drugs Act 1980,11. (1) says that no person shall label, package, treat, process, sell or distribute or offer for sale or advertise any drug in a manner that is false, misleading, deceptive or likely to create an erroneous impression regarding its character, value, potency, quality, composition, merit or safety. Critiques point out that all these legislations are nothing but attempts by the government to establish its hegemony over a site—the

Figure 9.6 Dusart's Syrup

DUSART'S Syrup of Lactophosphate
of Lime is Nature's Tonic Restorative.

It helps children teething, furnishes
the bone-forming material during the
growing period, developes contracted
narrow chests, weak lungs, feeble
constitutions and crooked legs.

BEWARE OF IMITATIONS !!!

Source: The Statesman, 1905.

body and its manifold processes—that many in power feared had long been forfeit to an underworld of advertisers. Moreover, the practice of using doctors in advertisements has, of late, been abandoned due to the notification in 2002 by Medical Council of India, prohibiting physicians to be part of any medical advertisement.[26]

Last but not the least, is the issue of supply. During late nineteenth to mid-twentieth century, address of the medicine shops and sometimes of the agents and the prices of the medicines are mentioned so that one can purchase it by mail, paying in advance the price and the extra postal charge. This is particularly true for ayurvedic and homeopathic medicines (for example *Amrita Bindu Salsa,* 1905). The need to mention the price, and the provision for mailing, even supply of bottles of medicine on application now give way to online buying facilities, multiple help-lines for consumers and cashless transactions through credit cards. Late twentieth century advertisements of Complan or Glucon D do not contain information regarding the price indicating formation of the capitalistic market network of corporate giants like Glaxo. As a standardized commodity the price labels are pasted on the container, which one can easily access in the market. Hence the need for mentioning price, and the provision for sending it by mail have largely disappeared.

Advertising in a Globalized World

A combination of content analysis and visual method of qualitative research brings out the underlying process of globalization. Globalization arises only when (*a*) activities take place in an arena which is global or nearly so (rather than merely regional, for example); (*b*) activities are organized, planned or coordinated on a global scale; and (*c*) activities involve some degree of reciprocity and interdependency, such that localized activities situated in different parts of the world are shaped by one another. Understood in this sense, the process of globalization is a distinctive feature of the modern world, and it is a process that has intensified significantly in recent decades.[27] In the 1960s and 1970s, the term cultural imperialism describes the assumption, held by many critical theorists, that the global spread of capitalism entails cultural homogenization. The consolidation of colonial power coupled with the process of industrialization creates a new pattern of world trade based on an emerging international division of labour. The claims of import from the West, of recommendations by foreign doctors, or the fact that it is manufactured and sold by multinational companies in an open capitalist global market prove the same. The only way an individual consumer can manifest his or her individuality in this society is to buy a mass-produced commodity. And this is called globalizing consumerism. Even in late nineteenth century there were quite a number of foreign companies who have agents in India to sell their products by dealers. Graefenberg Company of New York had B.S. Madan & Co. and

Nowrojee Bomanjee & Co. as their agents in Bombay. At present among the third world countries, India has been recognized by UNIDO, as one of the top ranking countries in terms of production and distribution of pharmaceutical products. At the time of Indian independence the value of pharmaceuticals output was only ₹ 10 crore bulk drugs into formulations with no production base. Today, the industry has grown in a gigantic way both in terms of output and product diversification. Following a report of 2005 there are over 15,000 drug manufacturing units in the country with a predominance of small-scale units. The relatively large scale units in the organized sector number about 250, including a few FERA companies and some units in public sector. There were 31 FERA companies with direct foreign equity exceeding 40 per cent in March 1978 on the eve of the announcement of drug policy (1978).[28] Since then most of them have diluted their foreign equity to 40 per cent or below. The Organized sector units account for nearly 70 per cent of the industry's total value of production. The national sector has witnessed a spectacular growth over the last two decades. It now accounts for 90 per cent of the production of the industry including that of small-scale sector.[29] Indian advertising industry was already 80 years old. Probably the first agency was the Indian-run B. Dattaram and Co. of Bombay, which was founded in 1905. But the multinationals soon followed like L.A. Stronach and Co. in 1926, Bomas Ltd. in 1928 and J. Walter Thompson in 1929. Since mid-1960s the Indian government tried to limit foreign equity in Indian operations, which was culminated in the Foreign Exchange Restraint Act of 1974, which virtually forced coco-cola to depart in 1977. The agencies, which stayed on during this period generally did so in 'Indianized' versions; JWT, for instance, became Hindustan Thompson Associates. In post-FERA period and particularly since 1991 there were many joint-ventures with multinational agency network.[30]

We can also locate the process of cultural globalization. For Mazzarella advertising business is a particularly compelling point of mediation between the local and the global, between culture and capital. The rise of mass consumerism in India in the 1980s as an explicit challenge to the developmentalist dispensation of the post-Independence years, the articulation of a concomitant social ontology around the 'commodity image', the crises of value brought on by the decisive opening of Indian consumer markets to foreign brands after 1991, and the associated re-tooling of Indian marketing professionals as cultural consultants are the important dimensions of it.[31] Even the expression of instrumental rationality in the language of persuasion of the advertisements, for example asking people to verify its worth by checking their body weight before and after the consumption signifies the impact of Western modernity. For example, the advertiser claims that consumption of two phials of Water of Life[32] within a month will produce at least five pounds of pure new blood and vigour of youth, a fact, which the advertiser claimed to be proved by weighing the body weight of the consumer.

Modernist preoccupation with self, identity and body in public space appears to be the major premise of the formulation of these advertisements. The advertisers try to entice their clients in the name of health, strength, energy, vigour and youth. Thus medical advertising laid the self completely open to commercial assault. It erodes the boundaries of the self by opening it up to various kinds of therapeutic intervention. It fragments the self by reducing selfhood to a series of acts of consumption and it tells consumers that the only way they can sustain a secure sense of selfhood is to consume more and more commodities. Thus body has become a field for advertised commodities. It appears that body's needs can best be met by consuming commodities. Advertisers simply capitalize words like health, beauty and strength—a strategy quite popular with the customers. Advertisements often elide distinctions between 'healthiness' and 'attractiveness'. Thus, for example the recent advertisement of Horlicks Lite mentioning its composition as 'zero added sugar, zero cholesterol and plenty of fibre', portrays the product as desirable both because it is 'good for you' in terms of promoting health and because it contributes to a slim body shape. In a full page advertisement in *Desh* (2 October 2006) a popular magazine in Bengal, we see nine boxes— four boxes contain images of an adult man with an athletic figure practising different free hand exercises, in the other three boxes a very slim woman does the same. In another box there is a text message—'Take a small step first' and in the last box there is the image of a bottle of Horlicks Lite. This ad implicitly advices the adult consumers to better have the health drink Horlicks Lite regularly, instead of taking plunge into the tough regime of daily exercise to maintain ones health as well as physique in good shape.

As this suggests, while health discourses are directed primarily at the 'inner body' in their emphasis on function and disease prevention, consumer culture discourses are directed at the 'outer body' in terms of its appearance.[33] Both public health media campaigns and commercial advertising campaigns address the same ideal of the body: as conforming to current global notions of attractiveness as youthful, vital and healthy.[34] These discourses are directed at the notion of the individual who is keen to engage in activities to care for, work upon, and improve the self and the body as well as indulging his/herself. As Featherstone has argued: 'Within this logic, fitness and slimness become associated not only with energy, drive and vitality but worthiness as a person; likewise the body beautiful comes to be taken as a sign of prudence and prescience in health matters.'[35]. The suggestion is that the pleasures of consumption are heightened by improved health and physical capacity for hedonism. In contemporary Western societies, therefore, notions of the ideal body conflate health, beauty, youth and normality. Health tends to be culturally linked to beauty, erotic attraction and truth as well as morality.

Preoccupation with self generates the desire to retain youth. The advertisers have intelligently manipulated this. Advertisements of Dr James Tonic Pills[36] *Mahashakti tonic* (*Bishudha Siddhanta Panjika*,1981), *Baidyanath Kesari Kalp Royal Chyawanprash* (2006)—all, though in different ways, guarantee youth and health even at 40, if not more. As early as in 1932 we come across an advertisement in *The Times of India*, of one Hakim Haji Nawab Ali Khan, who guarantees youthful appearance of his patients. To draw the attention of readers, his success in Europe and America is written in bold. To make his appeal even stronger the readers are informed of the fact that he had been awarded by Ottoman government of Turkey and late Caliph of Constantinopole (Figure 9.7).

Similar assurance of retaining youth, and physical strength for males is found in the advertisement of *Mahashakti Tonic* (*Bishudha Siddhanta Panjika*, 1981). Here a visual of a muscular male body is shown to portray the positive effect of having it regularly. In the same line, fitness and energy are projected as the key contributions of 'the only complete health drink'—the Complan.[37]

Figure 9.7 Hakim Haji Nawab Ali Khan

SUCCESSFUL IN EUROPE & AMERICA

Expert in Medicines for the treatment of dangerous diseases Has successfully relieved the sufferings of numerous patients The great Hakim Haji Nawab Ali Khan is well-known not only in Asia but also in Europe and America A trial will convince anybody of his great ability and healing powers He has been awarded the Majidiya Medal and several other certificates by the Ottoman Government of Turkey and the late Caliph of Constantinople

No Woman or Man of any station in life can afford to "LOOK OLD"

I GUARANTEE to make you RETAIN A YOUTHFUL APPEARANCE until an advanced Age and to help you to Restore and Improve Your Own Looks

Consulting hours :--7 A M to 12 Noon
4 P M to 9 P.M.

HAKIM HAJI NAWAB ALI KHAN

Cutch Castle Building, Sandhurst Bridge, Chowpatty, BOMBAY 4

6 AUGUST 1932

Source: *The Times of India*, 6 August 1932.

Related is the issue of nervous exhaustion or the drain of energy. Though the problem is not new but frequent reference to the association between modernity and escalation of work pressure on men is a typical feature of the contemporary way of life. Actually work or economic pursuit becomes the central social activity only in a capitalist social formation. In India change in this direction starts with the colonial advent and the pace of change has got a major boost in the 1990s as a result of adoption of the policy of economic liberalization by the government of India. The caption of the advertisement of Glaxose D[38] asks: 'Exhausted after a hard day's work?' The product is presented as an instant solution. More or less the same language has been used in the recent advertisement of Glucon D.[39] The possible moments of its use are specified like 'after a long sweaty day', or 'from football grounds to office, school to gym, you can take it anywhere to combat tiredness', etc. But as early as in 1906 in the advertisement of an imported medicine called Phosferine,[40] ceaseless activity is cited as a modern evil. It points out how in modern times both men and women suffer from excessive fatigue as a tremendous amount of nervous energy is spent in business as well as in the pursuit of pleasure.

For Giddens,[41] in late modernity self-identity becomes a reflexive project. Body and sexual identity are two central dimensions of self-identity. Modern individuals, under the condition of commodity capitalism, can choose a lifestyle to work upon body and to 'play' with sexuality. Advertising accentuates the process. But the choice of individual is not absolute, as he has to live under the standardizing effect of capitalistic market. As body and sexuality are matters of health, hence contemporary medical advertisements particularly that of various health drinks and tonics meant for vitality, physical strength, energy and sexual vigour manifest this typical trait of modern man.

Advertisement as a Discourse

The traditional materialist and moralistic interpretation of advertisement has been preoccupied with the notion of 'true' versus 'false' needs. For them advertisements divert people from a healthy or honest relationship with objects by encouraging unnecessary and harmful desires. The post-war paranoiac discourses on advertising projects it as a sinister centralized agency of mass manipulation. Structuralists, on the other hand, perceive goods and their representations as signifiers. As such they have no inherent meaning; rather, it is their positions within shifting structures of signification that render them meaningful in particular settings. The social constructionist perspective perceives advertisement and health care as socio-cultural products. An advertisement, taken as a commodity, is never finished. Its elements are sourced from an existing repertoire of resonances and meanings, and after being 'produced', it continues to be made and remade throughout its public career. The commodity image, projected in the advertisement, must be understood in this flow of practice.[42] Advertising makes sense because culture makes sense. Like other 'strong' constructionist approaches, post-structuralism draws particular attention to the role played by language in constituting notions of reality, including the advertising message. The concept of discourse brings together language, visual representation, practice, knowledge and power relations, incorporating the understanding that language and visual imagery are implicated with power relations and the construction of knowledge and practices about phenomena. The term discourse is commonly used in poststructuralist writings to denote the patterns of ways of thinking, making sense of, talking or writing about, and visually portraying phenomena such as human body, medical practices, etc. Cultural analysts adopting a poststructuralist perspective argue that there is an inescapable relationship between power, knowledge, discourse and what counts as 'truth'. The discourses that tend to dominate over others are those emerging from powerful individuals or social groups, helping to further their interests in shaping the ways in which phenomena are represented.[43] A great deal of corporate money and effort is spent on trying to establish authoritative—and legally protected—interpretations. The discourse of science in medical advertisements relies, in part, on the assumption that it is politically and culturally neutral, unlike some other knowledge, such as that articulated in homeopathic or *kabiraji* tonics and *salsa*s.

While looking into the way these advertisements work on individuals we find that the process of reception, interpretation and appropriation of media messages are much more complicated than Schiller's thesis of cultural imperialism. The process of reception was not a one-way transmission of sense but rather a creative encounter between a complex and structured symbolic form and the individuals, who belong to particular groups and who bring certain resources and assumptions to bear on the activity of interpretation. The appropriation of media products is always a localized phenomenon. And messages are often transformed in the process of appropriation as individuals adapt them to the practical contexts of everyday life. Hence process of appropriation remains inherently contextual and hermeneutic. Images of other ways of life constitute a resource for individuals to think critically about their own lives and life conditions. Thus this localized appropriation of globalized media products is also a source of tension and potential conflict. It is a source of tension partly because media products can convey images and messages, which clash with, or do not entirely support, the values associated with a traditional way of life.[44] Thus globalization is actually heightening rather than effacing the importance of locality and local identity. Thus local and global are not opposites, rather, they are mutually constitutive imaginary moments in every attempt to make sense of the world, whether for disciplinary, commercial, scholarly or radical purposes. Sociologist Roland Robertson speaks of 'the twofold process of the particularization of the universal and the universalization of the particular'.[45] Anthropologist Arjun Appadurai comments that 'the central problem in today's global interactions is the tension between cultural homogenization and cultural heterogenization'.[46] Global is constructed locally just as much as the local is constructed globally. Some sort of 'third-worldism' evident in the advertisements of ethnic medicines, herbal products or *ayurvedic salsa*s can be taken as a critique of the typical Western science-based health products. These may also signify a revivalist tendency to get back to ones root as these boast of the age-old indigenous composition. Actually dominant discourses are constantly subject to challenge. Hence advertisements of tonics based on allopathic medical knowledge of primarily Western origin has often been contested by counter advertisement-discourses expressed by proponents of alternative therapies, like the *homeopathic* or *ayurvedic* doctors or *kabiraj*s, who use the discourse of beneficent nature to oppose what they see as being the objectifying nature of scientific approaches in medicine.

All the economic decisions including that on marketing and advertisements are definitely subject to political feasibility. In the late 1990s, when the BJP government came to power at the centre, a new discourse of *swadeshi*[47] gained prominence. Here the influence of Swadeshi Jagaran Manch (SJM, or Forum for Swadeshi Awakening), which was part of a diverse coalition of BJP-affiliated groups collectively known as the Sangh Parivar, was evident. For them, Indian advocates of economic deregulation and globalized consumerism were simply victims of a postcolonial inferiority complex and therefore unable to recognize the superior value of their own heritage.[48] As a critique of this position the economic pragmatists tend to suggest that the *swadeshi* position is both unrealistic and, in the words of Cornell University economist Kaushik Basu, 'based on a bloated sense of national pride'.[49] Once in power, the mainstream of BJP had to take a middle path. The finance minister Yashwant Sinha, speaking to Indian-American and American business leaders in New York stated '*Swadeshi* is pro-globalization because it's pro-Indian without being anti-foreign'.[50] Thus cultural integrity and globalization seem compatible and even mutually reinforcing.

It must be recognized that biomedicine is a huge industry. Potential profit and eager market drive drug development. But unfortunately, the global diffusion of biomedicine is displacing local knowledge of remedies that could have enormously enhanced the pharmaceutical armamentarium.[51] The local does not easily give in. As early as in 1895 even in English language daily like *The Times of India* one can find advertisements of *Ashwagandha Rasayana* or *Binayaka Rasayana*—all, as the advertisers claim, are *ayurvedic* or '*Hindoo* medicines'. Interestingly as these local products meant for local market embrace a typically 'modern' form of advertisement in print media, the basic format and components of the text message become virtually the same as advertisements of Western allopathic medicines. The only difference is an emphasis on the Indian origin of the herbs used.

Advertising is one set of practices, among others, which contributes to the production of particular conceptualizations of the world and our place(s) in it. Like other social and cultural practices, therefore, it contributes to the production of subjects. It does not merely address already formed subjects and seek acceptance of its 'messages'. It actively contributes to their formation. At the same time, advertisers do not have unformed subjects to work on; they have to take account of what has already gone into the subjects they address and position.[52] The construction of subject position by the advertisements reflects the existing social divide, for example the hegemony of the British during the colonial times or the patriarchal bias throughout the period. An analysis of construction of subject position by the advertisements reveals that all advertisements are not meant for universal appeal. British appearance and dress of a boy and a girl in the advertisement of Dusart's Syrup (see Figure 9.6) indicate a preference for European clientele. Phosferine advertisement (see Figure 9.5) by (*a*) a picture of a British aristocratic lady acknowledging the contribution of the medicine, (*b*) a testimonial from one countess, and (*c*) the text narrating its regular use by European royal families, positions the subject as upper class Western elite. The exclusion of Indians reinforces the absolute social demarcation between the colonizers and the colonized. Typical dhoti-clad image of a male in the advertisement of

Manna's Cooperative Salsa (late nineteenth century) indicates a Bengali male subject position. In general the advertisements reveal a patriarchal bias. From the advertisement of Bovril (see Figure 9.2) to Glaxose D (*The Times of India*, 19 October 1975)—it is the same male image that predominates. Even when both genders are present the males are given an active role like in the advertisement of Dusart Syrup (see Figure 9.6), it is the elder boy, who holds the younger girl in one hand and the bottle of the syrup in the other. Girl's passive subject position is apparent from the fact that she requires support and, though present in the advertising space, has nothing to do. In the advertisement of Philco's Compound (*JogiSakha*, 1959, fifth year, 12th issue), the picture of a very weak lady with food served in front of her, does not only reflect a loss of appetite on her part but her helplessness and incapacity are explicit from her sitting posture—one leg stretched, and face—supported by palm. In the Complan advertisement we find two young housewives—one cooking with a smiling face, another tensed, and as indicated by written text, having a tough time managing her difficult-to-feed son. The liberated, employed women, capable of decision-making is still absent (*The Times of India* 3 October 1975). Only in the recent Glucon D advertisement (*Sukhi Grihokon,* June 2005), we find a young couple on an equal footing, along with their son, each having glassful of the drink happily. It corresponds to the contemporary projection of small nuclear family as the socially desirable unit for consumption.

In the analysis of advertising texts, spatial metaphors, that is positioning the product as well as the audience, are crucial. Here one may notice interpenetration between the physical and the social and cultural space. Since social and cultural space is not unambiguously unified and coherent, but complex, fluid, and to varying degrees contradictory, subjects are formed as complex and often contradictory unities. Positioning is always within a system, that is in relation to other objects in space. This space is not given but constructed and read on the basis of viewers' experience as a social being. How far the target audience of an advertisement understands the message depends on identifiability of various positions and relations between these positions. To position subjects or products as 'upper class' is to say where they are located in the system of social relations. To position the three subjects as family (for example, advertisement of Glucon D) or as siblings (Dusart's Syrup) is to locate the relationship between them within the range of human relationships. To position them as placing a value on good health is to place their attitude to health at a determinate point in the range, which extends from total disregard to chronic anxiety. In case of Phospherine advertisement, where verbal text simply locates its users as upper class, the positioning is determined by the literal meaning of the words used, which depends in turn on the position of those words in the language. Often it hints, suggests, or implies that someone is upper class. For example, in case of the same Phospherine advertisement, the beautifully maintained hands of the lady, which show no signs of having done manual work, her flowing gown, totally inappropriate in a work situation, frilled umbrella, again a proof of her preoccupation with fashion and style—all definitely suggest a life of luxury and comfort. In this case, the positioning of the person depends not only on the literal meaning of the words used, but also on the reader's knowledge of social structure and the kinds of hands, clothing, lifestyle, and so on, that go with being 'upper class'. Thus both visual items as well as words in a language are signifiers, bearers of signification, meaning. What they signify on a particular occasion is determined partly by their juxtaposition with other visual and verbal signifiers in the text, and partly by their position in relation to other signifiers in the system to which they belong.[53] Each item carries a range of significations. The specific meaning of it in a particular advertisement can only be understood if one can think of its possible substitutes (among the same category of objects), their meanings, and reasons for their exclusion from the advertising space and utilization of this particular item in the advertisement. The meaning of the advertisement may be varied either by replacing one or more of the signifying elements by other element from the same range, that is the paradigmatic dimension, or by rearranging the elements in the picture, that is syntagmatic dimension. Signifying elements are said to belong to paradigm(s) consisting of the elements, which could be substituted for them and with which they are contrasted, and the structures into which they may be slotted are called syntagms.[54] In the advertisement of Horlicks Lite adult male and female figures in different postures are used. The absence of children's images, so typical of Horlicks advertisement confirms an attempt to expand its market by incorporating the adult population as their new target consumers. The placing of each figure in a single box indicates the independence of adulthood and celebrates its capacity to make choice. And here the choice is right in front of them—the Horlicks Lite. The fact that both males and females are given similar private space also reveals the gender-neutral subject position of its viewer/reader.

Not only the characters or subjects, there are voices too. The only voices to speak are the voices of the subjects, as signified often by the quotation marks. In occupying the subject positions, in being drawn into the advertisement, we, the audience, address ourselves. The implication is that we do not need to be told what to do.[55] For example, the boy, in the advertisement of *Baidyanath Chyawanprash Special* is posing with a confident smile holding on one hand a huge Cup for, as text message says, being 'First in Sports and Exams'. In the days of cut-throat competition, every little boy who sees/reads this advertisement readily identifies with this image and wants to assert, just like the ad-boy—'I am the real champ!' Today's parents are even more likely to visualize their ward's image in the same. And if this really happens, the advertisers' aim has been fully accomplished. Thus advertisements actually intervene in the daily lives of consumers, shape their minds, alter their consciousness, and ultimately, circumscribe their most guarded lives in such a way that the most private cells of life becomes a repository, and finally a bastion, of commodity culture.[56] Advertised spectacle then can also be perceived as a coercive agent for invading and structuring human consciousness.

Identification with the advertising message on the part of target consumer is possible only through identification with the need projected in the advertisements. Advertising also creates new needs in the sense that it grafts new needs onto the existing ones. The aim of advertisements is to locate quite legitimate needs like the care of the body and redefine and constantly expand its boundary. The advertising message is by definition 'not disinterested'. It is in the advertiser's interest to lead you to conclude 'I want that'. The information the advertisement provides will be tailored to that end.[57] There is definitely a need for low cholesterol butter, which has been duly served by Prutina Peanut Butter. But through advertisements it creates the need for butter to be creamy, crunchy or chocolate, which the customers can choose from this 'cent percent vegetarian butter'.[58] But mere reference to need does not create the appeal an advertisement has for the people. Hence comes the issue of aesthetics.

Following Lukacs, attempt might be made to locate the commodified products on the threshold of culture and commerce. Analytical divisions of the structure of advertisements, between a rational core, that is its persuasive/informative appeal to consumers' calculation as a rational agent, and a decorative periphery, which gives pleasure to the consumer, that is when advertisement becomes a piece of art[59] is useful for the purpose. When you are about to buy a tonic or health drink its advertisements duly exhibit a much larger rational core (that is need to be fulfilled) compared to advertisements of perfume, for example. But above all, advertisements must please us, whether by amusing us, by being visually attractive or striking, or by presenting us with an occasion for fantasy. This is evident in the choice of beautiful faces and figures in the advertisements. Advertisers very frequently rely on the already acclaimed beauties, for example the well-established models or the film stars. Furthermore, bright and colourful images, stylized write-ups, intelligent use of words add its decorative content. In the face of new technologies, which allow advertisements to be avoided when not wanted, advertisements are bound to move in the direction of art. Richards calls it a spectacle, that is a set of aesthetic procedures for magnifying the importance of the most basic element of exchange, the commodity. For him this commodity spectacle has now become the dominant form of capitalist representation.[60]

Conclusion

Someone once defined advertising as 'the cave art of the 20th century'. It is possible to believe that the hunter in the stone age and the corporate in the information age, both have a common need—to publicize their core mission and achievements. This chapter shows how even health food and drinks, tonics and *ayurvedic salsas* have become consumer products for the purpose of mass consumption. In the world of advertising these definitely have acquired the quality of a fetish object. Sentiments of well-being and urge for long healthy life for self and dear ones on one hand, and anxiety, pain and insecurity vis-à-vis dreaded diseases and its probable sources on the other, are intelligently manipulated to expand the medical market to the poorest of the poor. To understand the cultural significance of advertisements this work acknowledges the journey of medical advertisements at different moments in the circuit of culture: moment of representation (verbal, written as well as visual) and moment of consumption. In an attempt to delimit this research I have mostly excluded an analysis of consumers' agency, though acknowledging their capacity to redefine the message. The focus is rather on how advertisement works on them.

Indian drug industry plays a determining role in the historical journey of medical advertisements over time. Before Independence, colonial India had to depend on imported basic drugs to produce medicines. An association between import from West and claim to purity of medicines can be located in the advertisements of colonial times. But there are always some advertisements, which boast of the indigenous composition of its products. And the numbers of such advertisements are growing rapidly in contemporary days. After Independence, to modernize the pharmaceuticals industry, government invites several multinational companies to manufacture basic drugs in India. Many Indian drug companies are now becoming multinationals. In tune with this, the reference to import has been replaced by a reference to the manufacturing company. Institutionalization of medical representatives has significant impact on the nature and the number of advertisements. Now it is the corporate advertisement of big pharmaceutical concern that dominates.

While analysing the meanings of advertisements and its changes over time, it is found that during colonial times advertisements of various health products primarily projected imperial images and themes. Power of the West is still felt in many advertisements as tonics are frequently prescribed by physicians, medical scientists or even common people of the first world countries basically to assure us about its quality. But more powerful impact of Western modernity has been located while deconstructing the advertising messages, which celebrate the Western values of instrumental rationality, individuality, and the centrality of body and appearance. Contrary to the traditional Indian perception of body as private, inhibited and potentially polluted zone, body has become a site for seeking pleasure and an asset to be cared, displayed and appreciated by others. Taking cues from Rolland Barthes'(1957) understanding of mythology, I consider these advertisements as important ingredients of the myth of modernity. Thus I find advertisements historical as well as cultural constructs. It gives historical intention a natural justification. Hence consumers take it as natural, and are not always alert about the underlying interest of advertisers. Its analysis then is certainly a political act.

Notes and References

1. D.T.A. Lindsay and G.C. Bamber, *Soap-making, Past and Present 1876–1976* (Nottingham: Gerard Brothers Ltd., 1965).
2. Thomas Richards, *The Commodity Culture of Victorian England: Advertising and Spectacle, 1851–1914* (London, New York: Verso, 1990).
3. Ibid., p. 169.
4. Ibid., p. 184.
5. Bill Bonney and Helen Wilson, 'Advertising and the Manufacture of Difference', in *The Media Reader,* eds M. Alvarado and J.O. Thompson (London: B.F.I. Publishing, 1990), p. 181.
6. Ibid, p. 182.
7. N.K. Denzin, and Y.S. Lincoln, 'Introduction: Entering the Field of Qualitative Research', in *Handbook of Qualitative Research*, eds N.K. Denzin and Y.S. Lincoln (Thousand Oaks, CA: Sage Publications, 1994), pp. 1–17.
8. E. Chaplin, *Sociology and Visual Representation* (London: Routledge, 1994), p. 16.
9. Advertising Age, quoted in Mohan Manendra, *Advertising Management: Concepts and Cases* (New Delhi: Tata McGraw-Hill Publishing Company Ltd., 1990), p. 2.
10. William Mazzarella, *Shoveling Smoke: Advertising and Globalization in Contemporary India* (Durham: Duke University Press, 2003), p. 4.
11. James Curran, 'The Impact of Advertising on the British Mass Media', in *Media Culture and Society: A Critical Reader,* eds Richard Collins, James Curran, Nicholas Garnham, Paddy Scannell, Philip Schlesinger and Colin Sparks (London, Beverly Hills, Newbury Park, New Delhi: Sage Publications, 1986), p. 310.
12. Ibid., p. 332.
13. Joseph Fernandez,*Corporate Communications: A 21st Century Primer.* (New Delhi, Thousand Oaks, London: Response Books [Sage], 2004), p. 100.

14. John B. Thompson, *Ideology and Modern Culture* (Cambridge: Polity Press, 1990), pp. 210.

15. Ivan Illich, *Medical Nemesis: The Exploration of Health* (New York: Pantheon, 1976), p. 76–88.

16. Richards, *The Commodity Culture of Victorian England*, p. 187.

17. *The Telegraph Magazine*, 26 February 2006.

18. Fernandez, *Corporate Communications*, p. 117.

19. *Suraballi Kashay, Grihastha Mangal*, 11th issue 29 February 1929.

20. *The Statesman*, 26 December 2005.

21. Advertisement in *The Times of India*, 28 September 1989, in Dileep Padgaonkar (ed.), *Brand New Advertising through the Times of India*, compiled and produced by Manjuliha Srivastava, Times of India Publication, 1989: 189.

22. Advertisement in *The Statesman*, April 1905 in Ranabir Raychoudhury (compiled). *Early Calcutta Advertisements 1875–1925: A Selection from the Statesman* (Bombay: Nachiketa Publications Limited, 1992), p. 473.

23. Interview with David Wheeler, Director of the Institute of Practitioners in Advertising, on 11 September 1980, quoted in James Curran, The Impact of Advertising on the British Mass Media', in Richard Collins, James Curran, Nicholas Garnham, Paddly Scannell, Philip Schlesinger and Colin Sparks (eds), *Media, Culture and Society: A Critical Readers* (London, Beverly Hills, New Delhi: Sage Publication, 1986), p. 318.

24. *Telegraph Magazine*, 26 February 2006.

25. *Times of India*, 6 January 1928.

26. Soliciting of patients directly or indirectly, by a physician, by a group of physicians or by institutions or organizations is unethical. A physician shall not make use of him/her (or his/her name) as subject of any form or manner of advertising or publicity through any mode either alone or in conjunction with others which is of such a character as to invite attention to him or to his professional position, skill, qualification, achievements, attainments, specialities, appointments, associations, affiliations or honours and/or of such character as would ordinarily result in his self aggrandizement. A physician shall not give to any person, whether for compensation or otherwise, any approval, recommendation, endorsement, certificate, report or statement with respect of any drug, medicine, nostrum remedy, surgical, or therapeutic article, apparatus or appliance or any commercial product or article with respect of any property, quality or use thereof or any test, demonstration or trial thereof, for use in connection with his name, signature, or photograph in any form or manner of advertising through any mode nor shall he boast of cases, operations, cures or remedies or permit the publication of report thereof through any mode (*MCI, Indian Medical Council [Professional Conduct, Etiquette and Ethics] Regulations, 2002. Gazette of India dated 06.04.02, part III, section IV*).

27. John O. Thompson, 'Advertising's Rationality', in *The Media Reader*, eds M. Alvarado and J.O. Thompson (London: B.F.I. Publishing, 1990), pp. 208–212.

28. The FERA companies are Alkali & Chemicals Ltd., (amalgamated with ICI), Bayer India Ltd., Johnson & Johnson Ltd., Roche products Ltd., Sandoz India Ltd., Wyeth Laboratories. The public sector units are Indian Drugs and Pharmaceuticals Ltd. (IDPL), the revival of which is under consideration of the Department of Chemicals and Petrochemicals (Ministry of Chemicals and Fertilizers, Government of India), Bengal Chemical and Pharmaceuticals Ltd. (BCPL), Hindustan Antibiotics Ltd., Bengal Immunity Ltd. (BIL) and Smithe Stainstreet Pharmaceuticals Ltd (SSPL).

29. Report of the fifth International Exhibition and Conference for the Pharmaceutical Industry, 1–3 October 2005.

30. Mazzarella, *Shoveling Smoke,* pp. 12–13.

31. Ibid., p. 3.

32. *Times of India,* 28 September 1899, Padgaonkar, *Brand New Advertising through the Times of India.*

33. M. Featherstone, 'The Body in Consumer Culture', *The Body: Social Process and Cultural Theory,* eds M. Featherstone and B. Turner (London: Sage Publications, 1991), p. 171.

34. Deborah Lupton, 'The Social Construction of Medicine and the Body', in *The Handbook of Social Studies in Health and Medicine*, eds Gary L. Albrecht, Ray Fitzpatrick and Susan C. Scrimshaw (London, Thousand Oaks, and New Delhi: Sage Publications, 2003), p. 60.

35. Featherstone, 'The Body in Consumer Culture', p. 183.

36. *Statesman,* April 1905, Raychoudhury, *Early Calcutta Advertisements.*

37. *Times of India,* 3 October 1975, Padgaonkar, *Brand New Advertising through the Times of India* 38. Ibid.

39. *Sukhi Grihakon* (Bengali monthly magazine), June 2005, Bartaman Private Ltd. Kolkata.

40. *Times of India,* 23 April 1906, Padgaonkar, *Brand New Advertising through the Times of India.*

41. Giddens, *Modernity and Self-Identity: Self and Society in the Late Modern Age* (Cambridge: Polity Press, 1991).

42. Mazzarella, *Shoveling Smoke*, p. 21.

43. Lupton, 'The Social Construction of Medicine and the Body'.

44. Thompson, 'Advertising's Rationality', pp. 176–77.

45. Frederic Jameson and Masao Miyoshi, *The Cultures of Globalization* (Durham and London: Duke University Press, 1998), p. xi.

46. Arjun Appadurai, *Modernity at Large: Cultural Dimensions of Globalization* (Minneapolis, London: University of Minnesota, 1996), p. 32.

47. Swadeshi, which literally means 'of one's own country' is a term used by Mahatma Gandhi since 1919 for a series of nationwide nationalist agitations against British industry, most notably the mill-woven cloth of Manchester. The term re-entered national political discourse in 1997–98 with the political rise of BJP, who, under the influence of Sangh Parivar raised the issue of desirability of consumerist globalization (Mazzarella, *Shoveling Smoke*).

48. Ibid., p. 8.

49. Kaushik Basu, 'Globalization and Swadeshi', *India Today*, 29 March 1999.

50. Narayan Keshavan, 'Swedish Goes Global', *Outlook*, 27 April 1998.

51. Zielinski Gutierrez and Kendall, 'The Globalization of Health and Disease: The Health Transition and Global Change', in *Handbook of Social Studies in Health and Medicine*, eds Gary L. Albrecht, Ray Fitzpatrick and Susan Scrimshaw (London, Thousand Oaks, Delhi: Sage Publications, 2003), p. 95.

52. Bonney and Wilson, 'Advertising and the Manufacture of Difference', p. 191.

53. Ibid., p. 188.

54. Ibid., p. 189.

55. Ibid., p. 187.

56. Richards, *The Commodity Culture of Victorian England*, p. 204.

57. Thompson, 'Advertising's Rationality', p. 209.

58. *Sunday Statesman*, 8 August 2000.

59. Thompson, 'Advertising's Rationality', p. 208.

60. Richards, *The Commodity Culture of Victorian England*, p. 195.

Chapter 10

Just for Fun

Changing Notions of Social Forms of Leisure

Nilanjana Gupta and Devlina Gopalan

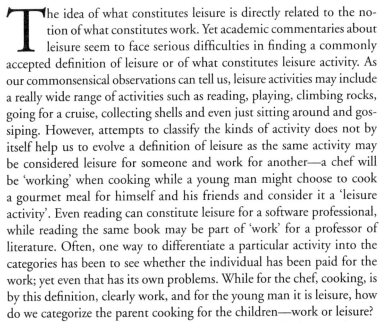

The idea of what constitutes leisure is directly related to the notion of what constitutes work. Yet academic commentaries about leisure seem to face serious difficulties in finding a commonly accepted definition of leisure or of what constitutes leisure activity. As our commonsensical observations can tell us, leisure activities may include a really wide range of activities such as reading, playing, climbing rocks, going for a cruise, collecting shells and even just sitting around and gossiping. However, attempts to classify the kinds of activity does not by itself help us to evolve a definition of leisure as the same activity may be considered leisure for someone and work for another—a chef will be 'working' when cooking while a young man might choose to cook a gourmet meal for himself and his friends and consider it a 'leisure activity'. Even reading can constitute leisure for a software professional, while reading the same book may be part of 'work' for a professor of literature. Often, one way to differentiate a particular activity into the categories has been to see whether the individual has been paid for the work; yet even that has its own problems. While for the chef, cooking, is by this definition, clearly work, and for the young man it is leisure, how do we categorize the parent cooking for the children—work or leisure?

Considering the fact of payment does not by itself help us to demarcate between leisure and work. Some theorists have suggested that 'use' is a better way of distinguishing between the two. In the example above, the father cooking for his children is clearly 'useful', and though unpaid would probably not seem like leisure to him. However, even this has its limitations if we consider voluntary activities that individuals engage in by choice, such as running literacy camps or caring for stray dogs.

While such activities may be non-paid and seem to be of no immediate usefulness, they may give immense pleasure to the one 'hard at work'. What then may be said is that leisure is whatever activity the individual chooses to do as opposed to the activity that one has to do in order to earn a wage or run the family or for some other socially determined goal—such as attend a dinner party to celebrate a niece's engagement. In fact, leisure itself is often easier to define in terms of what it is not, rather than what it is.

However, as any historical survey of leisure practices shows, the notion of what constitutes leisure is also determined in different ways at particular historical moments. In contemporary times, as in the globalized work arena the structure and nature of work itself is being redefined, so the ideas of what constitutes leisure begin to change. Studies have traced the changes that took place when society moved from a rural economy to an industrial economy—cycles of work changed from seasonal to weekly and hourly, the nature of activities changed, and so on.[1] Theodore Adorno and Max Horkheimer's canonical study *Dialectic of Enlightenment*[2] characterizes leisure as an 'escape from the mechanised work process' but raises a new dimension when it argues that 'what happens at work, in the factory, or in the office can only be escaped from by approximation to it in one's leisure time.' The impact of literacy on leisure activities has also been studied with particular emphasis on the working class habits.[3] Activities that constitute leisure are not defined exclusively by changes in the constitution of work; Adorno and Horkheimer emphasize the role of technological inventions, such the cinema, the television or the movie camera and work practices, such as the division of labour as equally important.

Other factors that define or determine the constitution of leisure are the social, cultural and ideological shifts in social organization. Rudy Koshar reminds us in the Introduction to the volume *Histories of Leisure*[4] that 'Leisure time was relatively strictly tied to the dominant social hierarchies in earlier historical periods, just as clothing and other objects were'. This chapter will suggest that even this statement, while it draws our attention to the issue of social hierarchies, does not interrogate the fact that the constructions of leisure spaces and the delineations of leisure activities can actually become strategies that define, create, reinforce and determine social hierarchies that exist and act through the existing categories of class and privilege. There is a tendency to view leisure as a 'private' act—an act where neither the state with its regulatory tendencies nor the market with its own logic—can intervene. Because leisure—as opposed to work—is seen as a private act and a private decision, it is often presumed that the ideologies of the state and society are absent from the acts of individuals when they are engaging in acts of leisure.

This chapter will look at constructions of leisure communities and the ideologies implicit in the ways in which a particular aspect of leisure is defined, constructed and participated in by looking at the phenomenon of the social clubs of Kolkata. This discussion looks at the changes that took place during and after the period of British colonization in Kolkata and argues that in contemporary times, changes in patterns of leisure spaces, their organizational structures and the range of activities are taking place that are related to the larger ideological changes due to the historical trajectories of the nationalist movements and the current era of globalization of work, society and leisure.

While work or occupation is usually the most important determinant of an individual's position in social structures, other factors have always been important in creating what can be called the social elite in any society. In *The Poetics and Poetics of Transgression,* Peter Stallybrass and Allan White argue that in certain spaces such as museums, strict codes of behaviour which emphasized decorum and restraint had been enforced as 'part of an overall strategy of expulsion which clear[ed] a space for polite cosmopolitan discourse by constructing popular culture as the "low-Other", the dirty and crude outside'.[5] While their argument is related to the way in which a class imposes its viewpoints on other social classes, this comment sounds equally relevant for understanding the process of creating an exclusive leisure space during the period of colonization in India.

The idea of the club is seen to be a particularly British invention.

Marx considered British working men to be great 'joiners': their support for clubs of all kinds outstripped even that of their mutualist-inclined French counterparts. It was a habit that prompted the French literary brothers Goncourt to remark that the first thing two

Englishmen would do if cast away on a desert island would be to form a club.[6]

However, there are important issues that are raised the moment we try to define the notion of 'club'. For the purposes of this chapter the broad definition that commentators on the club phenomenon agree on can be used: an association created for the purposes of sports or other leisure activities which submits to principles of democratic governance. Analysts who have researched the composition and structures of these clubs have concluded that the kind of clubs that Marx had spoken about—with largely working-class memberships—provided a form of sociability that was an extension of locality-based sociability. Later, with the growth of housing estates and compounds for the middle classes and above, the golf club began to represent a different kind of sociability where 'a small group of industrial and public service managers, with no local background and few social connections in the town, colonized a series of clubs through which they preserved their social separateness; the golf club was the prime example'.[7] Yet this use of social spaces for creating separateness was already prevalent and established in the British colonies. Hill mentions C.L.R. James' book *Beyond the Boundary* which describes the carefully segregated cricketing clubs that existed in the colonial Caribbean. As he mentions, there is very little work on the patterns of leisure during the colonial age.

This chapter will first look at the ideology of the original social clubs created by the British and what may be called the nationalist response to them and then end with a brief discussion of the new generation of clubs. It will argue that choices and decisions about spending leisure time are simultaneously indicators and determinants of larger social and ideological frameworks. Yet because pleasure, leisure and apparently empty space and time have not engaged social commentators as much as work spaces and practices have, there has been relatively little academic enquiry into the indirect ways in which the social hierarchies that are necessary for the existence and upholding of social, political and ideological structures function. 'The history of leisure culture is clearly also the history of political culture, indeed of citizenship in the broad sense of social participation.'[8] Kolkata as the centre of the British Empire in India is an apt place to see how the social clubs have functioned during the colonial period and then later as a very different set of work and living conditions, and indeed political citizenship are evolving in contemporary moments of time. These leisure practices both construct and enact several dimensions of social history.

The clubs that have been surveyed for this study are some of the social clubs that were established during the British period in India as well as some of the more recent clubs which have been established in the postglobal period. Clubs that were primarily formed by the rationale of linguistic or religious groupings, such as the Malayalee Club, Maharashtra Club or Parsi Club, have not been included under this study, as those organizations have objectives other than organizing leisure. Also organizations, including locality-based clubs, which have social service as their main objective have not been considered in this discussion. This discussion focuses only on those clubs which have general forms of relaxation, leisure and recreation as their only objectives—rather than a tennis club or a club for stamp-collectors, for example, which have a specific shared passion—and have strict norms regarding the enforcement of certain notions of exclusivity, in other words clubs which one cannot enter merely because one would like to do so.

The phenomenon of clubs was an important part of the Raj society. Several novels located in those times depict the centrality of the club in the social and even political life of the British in India. Paul Scott's *The Jewel in the Crown*,[9] for example, describes club culture very vividly even though the novel is set in the imaginary Mayapore in West Bengal. There is an entire chapter entitled 'An Evening at the Club'. The scene describes an Englishwoman sitting with another lady in the 'lounge-bar of the Gymkhana Club, turning over the pages of a none-too-recent issue of the *Sunday Times* Magazine—"today's fashionable equivalent of the *Tatler* or the *Onlooker*..."'.[10] Apart from this Englishwoman and her companion there are several other English men and women in the lounge. 'But Lady Chatterjee is the only Indian...'.[11] Terry Grigson, an English gentleman and club member has invited Lady Chatterjee for a drink. While he goes to change his tennis clothes, he leaves her and a companion at his wife's table. Mrs Grigson ignores the guests, is hostile and rude. Lady Chatterjee ponders on how much the club has changed since 1942 (this scene is set in 1964) as she notices her surroundings minutely:

> The servants still wear white turbans beribboned to match the wide sashes that nip in the waists of their knee-length white coats. White trousers flap baggily above their bare brown feet, and stir old memories of padding docile service. Perhaps in the décor of this particular lounge-bar, change of an ephemeral nature may be seen: the formica-topped counter instead of the old wood that needed polishing, glazed chintz curtains decorated with spiral abstractions instead of cabbage roses, and chairs whose severe Scandinavian welcome brings the old cushioned-wicker comfort gratefully back to the mind.[12]

The Englishmen didn't sit with the women but preferred to talk with Indian men in the other room where drinks were served. They seemed to display an 'old-maidish decorum and physical fastidiousness'.[13] The chapter continues with a detailed description of the Tudor fireplace, the dining room and smoking room, dances, seats under trees, tennis and a floodlit pool. Mr Srinivasan was the first Indian Secretary of the Gymkhana Club. The membership records maintained during 1939–45 show only one or two Indians. The Indians who were the 'King's officers' were entitled to join the club but they made excuses not to remain too long or cause embarrassment. Finally a rule was passed which enabled these men to have Special Membership or Privileged Temporary Membership. They paid a subscription and ultimately only Anglo Indian guests were forbidden as unsuitable. In 1939 the Deputy Commissioner of Mayapore caused a social solecism by inviting three Indians to the club. One of the invitees humourously recalls that it was '...the first time any Indian civilian had entered. Also it was the last because Mr White was stopped by the committee from repeating his social indiscretion.'[14] He sums up by saying: 'A club was a club, a private institution no outsider could enter, even as a guest of the Deputy Commissioner unless a club official allowed it.'[15] Apart from the Gymkhana Club, there is mention of the Mayapore Club (originally the MHC, then MC), the Willingdon Club and the Royal Yacht Club.

> Willingdon Club was founded by the Viceroy Lord Willingdon in a fit of rage because the Indian guests he invited—in ignorance—to

a private banquet at the Royal Yacht Club were turned away from the doors in their Rolls-Royces before he cottoned on to what was happening.[16]

The Mayapore Club was supposed to have been the Mayapore Hindu Club—MHC—but remained MC. 'It was originally meant to be an English-type club for Indians who were clubbable' and was taken over by 'Hindu Banias' who sat with their feet on the chair and only understood money.

This description, fictional though it claims to be, has too many parallels with the real history of real clubs to be dismissed as fiction. The role of the social club in E.M. Forster's *A Passage to India* disgusts both Mrs Moore and Fielding—the British characters who see British Indian society in terms outside those set by the colonial administrators who must follow all injunctions which go well beyond the boundaries of work. Ruth Jhabvala's *Heat and Dust* also has several scenes in which the centrality of the social club is highlighted.

British men who had left home created for themselves a convivial atmosphere in these social clubs, a place where a drink was accompanied with smoking and choice cooking appropriate to the British palate, good conversation and masculine games and sports (like billiards, cards or a round of golf). However, it was also important that these clubs provided a space from which natives were excluded. Thus, from the very beginning, the issue of who was not allowed was as important as who was allowed into the clubs. Jug Suraiya described this phenomenon in the July 1990 issue of the *Calcutta Club Magazine* thus:

> Building an empire was a bothersome business, calling for British bluff, a stiff upper lip and other uncomfortable angularities designed to awe the native population and keep it in its place. Much more than his counterpart at home, the Englishman abroad needed a place where he could seek sanctuary from the high noon of Empire, momentarily forget his white man's burden, put aside his sola topi, down a couple of gins and tonic and generally unbend a bit...[17]

Most accounts of the establishment of the club culture of the Raj period emphasize these elements of nostalgic creation of a home-like atmosphere. Yet this sort of description seems to downplay the role of the social club in the ways in which the clubs were always and still remain one of the ways by which hierarchies of social and cultural power are created and sustained. It is certainly not just enough to say that these clubs were racist in nature, because membership to them was not only on the basis of race. The white man had to belong to a particular social class and engage in particular professions. They were 'exclusive' in the sense that the club rules were very clear about whom to include and whom not to include and usually applicants had to go through several rounds of interviews and interactions to prove that they were 'the right sort' before being enrolled.

Social institutions like these clubs serve several purposes. On the one hand they define the 'desirable' and the undesirable in terms of who is allowed access and who is not. For instance, the members of the Bengal Club were all British men, most of them drawn from the 'service of the John Company', but the club did not include all British men. It selected the desirable in terms of 'a command of character and friends', and strove to create, for those who 'constitute the society of Calcutta', a place to spend 'an idle half hour agreeably' and meet old friends and acquaintances.[18] The number of members was limited to 500, 100 of which was drawn from 'Gentlemen not in the service of His Majesty or the Company', which meant members of the 'Bench, Bar and the Clergy'. By creating a list of who was considered desirable, the club rules endowed a sense of exclusiveness and by the very phrase 'constitute the society of Calcutta', the club decrees itself as the arbitrator or determinant of what constitutes the 'society'. Yet, the notion of exclusiveness works successfully only if everyone, not only those who are included, but also those who are excluded, accept the legitimacy of the institution to act as the arbitrator of defining the exclusiveness. A point from which to begin this discussion could be a more detailed description of Bengal Club, one famous for its exclusive and high social status.

The Bengal Club House, No. 33 Chowringhee was the Calcutta residence of Thomas Babington Macaulay, Law member of the Supreme Council from 1834 to 1838. The club originally consisted of five houses at 33 Chowringhee Road, No.1 Park Street, Nos.1 and 2 Russell Street. 'The management of the club is vested in a President, Vice-President, and seven other Members of Committee, who are elected annually' and

'All gentlemen received in general society in Calcutta are eligible' as members.[19] However, the Bengal Club was so named 'only by virtue of its geographical location'; according to Bharati Ray it could have been named more appropriately 'ECEB' Exclusive Club for Europeans in Bengal.[20] 'It was an exclusive club in two senses—exclusively European and exclusively selective.'[21]

The club carefully created an exclusive space where the architecture, the décor, the food and drinks could replicate, as far as feasible, the lifestyle of the English gentleman. Indigenous practices were banned, sometimes by rules. William H. Russell (a *London Times* Correspondent) noted, for example, that 'By 1857, hookah smoking in the club was replaced by pipe and cheroot smoking'.[22] This injunction suggests that *hookah* smoking had been a practice prior to 1857, but after the establishment of the British Raj, the tendency to proscribe all things Indian and replace them with English practices probably prompted the framing of this rule. Of course, natives were allowed in, only as serving personnel and to provide other necessary support for the members and their activities. By the creation of such a space—both physical and social—the activities of the English gentleman become coded as the desirable. The elaborate dress codes and other rules serve not only to legitimize the power of the English in the social sphere, but also to legitimize the cultural styles of a particular class of Englishman as the desirable, elite and dominant.

Accordingly, dress codes were strictly enforced in the Bengal Club, as they still are. The rules stipulated that a tie and jacket should be worn throughout the year. The dress code was more formal for the evening. At dinners the standard attire was 'black tie' (short dinner jacket with dress tie); a 'white tie' (tailcoat) was worn on special occasions. Black trousers and a black cummerbund compensated for the discarded jacket in hot summers. This was despite the heat and humidity of the Indian climate. However, the aura of power that surrounded the British needed to be reinforced by such rules and codes that created several layers of distinction between the British administrators and the Indians, who were often richer and more influential in their own social and cultural spheres. The success of social, cultural and linguistic institutions in creating or reinforcing hierarchies of domination lies precisely in the fact that the higher strata enforces codes, and behavioural norms such that outsiders will always feel incompetent.[23] Thus, the establishment of clubs was not only about race, as even less powerful members of the ruling race were clearly not deemed competent enough to be allowed entry into these spaces.

The first President was Lt. Col. J. Finch and Charles Metcalfe, the Governor, was the club President for 10 years. Gradually the Bengal club members were drawn from the British ICS officers, high court judges, leaders in the legal and medical professions, and the *burra sahib* representatives of commercial houses. 'The club had opened its door to Indians only in 1959';[24] however, care was taken to ensure that 'the Indian entrants came from the highest echelon of the corporate world'[25] and they had one common trait—they were either educated in the United Kingdom or trained in British corporate ethics. These men were competent enough in British culture and could thus follow the complex rules—both written and unwritten—with élan. Yet these men were instrumental in gradually Indianizing the Club.[26] From 1988 women could become members in their own right and the club became a proper social club. 'Between 1969 and 1979 the club became almost totally Indianised.'[27]

The large club house in Esplanade Row contained residential accommodation for the members. Breakfast, tiffin and dinner were offered to residents and non-residents. In the past, the food served included roast beef, sea fish, mangoes and apples. The nostalgic British gastronomy-inspired menu included dishes like 'Toad in the Hole, Lancashire Hot Pot, and Roast Lamb served with boiled potatoes and boiled cabbage'.[28] Continental dishes were also served alongside. A curry lunch was sometimes served as a Sunday treat. However, the description offered reflects the British contempt of the Indian traditions of food and eating practices:

> The manner of eating the curry would seem today to be funny. Rice was heaped on a plate in a mound with a shallow depression on the top like a crater of a volcano. Into this crater was poured 'Dhawl curry', superimposed on which came the main mutton curry, accompanied by sweet mango chutney and chopped raw onions. The final

topping was of 'Papadams' crushed in the hand and sprinkled. This somewhat weird mixture was consumed with great relish.[29]

Now the 'Wednesday buffet lunch is of fish curry along with five types of vegetables and three types of sweets, all done in the Bengali style, Friday buffet lunch presents a continental spread and Saturdays are for Mughlai kabab and tandoori dishes. For dinners, Indian gourmet has found a favoured place by the side of the Western...'.[30] During the celebrations of 150 years of the club in 1977, the dishes on the menu cleverly incorporated the names of the founders and past presidents of the club. By such strategies, the history of the club is remembered and commemorated so that a continuity of the basic ideology of the club is ensured. Membership is still selective in this 'prestigious' club. The club has a well-stocked library adjoining the Reading Room (the Club was formerly described as a 'very pleasant resort; and the reading-room is kept well-supplied with the best periodicals, etc., from every part of the world')[31] but the Barber's Shop remains a favourite with the members. The Bengal Club had a reciprocal relationship with the 'Bombay (Byculla) Club, the Madras Club and the Hong Kong and Shanghai clubs, in admitting the members of those clubs, if visiting Calcutta, to all the privileges of Honorary membership for the time being'.[32]

Another of the older elite clubs in Kolkata, the Calcutta Club was founded in 1907. According to legend, the club was born out of an incident that took place in the early twentieth century when in a club in Calcutta meant for whites only, Sir Rajen Mookerjee, a guest of the Viceroy had to dine in a shamiana put up for the purpose, as non-whites were not allowed entry in the Club building. This led to the birth of Calcutta Club as the first multiracial Club in India, a character which it has maintained all along.[33] It shifted from 17 Elysium Row to its present position in the early part of the twentieth century. The Calcutta Club founding committee consisted of 11 Indians and 11 Europeans and the patron was Lord Minto, the Viceroy. As early as 1907 the President of the club was His Highness the Maharaja of Cooch Behar.

The Club was thus established out of a need felt for a place where people could meet for social intercourse, without frontiers of community, race or religion. It was the result of a conviction that in a composite society, an understanding of the way of life and culture of the constituent communities living in Calcutta could be gained by personal contacts.[34]

However, this Club, while it insisted on removing the barriers of race, seemed to adhere to the class and social requirements of the social elite of the times. Indians who were educated in Britain or in British ways were the ones who felt the need of a public social place where drinks, good food and conversation could be indulged in. This replaced the earlier such public spaces in feudal houses. The British concept of the social club was something that the Indian elite felt it needed. However, these elite did not try to establish any Indian character in this new club. Rather, the description of the club in the Centenary Volume reflects the pride in the fact that it was, and still is, so British in character: It is 'full of old fashioned elegance, with Chippendale chairs and staff dressed in traditional white uniforms, which impresses deeply those walking into the club for the first time, particularly foreigners'.[35]

Ladies were originally not allowed in the club but in 1909 they were permitted to play tennis on two days. A Lawn House 'where ladies could come and enjoy the facilities of the Club' was donated and renamed the Ladies Annexe. It was formally inaugurated on 12 January 1920. In 1954 ladies were allowed to use the main entrance and the ground floor of the club was completely opened to them. In 1979 only the Men's Bar denied entry to ladies.[36] Today ladies are integral to the Club. They help organizing most Club events and the Ladies Advisory Committee, headed by the President's wife, is constituted 'for planning, implementing and supervising the different activities of the Club'.[37] The article concludes on the note that '…ladies can contribute to making the Club institution economically more viable, with a more assured future'.[38]

In another article in the same magazine[39] by Manishankar Mukherjee, better known as the Bengali author 'Shankar', entitled '50 Years of *Kata Ajanarey*' the author reminisced about his association with the Calcutta Club through his acquaintance and association with the famous Mr Noel Barwell, the last European Barrister practicing in the Courts of Calcutta. Shankar shared his 'nostalgic memories' of Mr Barwell who had spent the last three years of his life (1951–53) in Calcutta Club, where 'he used to reside in a suite which is now known as Room No. 7 of the club'.[40] Room No. 7 has since been converted into an air-conditioned Mixed Card Room, Lounge and Cocktail Bar. Shankar describes the emotions that he had felt the first time he had passed the Calcutta Club building 55 years ago:

> Once on my way to the PG Hospital, later renamed as SSKM, I had seen this building from the footpath and had wondered what happens here? I was told that this was a 'Club'. Earlier during my job-hunting days, I had seen from [a] distance the magnificent dome of the Bengali Club on Chowringhee, which alas! does no longer exist. What did people do in Calcutta Club was a well-kept secret; having failed to collect more information, I had presumed that Calcutta Club can only be a smaller part of the bigger Club representing Bengal.[41]

Barwell used to meet his lay clients in the club; these often included ladies seeking counsel for matrimonial jurisdiction. Shankar recalls, 'Since ladies were not allowed entry through the main gate, the backdoor on the east came in handy to welcome, or should I [Shankar] say "smuggle" the ladies in the lawyer's sitting room.'[42] The club in the 1950s was full of 'sahib' members and Barwell loved to introduce his clerk or Shankar to them as his 'highly talented' friend. Thus Shankar came to identify 'almost all the *burra, mejo* and *chota sahibs* of Bird & Co., Heilgers, Gillanders, Arbuthnot, Jardine & Henderson, Dunlop, CESC, Mackinon Mackenzie, Metal Box, etc.'.[43] He concludes by paying tribute to the club by describing the club building as a shrine which allowed him to 'enter on compassionate ground the temple of creativity'.[44]

Among the many accounts of the Club that exist, the account written by Shankar is perhaps the most interesting as it clearly captures the way an 'outsider' to the elite class that comprises the Calcutta Club membership sees the club and its activities. The use of the word 'shrine' is particularly significant as the Club does indeed, like all shrines, appear to be the home of the powerful, the dominant, the ones who control the world as we know it—the gods of our society. To the outsider, the sense of the aura is overwhelming indeed.

The Club Magazines and volumes still carefully and perhaps in-
tentionally create a picture of what is often called 'old world charm'.
In 'Nostalgia Unlimited', for example, Dr Dhrubajyoti Banerjea nar-
rates how at the time of the club's Diamond Jubilee in 1967, Mr Ashok
Chandra Gupta was the only Founder member alive at the time. He
had retired as the Accountant General of Punjab in 1936, and was a
bachelor, who chose to stay in Room No.1 of the club. He was a patient
and was 'well-looked after by two bearers, one of them was Majid Khan,
Abdar in the Main Bar'.[45] The legendary aviator Mr Biren Roy was also
a member of the club. In 1987 there used to be an Octogenarian's Corner in the Men's Bar in the afternoon. Two of the men, over 90, Sachin
Bando and Sisir Mullick as well as some others—'Come rain or shine,
bandhs or dislocations these gentlemen would meet everyday, have their
varied drinks and go back home around 3-30 p.m.'[46].

Haraprasad Mitra in 'Dakshiner Baranda' [Bengali] fondly recalls
the tea drinking, addas, business discussion, gossiping and leg pulling
that took place on the balcony. In the evenings one would take drinks
with shami kabab, finger food, etc. He speaks of the excellent toast,
tennis lawns and giant trees. Shankar had praised the club's inimitable
'Beckti' fish preparation. Mitra also praises the wonderful library which
contains 30–35,000 books. Some of these books are rare gems. At one
time, he reminisces, High Court judges used to meet in the library and
drinks were allowed in there. Now, on the huge round table, India's daily
newspapers and magazines, like the *Times, Economist, Newsweek* and
India Today lie scattered. One of the changes in the last five years is that
Bengali books have begun to be stocked though no Bengali magazines
as yet. He complains that despite computerization the books are not
shelved properly making them difficult to find.

Yet alongside the invention of the traditions there is also a rapid
modernization programme happening in all the clubs. Whereas generous donations and contributions from the wealthy members would be
enough to meet the Clubs' extra expenses, and tradition was left largely
untouched, today things are changing. New foods such as pizzas and
Chinese cuisine have been introduced; new events which corporate
houses are only happy to sponsor, knowing that they will be able to
reach the wealthiest of consumers and therefore will get more focused

target groups; and new activities have come to dominate the club culture.

Thus, Calcutta Club like the Bengal Club has taken pains in recent years to preserve its furniture, oil paintings, lithographs and photographs. Simultaneously, an outlet of Don Giovanni's has been set up in the club to cater to the new demand for pizza. The club's national debate in February is open to eminent speakers and some prominent politicians also grace these occasions. Events like these are increasingly dependent on sponsorship with corporate houses, alcohol manufacturers and other consumer goods manufacturers paying good money for the privilege of seeing their names on show during these events. Bhaskar Gupta finds it incongruous to have the sponsor's name, in the banners and invitation cards, as presenter of a club event instead of the club just acknowledging their help indirectly with gratitude. 'Sponsors we need and the club has to be thankful to them for their generous help';[47] yet, there seems to be a note of sadness in these words, and nostalgia for the days when such crass commercial intrusions were not part of the elite ethos of the club culture.

The histories of most of these older clubs of Calcutta are similar. In the Calcutta Swimming Club the first Indian member in 1964 was the Maharaja of Cooch Behar, while the first Indian President was the Late P.T. Basu. He was elected to the post in 1976. The exclusion principle worked till the last quarter of the previous century. The Calcutta Swimming Club was established on 24 May 1887 and it was inaugurated by the Lieutenant General of Bengal Sir Stewart Bailey. In the days of the 'Raj' CSC was called 'The Calcutta Swimming Baths'. From the 1920s, days were fixed for ladies only at the club and they had separate cubicles for changing—the galleries were allotted for the men and slips for the women. Post-World War II, the club had 1,500 families and celebrated a 'golden period'. In recent times the membership has doubled. Nafisa Ali, Amitabh Bachchan, several MLAs and MPs patronize the club. The patrons of the club include top corporate businessmen, professionals, intellectuals and eminent sportspersons. The club has a Rajasthani Room serving good vegetarian cuisine to cater to 'lots of Gujarati and Marwari members'[48] and there is a Health Parlour. An interesting category in the types of members the club allows is 'missionaries' and includes Armenians. The club has links for accommodating members in places in India and abroad like Dubai and Colombo. There are provisions for karaoke sessions in the pub bar, swimming, billiards, cards, carom, chess, darts, pool, table tennis, a gym with a sauna and modern equipment and a saloon. Successful representatives of the club in various sporting events receive cash rewards to the amount of ₹ 20,000. Yet the effects of the changes are felt here too, and are not always for the better. A staff member, however, felt that the atmosphere in the club had changed with some people treating the club like a hotel—they arrived during lunch and left shortly after, or arrived during dinner had a couple of drinks, ate, and then left.

The Tollygunge Club was established in 1895 by British Executives and is now open to senior executives, bureaucrats, defense personnel, police, customs, excise officials and entrepreneurs among others. A country club, it has facilities for horse riding and annual equestrian and golf tournaments are held. Sporting facilities like billiards, pool, table tennis, swimming, squash and tennis attract the members. In some clubs members vary from 2,500–4,000 but till 2003 the Tolly Club restricted its members to 1,500.

The Royal Calcutta Golf Club (RCGC) was established in 1829 (it celebrated 175 glorious years of golfing history in 2004). It was initially located at Dum Dum, then a small suburb to the north-east of Calcutta. At a later date it removed itself to the Maidan until, in 1903, land for the new course was found near the Tollygunge Club. The links in the maidan made way for the construction of Victoria Memorial.[49] 'The club has always believed in nurturing talent but more importantly it is a members club.'[50] The club boasts of a Junior Training programme in golf. Already members have won several international awards over the years. Member Arun Shroff fondly recalled the fine discipline, foot massage in the dressing room, delicious brownies, 'gol toast and jam' and the delicious Christmas lunch with Rum and Raisin Pudding.[51] Cotton writes:

> The links are extensive, and much has been done to improve the *maidan* over which the 'Golfers' have to travel in a game. There is also a piece of turf used by the members for Bowls. The Club is the

possessor of a handsome pavilion, which, however, according to Fort regulations, is deemed a portable building only, and as such, subject to removal at short notice. During the year several prizes are competed for, the most important being the Club Gold Medal; Cashmere Silver Cup; Blackheath Gold Medal; Madras Silver Medal; Bombay Medal; St. Andrew's Silver Challenge Tankard; Silver Challenge Cup.

In May 1891, a Ladies' Golf Club was founded and a course was laid out for them, on the opposite side of the Casuarina Avenue.[52]

Dalhousie Institute (better known as D.I.) was founded in 1859. Its original premises had been at 34 Dalhousie Square. H.E.A. Cotton describes the Dalhousie Institute as:

Externally it has no pretensions to architectural beauty, but it contains a handsome hall, 90 feet by 45 feet, the walls of which are lined with marble, with a semi-circular roof, richly decorated. It also contains a library, reading-rooms and a billiard room. It was erected 'as a monumental edifice, to contain within its walls statues and busts of great men'...The Hall is available for Lectures, Concerts, and other entertainments.[53]

The members were composed of a large number of Freemasons and other citizens of Calcutta. After the Central Government took the plot in 1948, D.I. arrived at its present location opposite the Modern High School (42 Jhowtalla Road) on 21 December 1956. The President was Mr P.E. Walde. A cosmopolitan club, children are welcomed on all days. There is badminton, beauty pageants and the club holds an annual picnic and a jazz fest. The club is famous for its quizzing activities and houses a cyber café. The types of members include married couples with children below 18, married persons with children wishing to join in an individual capacity; individual gent or lady above 21 years; junior members between 18 and 21 years; temporary members; corporate members (four nominees for five years) and life members.

It is CC&FC, the Calcutta Cricket & Football Club, however, which lays claim to being the oldest club in Calcutta. Founded in 1789, it was originally known as the Tea Planter's Club. CC&FC is the oldest rugby and cricket club in Kolkata and one of the oldest in Asia as well. Football, cricket, swimming and table tennis are the main sports played. The Merchants Cup for cricket and football and New Year celebrations are important events in the club calendar. The Saturday Club at No. 7 Wood Street was established in August 1875. Cotton writes in his book:

> The amusements most popular with members are Dancing, Concerts and Amateur Theatricals, and some excellent entertainments have been given from time to time in the Club Rooms. There is an excellent supply of newspapers and periodicals. Lawn Tennis forms a special feature, and there are several well-kept courts. The Committee [has] power to admit as Temporary members, persons proposed and seconded and temporarily residing in Calcutta. All ladies and gentlemen received in general society in Calcutta are eligible for admission as members of the Club.[54]

There is a health club, a library, a swimming pool, a billiards room, beauty parlour, barber's shop and general store in the club itself. The club is affiliated to many clubs abroad and members enjoy joint membership in Asia, Europe and the US.

The Royal Calcutta Turf Club at Russell Street—predominantly a horse-racing club—was one of the first clubs to have its office in London. Cotton goes on to mention two other clubs—The United Service Club, formerly the Bengal Military Club in 1845 which was turned into a 'Limited Liability Company'; and the New Club in Park Street in 1884. The attractions were the residential quarters, the Library, Lawn Tennis, Billiards, Smoking Concerts, House Dinners, Dances and others. They no longer exist. A few other clubs which shut down are the Jodhpur Club, an old German Club, the Bengal Gymkhana, the Delta and the 300 Club on Theatre Road. These were clubs that could not change with the times. With the end of the Raj, the political, social, cultural and economic discrimination on the basis of race alone disappeared, but was replaced by a subtler form of social discrimination.

These clubs were unquestioning in their attempt to create a space—physical, social, gastronomical and cultural—which allowed only the rituals and activities of the British gentleman to be emulated. It is significant that the early history of even those clubs which were created in response to the policy of racial exclusion of Bengal Club and others also insisted that members were either educated in England or had worked long enough in British corporations to have imbibed the British ways. The elaborate dinners and conversations were part of the process of applying for membership, which could only be considered if recommended by existing members. These elaborate rituals also ensured that the 'right' kind of men were included. A person had to have mastery over the rituals of dining correctly, of speaking correctly and of belonging to the desired social class. The sociologist, Pierre Bourdieu writes about the circumstances under which those who are not competent in particular ways of speaking are forced to become silent. The exclusivity of membership procedures ensured that only that section of society that was fluent in the desirable social codes were allowed membership into the hallowed clubs.

The kinds of events that were organized by the clubs also, as detailed earlier, reveal the cultural politics inherent in these clubs. In the area of sports, for example, the more 'elite' sporting activities like golf, tennis and horse riding were the mainstay of these clubs while, apart from CC&FC, more plebeian activities such football or rugby were not part of their programme. Balls, cocktail parties and formal dining were contrasted to the more 'native' habits of 'adda' where some friends would get together to chat about whatever caught their fancy. In fact, Rudrangshu Mukherjee, in the Centenary Volume points out that while the Tagore family was an important patron of the Calcutta Club, Rabindranath Tagore himself never visited the Club and Abanindra and Gaganendra became members, only to resign soon after. Mukherjee points out that these Tagores, with their vision of a nationalist, Bengali culture probably deliberately kept away from these institutions which were founded on mimicking British culture.

Yet for the first 50 years after Independence we find the trend is towards substituting the British culture of these clubs with an 'elite' Indian culture. Post-Independence India in its eagerness to create an elite culture which still distinguished itself from the popular culture of the streets began to introduce programmes which highlighted a new form of cultural eliteness. Thus, classical Indian music or Tagore evenings began to make their way into the cultural calendar. Events like the Bengali New Year, originally not a social event, became ways in which a burgeoning sense of nationalism found expression. On the Calcutta Club calendar there are Christmas Carols, sumptuous Christmas lunch, and the New Year's Eve Dinner and Dance alongside Poila Baisakh (the Bengali New Year) and Bijoya Sammelani (after Durga Puja get-together). Calcutta Club produced its first dramatic production in 1976 with the staging of Tagore's 'Sheshraksha'. This successful event was followed the production of several other plays by Tagore and other Bengali writers. Ironically, Tagore provided the local Bengali *bhadralok* or gentleman the means by which he could create a new 'elite' culture. Local festivals and rituals also begin to appear on the club calendars. Several clubs, for example, make arrangements for playing Holi.

However, what is particularly interesting is the fact that there is another shift taking place in the club culture of Kolkata. It is only in the very recent times that we find the introduction of truly popular cultural programmes such as Hindi film related events beginning to enter and even dominate the cultural calendars of several of these clubs. So Christmas parties and carnivals, New Year's Eve dancing and dinner parties, May Queen and other beauty pageants which have colonial origins, are now side by side with Disco nites and rain dances which are attended by Bollywood film stars (or at least wannabe stars). Events like Dandiya dancing, heavily influenced by popular Hindi films, are among the most popular events in terms of member participation. A local newspaper report[55] notes that the Christmas Celebrations of the four clubs visited—Tolly Club, CC&FC, RCGC and Saturday Club—'All clubs had a Mumbai element to their song and dance routine. A far cry from the formal Balls of the Raj! In fact, the older members of these clubs do not seem to be very happy with these changes as can be found in the words of Bikash Sinha when he writes: 'Film stars are at the focus, a bit of razzle here and a bit of dazzle there seem to make the members so very happy.'[56] Another event that has entered the calendar of almost all clubs in recent times is the observance of Valentine's Day.

Bengali music is now also popular, but whereas it used to be Tagore and sometimes the more traditional kind of songs, increasingly Bangla rock bands are invited to play, which may not be as accepted by the older and more orthodox club members. While these changes reflect contemporary changes in cultural taste, there is also a recognition that the changes are not limited to the issue of what kind of programmes should be organized. The changes also represent the ways in which the concept of Calcutta's once elite clubs are changing. While 'global' cultural events like Valentine's Day are being celebrated, a conscious cultural 'local' is also being created as if to emphasize a balance that the 'new global Indian' is searching for—a culture in which both the local and the global can exist side by side in comfort.

During the early period of the history of club culture in Kolkata, the clubs provided a public space which was also exclusive. Thus, membership rules and rituals were highly formal and controlled. A new membership could only be processed if an existing member sponsored it. The aspiring member had to provide evidence that he was the right kind of person in terms of profession, social class and cultural ethos. Thus, the process was long and elaborate and designed to check the claim of the aspirant. Drinks, dining and social situations were essential rituals during which the existing members decided whether the aspirant was truly 'one of us'. Only money, or only the proper job description could not ensure that the person had the desired social and cultural qualities that the club insisted on. Dress codes were considered one important way of distinguishing between the proper gentleman and the aspiring gentleman. For the Bengali gentleman, the membership of a club ensured his entrance into a social and cultural practice that was different from his traditional one. In this new social space, the idea of leisure became entwined with the sense of belonging to a community which was not defined by traditional social forms, such as family or caste. In fact, the multi-religious nature of the membership of these clubs also indicated a new Westernized sensibility in a society where there were few places that could be shared by the various religious groups.

The issue of the gradual inclusion of women is also connected to the evolving ideas of the ways in which women were first excluded from public spaces in India. Leisure is traditionally a gendered activity and women have had different ways of finding spaces and activities which provide them with leisure. Gradually, as the modern notion of family came to be more acceptable and even desired, the entrance of women into public spaces of leisure began to become acceptable. A couple was recognized in Indian society as a unit which could spend time in public engaging in leisure activities. Before this, the public spaces designated for leisure activities were highly gender segregated. Thus, women emerged onto tennis courts, swimming pools and dining halls only gradually with a change in social mores.

The entire family, i.e. inclusive of children, enters into the clubs even later, only when the unit of the family as a unit of sharing leisure activities enters into social conventions. In fact, children's corners and children-oriented activities are only relatively recent events in the club calendar. As the modern nuclear family unit becomes the norm, spending time together with the family becomes desirable and the club adjusts to provide space and activities where the parents and children may publicly enjoy their leisure.

In recent times, these ideas of leisure, of leisure communities and perhaps, even of social hierarchies of distinction are rapidly changing. Older social codes which were represented through the complicated dress codes are no longer valid. Increasingly, social hierarchy and cultural elitism is being replaced by simpler equations of wealth and income.

Space Circle is one of the new types of clubs that is increasingly becoming popular in the city's social scene. To be a member of this or others like Princeton Club, Spring Club or Ibiza, the elaborate social and cultural examination of the past is no longer required. Mostly these clubs are part of a large apartment complex and apartment owners are automatically members. Outsiders can become members by paying the required sum of money. There is no prolonged social vetting process to gain membership here.

One important change that can be noticed is that these are all professionally managed—unlike the older clubs which were largely self-managed and members voluntarily gave their time to organize the events of the clubs. These clubs are owned and managed by the promoters of the apartment complexes who are interested in running their institutions as profit-oriented corporations. In this connection one may mention Mr Gordon D'Mello of the Dalhousie Institute club, who conducted a survey (2003) where he showed that most clubs were incurring huge financial losses and unable to generate enough funds for proper management.

The Bengal Club may also be mentioned here as they were forced to sell off club land to pay off debts. The Chatterjee International Centre stands on their former club grounds. Clubs which were in a fairly healthy state, according to the survey, were Space Circle, the Calcutta Swimming Club, the Punjab Club and Hindusthan Club. For these new clubs, the issue of creating a community of members from the 'proper' social and cultural strata does not exist. The willingness and ability to pay for the membership and then the various activities are the main points of consideration.

These clubs offer various facilities to all its members. Space Circle has a gym, a library, a rock climbing facility, a rifle and pistol shooting range, a bowling alley and an indoor cricket stadium where badminton, basketball and soccer are played. The Merlin Group which set up Club Ibiza and the Princeton Club in 2004, felt that 'offering complimentary club membership made selling flats a lot easier'.[57] In the Princeton Club, there is a reading room, a kids' playing zone, two residential facilities and a banquet hall. Conference and Banquet halls are part of the club's 'survival strategy' as they are regularly rented out for specific corporate or social events to non-members. 'Surprisingly Bengali cuisine is not on the club menu, despite 60 per cent of the members being Bengali'. At the lounge bar a live band plays classic rock on Fridays and jazz and classical fusion on Thursdays which, interestingly, both members and non-members can attend. The formal bar is used to finalize business deals over a drink. A rooftop swimming pool, a spa, a ladies' massage parlour is available, as is a modern gym with the latest equipment. Sports like squash, table tennis, billiards, cards, badminton and darts are on offer. Children have a play-pen and maids are allowed to accompany them. The club holds Food Festivals, X-Mas Carnivals and New Year's Eve Celebrations, and Valentine's Day is a huge affair.

The advertisements, website and other promotional material that the Princeton Club uses capture some of the changes in the creation, profile and activities of these new generation clubs. 'Princeton club has arrived for those who aspire for the best in life. For those who want a club to be a place of their own…to socialise with like-minded people or simply be by themselves' is how the club describes itself. It continues: 'Princeton is new, informal with amenities of international standards.' While the clubs discussed earlier, like the Calcutta Club or the Tolly Club or the Bengal Club are anxious about their credentials of age and tradition, this club proclaims the qualities *new* and *informal* as desirable qualities. Perhaps even the name 'Princeton' is a sign that this club chooses to align itself, not with the tradition of the English social club for the stiff-upper lipped Britisher, but the more egalitarian social codes of America. This is reflected in the fact that while the Princeton Club does have a dress code, it is much less formal and stringent than that of the older clubs.

The list of facilities offered show not only the changes that have taken place as to what constitutes leisure, but also a much greater emphasis on the notion that these clubs are offering families the physical space and the facilities to spend time together and pleasurably. Traditionally the clubs were all part of the male prerogative to spend time apart from the family in peace and comfort. Gradually, the wife entered the space as companion to the male, but now the entire family is the target of the clubs' activities. As traditional Indian social spaces shrink, large families, close-knit localities and ritual observances are disintegrating. The need for organising leisure as a business proposition has emerged and it seems that these new clubs are able to define and cater to new needs in today's global times. For example, while the older clubs offer some outdoor sports facilities such as tennis, or golf or badminton, here the sports facilities are all related to indoor sports which include squash, croquet, pool and a small indoor swimming pool.

Another such club—The Spring Club, which is also attached to a new apartment complex, is currently advertising and inviting people to become members. Of course, this means of attracting membership through placing advertisements in newspapers and magazines would have been unthinkable in the days of the older social clubs, where membership was deliberately kept exclusive. The photographs and text that constitute the advertisement too evoke a young, active family who are enjoying the facilities. The club is a place where people go as a family to enjoy facilities offered there in a safe and secure environment—this seems to be the message of these advertisements.

Social exclusivity is no longer the *raison d'être* for social clubs. As the logic of the market begins to dominate all aspects of life in our globalized, post-liberalization world, leisure too becomes a commodity which is available for the right price. These new clubs will offer whatever is popular and will draw members to participate, unlike the dilemma of the more established clubs which have traditions and history to answer to. Kolkata with a long and deep Raj influence had evolved leisure communities which responded to the rules established by the British. Through the second half of the twentieth century, a period of Indianization can be traced in the activities of these social clubs. The era of globalization has changed social structures in many ways and it appears that the idea of leisure, the ways in which leisure activities are organized and leisure communities are constructed are changing every day.

Also interesting is the fact that while the older clubs were all run on a voluntary basis, that is the members would elect from amongst themselves an Executive Committee and other Office Bearers and there would be Annual General Meetings and the other paraphernalia of democratic functioning, the more recent clubs follow a corporate model of organization. In this trend the broader trajectory of recent times for the individual to redefine him/herself as the consumer, rather than the citizen can be seen. Leisure, which used to be seen as a place and time in which one could escape the contours of work and the market is itself becoming marketized and commercial, as clubs are seen increasingly as places which provide just another service and individuals 'buy' the package which suits them the best. With the changing times and ideological frameworks, the clubs of Calcutta are recreating themselves to fit into a new global time and space far from the panelled smoking rooms of the Raj.

Notes and References

1. Michael Argyle, *The Social Psychology of Leisure* (London: Penguin, 1996).
2. (New York: Continuum, 1999), p. 199.
3. Richard Hoggart, *The Uses of Literacy* (Harmondsworth: Penguin Books, 1957).
4. Berg, 2002, p. 4.
5. London: Methuen, 1986, p. 87.
6. Jeffrey Hill, *Sport, Leisure & Culture in Twentieth Century Britain* (Palgrave: 2002).

7. Ibid., p. 138.
8. Rudi Koshar, p. 21.
9. Paul Scott, *The Jewel in the Crown* (Great Britain: Pan Books, 1966).
10. Ibid., p. 204.
11. Ibid.
12. Ibid., pp. 205–06.
13. Ibid.
14. Ibid., p. 231.
15. Ibid., p. 232.
16. Ibid., p. 214.
17. Kamalika Bhattcharjee, 'Ladies and the Calcutta Club: A Journey through the Ages: Now and Then!', *The Elite* (Winter, 2003–04), p. 2.
18. Bharati Ray, 'The Bengal Club in History: Birth and Survival', *The Bengal Club in History*, Kolkata Bengal Club Ltd., 2006), p. 3.
19. H.E.A. Cotton. *Calcutta: Old & New* (Calcutta: General Printers & Publishers Pvt. Ltd., 1909. Rev.ed.1980), p. 753.
20. Ray, 'The Bengal Club in History', p. 1.
21. Ibid., p. 3.
22. Ray, pp. 6–7.
23. Several of the theoretical concepts used in this chapter have been derived from Pierre Bourdieu's analysis of competence.
24. Following quotations taken from Ray, 'The Bengal Club in History', p. 10.
25. Ibid., p. 11.
26. Ibid., p. 11.
27. Ibid.
28. Ibid., p. 5.
29. Ibid., p. 7.
30. Ibid.
31. H.E.A Cotton, *Calcutta: Old and New* (Calcutta: Hartly Home).
32. Ibid.
33. Bhaskar P. Gupta, 'International Evening—A Retrospective', *The Elite* (Summer, 2006), p. 18.
34. Ibid, p. 19.
35. Ibid., p. 18.
36. Bhattacharjee, 'Ladies and the Calcutta Club', pp. 3–4.
37. Ibid., p. 5.
38. Ibid.
39. *The Elite*, The Calcutta Club Magazine, Summer Issue 2006. Mr Kallol Basu—Chairman, Library and Publication.
40. Ibid., p. 30.
41. Ibid.

42. Ibid., p. 31.
43. Ibid.
44. Ibid., p. 33.
45. Ibid., p. 34.
46. Ibid.
47. Bhaskar P. Gupta, 'International Evening', p. 19.
48. *The Telegraph*, 8 December 2006.
49. *Royal Calcutta Golf Club: 175th Anniversary 1829–2004*. Text and editing Arjun Mukherjee, N.K. Gossain & Co. Ltd.
50. Ibid., p. 72.
51. Ibid., p. 87.
52. Ibid., p. 758.
53. Cotton, *Calcutta: Old and New*, p. 741.
54. Ibid., p. 757.
55. *The Telegraph*, 26 December 2006.
56. Bikash Sinha, 'Calcutta Club-Now and Then!', *The Elite*, A Special Issue (2002–03), pp. 29–30.
57. Karo Christine Kumar, 'Old vs New' *The Telegraph*, 18 April 2008.

About the Editors and Contributors

The Editors

Partha Pratim Basu is Professor at the Department of International Relations, Jadavpur University, Kolkata. He has been a Fulbright Fellow at American Studies Institute in Southern Illinois University at Cambridge, USA (2001).

He has contributed a number of research articles and book chapters in the area of culture studies and is presently completing a UGC-supported Major Research Project on *India's Trade Policy, WTO and the Print Media*. His areas of expertise include media and politics/ international relations, politics of non-governmental organizations, religion and politics and human rights.

He has published books/journals such as *State Nation and Democracy: Alternative Global Futures* (2007), co-edited with Purusottam Bhattacharya, Rochana Das, Anjali Ghosh and Kanak Chandra Sarkar, *The Press and Foreign Policy in India* (2003).

Ipshita Chanda is Professor at the Department of Comparative Literature, Jadavpur University, Kolkata. She has been member of Faculty Team in the International Faculty Exchange Programme of the Virginia Council for International Education and the Virginia Community College System, 2008–2009, tenable at the John Tyler Community College at Midlothian and Chester, USA. Her list of books/journals includes *Packaging Freedom Feminism and Popular Culture* (2003), *Selfing the City: Single Women 'Outsiders' and the Practices of Urban Life* (forthcoming).

The Contributors

Dalia Chakraborty is Reader in Sociology at Jadavpur University. She was educated in Presidency College, Kolkata, and JNU, New Delhi. She obtained her Ph.D. from Calcutta University. She has published a book *Colonial Clerks: A Social History Of Deprivation And Domination* (2005). She has also contributed to books titled *Political Sociology* (2005) and *Sociology in India: Intellectual and Institutional Practices* (2010).

Sayantan Dasgupta is Lecturer in Comparative Literature, and Co-ordinator, Centre for Translation of Indian Literatures (CENTIL) at Jadavpur University. His areas of interest include modern Indian literature, translation and South Asian literatures and cultures.

He is author of *Indian English Literature: A Study in Historiography* and *Shyam Selvadurai: Texts and Contexts* and has a Ph.D. on contemporary English language fiction from South Asia.

Manas Ghosh is Lecturer in the Department of Film Studies, Jadavpur University. He has completed his Ph.D. from the same university. He has contributed articles to the *Journal of the Moving Image,* which is an annual publication of Department of Film Studies in Jadavpur University.

Devlina Gopalan is Reader in the Department of English, Women's Christian College, Kolkata.

Nilanjana Gupta is Professor in the Department of English, Jadavpur University. Her revised edition of the textbook *English for All* (2000), produced as a departmental project under her supervision, has achieved wide recognition. She is also an authority on media studies, having published widely on this subject in India and abroad. She has contributed to a forthcoming book, *The Enabling Environment: Media, Reform and the Democratisation Process in Societies in Transition.*

Abhijit Roy is Reader in the Department of Film Studies, Jadavpur University. Currently, he is also Joint Director at School of Media,

Communication and Culture, Jadavpur University, and Joint Coordinator at The Media Lab, Jadavpur.

Modhumita Roy is Associate Professor in Department of English, Tufts University, Medford, USA, since 1998. Some of her publications include *The Sun Never Sets: Imperial Ideologies and Indo-British Fiction* (forthcoming), *The Pledge of Intellect: Selected Writings of Michael Sprinker*, Fred Pfeil and Modhumita Roy (eds, forthcoming).

Rajdeep Roy, a former Research Fellow at School of Media, Communication and Culture, Jadavpur University, is presently pursuing his doctoral research in Cinema Studies at the School of Communication, Arts and Critical Enquiry, La Trobe University, Melbourne, Australia.

Index

Index

Index

Index